Clare's Letters to Agnes

Texts and Sources

Joan Mueller

Clare's Letters to Agnes

Texts and Sources

Joan Mueller

The Franciscan Institute
St. Bonaventure University
St. Bonaventure, New York
2001

Cover Design

The cover features a miniature taken from the feast of Saint Agnes of Rome in the Osek Lectionary, circa 1270. Inside the "S" is Saint Agnes of Prague dressed in the habit of the Poor Ladies (bottom) imploring the intercession of Saint Agnes of Rome holding the palm of martyrdom (top). Used with permission of the State Library, Prague.

Library of Congress Catalog Card Number

00-111769

ISBN: 1-57659-176-X

Printed and bound in the United States of America

BookMasters, Inc.
Mansfield, Ohio

In Grateful Memory of

Margaret Halaska, OSF

Table of Contents

Abbreviations

Writings of Saint Clare

1LAg	First Letter to Saint Agnes of Prague	*4LAg*	Fourth Letter to Saint Agnes of Prague
2LAg	Second Letter to Saint Agnes of Prague	*RCl*	Rule of Saint Clare
3LAg	Third Letter to Saint Agnes of Prague		

Source Material for Saints Clare of Assisi and Agnes of Prague

LegCl	The Legend of Saint Clare of Assisi	*Proc*	Acts of the Process of Canonization of Saint Clare
LegAg	The Legend of Saint Agnes of Prague.		

Cited Writings of Saint Francis

Adm	The Admonitions	*LtL*	A Letter to Brother Leo
CtExh	The Canticle of Exhortation	*LtMin*	A Letter to a Minister
ER	The Earlier Rule (Regula non bullata)	*LtOrd*	A Letter to the Entire Order
LR	The Later Rule (Regula bullata)	*LtR*	A Letter to the Rulers of the Peoples
1LtF	The First Letter to the Faithful	*OfP*	The Office of the Passion
2LtF	The Second Letter to the Faithful		

Cited Franciscan Sources

AC	The Assisi Compilation	*LMj*	The Major Legend by Bonaventure
AP	The Anonymous of Perugia	*LMn*	The Minor Legend by Bonaventure
1C	The Life of Saint Francis by Thomas of Celano	*L3C*	The Legend of the Three Companions
2C	The Remembrance of the Desire of a Soul	*1MP*	The Mirror of Perfection, Smaller Version
3C	The Treatise on the Miracles by Thomas of Celano	*2MP*	The Mirror of Perfection, Larger Version
ChrJG	The Chronicle of Jordan of Giano	*ScEx*	The Sacred Exchange between St. Francis and Lady Poverty
LJS	The Life of Saint Francis by Julian of Speyer		

Breviary Manuscripts

Assisi, Sacro Convento , 693
Assisi, Sacro Convento, 694
Assisi, San Damiano, *Breviary of Saint Clare*
Assisi, Santa Chiara, *Breviary of Saint Francis*
Chicago, Newberry Library, 24
Paris, Bibl. Nationale, lat. 4162[A]
Prague, Národní knihovna České republisky, Osek 76

Standard Works and Periodicals

ABR	*American Benedictine Review*	*LTK*	*Lexikon für Theologie und Kirche*
AF	*Analecta Franciscana*		
AFH	*Archivum Franciscanum Historicum*	*MGH*	*Monumenta Germaniae historica*
AASS	*Acta Sanctorum*	*MGH SS*	*Monumenta Germaniae historica, Scriptores*
BF	*Bullarium Franciscanum*		
CDB	*Codex Diplomaticus et Epistolaris Regni Bohemiae*	*Niermeyer*	*Mediae Latinitatis Lexicon Minus*
CF	*Collectanea Franciscana*	*OLD*	*Oxford Latin Dictionary*
DS	*Dictionnaire de spiritualité, ascétique et mystique*	*PL*	*Patrologia Latina*
		SF	C.D. Lanham, *"Salutatio" Formulas in Latin Letters to 1200: Syntax, Style, and Theory* (Munich 1975)
FranzStud	*Franziskanische Studien*		
FRB	*Fontes Rerum Bohemicarum*		
FS	*Franciscan Studies*		
GR	*Greyfriars Review*	*Souter*	A. Souter, *A Glossary of Later Latin to 600 A.D.* (Oxford 1949)
Latham	*Revised Medieval Latin Word-List From British and Irish Sources* (London 1965)		
		ST	*Studi e Testi*

Scripture

Scripture abbreviations in English texts are taken from the *New American Bible*. Scripture abbreviations in Latin texts referring to books of the Vulgate Bible are taken from *Biblia sacra iuxta Vulgatam versionem*, ed. R. Gryson *et al.*, 4th rev. ed. (Stuttgart 1994).

Introduction

Clare's Letters to Agnes

The four letters attributed to Clare of Assisi and addressed to Agnes of Prague are documents of primary importance for the study of the early Franciscan movement and, in particular, for the history of early Franciscan women. Through Clare's letters, one can ponder the thoughts, issues, evolution, and spirituality of the early Poor Ladies. Written between 1234-1253, Clare's letters serve as source material documenting a pivotal moment in the history of medieval women.

The Legend of Saint Agnes of Prague attests to the correspondence between Clare and Agnes: "By her frequent and gracious letters, Clare consoled her [Agnes] maternally, reverently, and most affectionately, and enthusiastically encouraged her in her holy purpose."[1] Of this mutual correspondence, only the letters of Clare are preserved. The content of Agnes's letters is known only insofar as Clare addresses this content in her letters.

Important new discoveries of manuscripts that include Clare's letters have eased doubts regarding their authenticity. In 1896, Dr. Achille Ratti, who was archivist of the Ambrosian library and who later became Pope Pius XI, discovered a manuscript in the archives of the Basilica of Sant'Ambrogio in Milan that contained the four letters of Clare to Agnes in Latin as well as a Latin version of *The Legend of Saint Agnes of Prague.* Ratti reported that he uncovered the Milan manuscript through investigating a faithful seventeenth-century transcript of it in the Ambrosian library. Upon examination of the writing and ornamentation of the older manuscript, he decided that it could not have been written later than the beginning of the fourteenth century. He hypothesized that the Milan manuscript contained a version of Clare's letters that was certainly much earlier and more reliable than the manuscripts known at the time.[2]

Although Clare's four letters were first published by the Bollandists in 1668,[3] and were therefore known before Ratti's discovery, the Milanese manuscript represented their earliest and most complete form. Clare's first letter was also known before Ratti's discovery through its inclusion in the Hall Manuscript of *The Chronicle of the Twenty-Four Generals*, which was written by Nicholas Glassberger, dated 1491, and published in 1897.[4]

In 1915, Walter Seton, unaware of Ratti's work, published an edition of Clare's letters in his thesis *Some New Sources for the Life of Blessed Agnes of Bohemia*.[5] Seton based his research primarily on a late fourteenth-century manuscript housed in the Royal Library of Bamberg, which contained a German text of Clare's letters. He also consulted a second German language Bamberg manuscript containing Clare's letters from the late fourteenth or early fifteenth-century, a German language edition of Clare's four letters in a fifteenth-century Wolfenbüttel manuscript, a fifteenth-century Dresden manuscript written in German, and a German fifteenth-century Berlin manuscript.[6]

From a note on the last folio of the first Bamberg manuscript, Seton postulated that this manuscript had been written in Nuremberg before 1380. About 1600, when the Nuremberg convent was dissolved, the manuscript was given to the Convent of Banz near Langheim in the Diocese of Bamberg. In 1802, the convent libraries in the Diocese of Bamberg were merged into the Royal Library of Bamberg.[7] Through the Bamberg text, Seton was able to date the manuscript tradition of Clare's letters back from the Bollandist date of 1668 to about 1380 making their authenticity more certain.

Seton became convinced that the Bollandist's Latin version was a translation of the German texts, and that the German manuscripts were a translation of an earlier Latin text. In June,

Introduction

1922, Professor Josef Susta of Charles University in Prague sent Seton a review of Seton's book which Susta had published in *The Czech Historical Journal.* While reading Susta's review, Seton learned of Dr. Achille Ratti's 1896 article that had reported a Latin manuscript of Czech origin that contained Clare's letters as well as the Latin *Legend of Saint Agnes of Prague.*[8]

In examining photographs of the Milan manuscript, Seton concurred with Ratti in regard to its dating, postulating that it had been written between 1280 and 1330. By studying *The Legend of Agnes of Prague* in tandem with Clare's letters, Seton suggested that the Milan manuscript was written prior to 1328 for the initiation of Agnes's canonization process, placing the text within seventy-five years after the death of Clare, and fifty years after the death of Agnes of Prague. Because Glassberger's copy of Clare's first letter in *The Chronicle of the XXIV Generals* corresponds almost verbatim with the Milan manuscript, Seton postulated that Glassberger had access to early and reliable sources.[9]

A fourth Latin manuscript discovered by Dr. Krsto Stošič in the Minorite monastery in Šibenik, Dalmatia, contains the second half of the second letter, as well as the third and fourth letters. This manuscript, besides omitting the complete text of the first letter and part of the second, is not as legible as the Milan manuscript.[10]

In 1932, Jan Kapistrán Vyskočil published a critical edition of Clare's four letters to Agnes of Prague.[11] After meticulously studying both the German and Latin manuscripts, Vyskočil concluded that: 1) the Šibenik manuscript was copied from the Milan manuscript; 2) the Bamberg manuscript was probably influenced by the Šibenik manuscript; and 3) the Milan manuscript was most likely written in Prague in preparation for Agnes's canonization process.[12]

In 1978, in his work *Opuscula S. Francisci et Scripta S. Clarae Assisiensium* (Assisi: Biblioteca Francescana Chiesa Nuova), 410-47, Giovanni M. Boccali, OFM, reedited the

Clare's Letters to Agnes

Latin text of Clare's letters based on the Milan manuscript. Ignacio Omaechevarria, OFM, in his second edition of *Escritos de Santa Clara y Documentos Complementarios* (Madrid: Biblioteca de Autores Cristianos, 1982), 317-42, bases his Italian text on Boccali's 1978 work.[13] The critical edition of Clare's letters in the *Sources Chrétiennes* series by Marie-France Becker, Jean-François Godet, and Thaddée Matura entitled *Claire D'Assise: Écrits* (Paris: Les Éditions du Cerf, 1985), 82-119, relies on Vyskočil.[14] The Latin text of Clare's letters presented in this book is based on the work of Boccali found in *Fontes Franciscani* (S. Maria degli Angeli—Assisi: Edizioni Porziuncola, 1995), 2263-84, but when there are differences between the texts, preference is given to Vyskočil.

The Dialogue Partners

The life of Clare of Assisi is relatively well-known and available in English.[15] Born in 1193 or 1194, Clare was the daughter of Offreduccio di Favarone and his wife, Ortolana. During her early years, Clare and her family took refuge in Perugia during a time of civil unrest in Assisi, but later returned to their home next to the Cathedral of San Rufino.[16]

After Francis returned to Assisi with oral approval from Pope Innocent III for his form of life, Clare heard Francis preach. Convinced by his message after a series of conversations,[17] Clare escaped her family home and was tonsured at the hands of Francis in the small church of Saint Mary of the Angels.[18]

After her tonsure, Francis and the brothers took Clare to San Paolo delle Abbadesse, a Benedictine monastery whose privileges included the threat of excommunication towards anyone who dared molest the inhabitants of the monastery.[19] The seven knights of her family came to the monastery to threaten Clare, but Clare stood her ground showing them her shorn hair. Seeing that she could not be persuaded, and

Introduction

realizing that because of her hair she could not be wed to a nobleman, Clare's family disowned her.[20] With her safety thus assured, Francis took Clare to the Monastery of Sant'Angelo di Panzo which was a smaller and simpler monastery and was nearer to San Damiano.[21]

Clare's sister Catherine joined Clare at Sant'Angelo. The wrath of the Offreduccio knights followed and, as a result of their physical abuse, Catherine nearly died in the struggle. Clare nursed Catherine back to health and the two settled shortly after in the Monastery of San Damiano just outside Assisi.[22]

All her life, Clare struggled to obtain papal recognition for her Franciscan form of life. The popes, whose agenda at the time was to try to amalgamate and codify the diverse expressions of religious life for women, had little sympathy for Clare's novelty. Rather, they imposed on her and her sisters The Rule of Saint Benedict. Clare negotiated the Privilege of Poverty,[23] which guaranteed that the sisters living within the Monastery of San Damiano would not be forced to accept possessions. Clare's refusal to accept endowments for her monastery along with the accompanying privileges that property entailed kept the sisters of San Damiano close to the experience of those who were poor and outcast in society. Agnes of Prague worked in tandem with Clare to negotiate not only for the Privilege of Poverty, but also for a Rule that would acknowledge the place of the Poor Ladies within the Franciscan movement.[24] On August 9, 1253, Clare received papal approval of her Rule in which she placed poverty at the center.[25] She died two days later on August 11, 1253.

Agnes of Prague,[26] (1211-1282),[27] was the youngest daughter of King Přemysl Otakar I and Queen Constance of Hungary. Agnes's mother was a sister to Andrew II of Hungary, the father of Saint Elizabeth.[28] Constance was the second wife of Otakar; the first, Adele, was the daughter of the margrave of Meissen. Otakar and Adele had four children. As time passed, Otakar grew tired of Adele preferring the younger

Constance. He used the fact that Adele was a distant relative as grounds for dispensation, and convinced Bishop Daniel of Prague to annul the marriage. Adele appealed to Pope Innocent III, but died before the matter was settled. Constance and Otakar had nine children. Otakar's oldest living son from this second marriage, Wenceslas I, became his successor.[29]

Agnes's father was a master politician who secured for Bohemia its hereditary dynasty.[30] Anxious to expand and protect his kingdom, Otakar betrothed his daughters diplomatically. At the age of three, Agnes was sent to Silesia with her older sister, Anna, who was to be engaged to Henry II, son of the duke of Silesia.[31]

Anna and Agnes were placed under the care of their aunt, Duchess (Saint) Hedwig of Silesia (1174-1243).[32] Hedwig arranged that the young Agnes be cared for by the Cistercian nuns of Trebnitz.[33] Anna stayed in Silesia and was married to Henry II in 1216.[34]

Upon her return to Prague, Agnes was sent to the Premonstratensian convent of Doxany in Bohemia.[35] In 1143, this convent had been founded by Queen Gertrude, Agnes's grandmother, for the purpose of educating daughters of the aristocracy. Its nuns were daughters of the highest nobility, and the convent was known for its pedagogical excellence. It was here that Agnes learned to read.[36]

Sometime during 1219-1220, Agnes was betrothed to Henry VII, son of the German emperor Frederick II. Since Henry was in residence with Duke Leopold VI of Austria, Agnes was sent to Vienna to begin her formation as queen.[37] Taking advantage of changing political situations, Leopold VI, however, undermined Otakar's agreement with Frederick and negotiated a wedding between his own daughter Margaret and Henry.[38] This arrangement threatened Otakar's regional dominance and offset the delicate political equilibrium in Europe. Agnes returned to Bohemia[39] and Otakar declared war on the duke of Austria. Although Otakar I negotiated an armistice with the Austrian duke, the Bohemian/Austrian conflict continued during the reigns of Otakar's successors.[40]

Meanwhile, Agnes was designing a plan of her own. The Franciscan spirit was welcomed not only by Agnes, but also by a substantial number of the royal family of Premyslids,[41] including Agnes's cousin, Elizabeth of Hungary. In Eastern Europe, the Franciscan movement initially had its greatest impact on the upper classes of society, a phenomena opposite that which happened in Italy.[42]

After the marriage between Henry VII and Leopold of Austria's daughter Margaret, Otakar focused his efforts toward obtaining a political alliance with England, again taking advantage of Agnes's marriageable status. Talks began which proposed Henry III, king of England,[43] as a possible suitor for Agnes.[44] These negotiations proceeded slowly perhaps because of Agnes's reluctance, and also perhaps because Otakar preferred to wait for a more advantageous political alliance.[45]

In 1231, Emperor Frederick II, who had been recently widowed, asked for Agnes's hand in marriage.[46] At this last proposal, Agnes appealed to Pope Gregory IX. In the end, her brother, King Wenceslas I rejected the emperor's request. *The Legend of Agnes of Prague* 2:2, describes the dynamics of the scene:

> And in order that she might more surely persevere in her resolution, which she conceived through God's inspiration, putting her hand to strong things, through trustworthy and discreet messengers, she made known her intention to the noble vicar of Christ, the Lord Pope Gregory IX. This felicitous pope rejoiced at the most generous devotion of the virgin, encouraged her by his gracious letter which he sent back by the same messengers, commended and confirmed her holy resolution, and with many spiritual gifts invited her to be his adopted daughter and accorded her his devoted paternal affection all the rest of his days.

Clare's Letters to Agnes

The daughter of Christ was filled with spiritual consolation by these things that she received by way of reply from the High Pontiff, and immediately, fearlessly explained her resolution to her brother the Lord King Wenceslas I. When the king heard this, he was not without great anxiety, as would be expected, about how to excuse himself, and he dispatched messengers to disclose to the emperor what his sister had resolved to do.

It is said that the emperor replied to their message in the following manner: "If this affront had been committed against us by any man, under no condition would we desist from avenging the insult of such contempt. However, since she has rather chosen a Lord who is greater than we, we do not consider this to be any insult against us, for we believe that this thing has been done through divine inspiration." Therefore, with words of praise he highly extolled the virgin's good intention and sent her rich gifts and many relics, exhorting her to bring to a fruitful end what she had happily begun.[47]

On November 17, 1231, Agnes's cousin Elizabeth of Hungary, who was only a few years older than Agnes, died at the age of twenty-four. Elizabeth's care of famine victims, her founding of a hospital out of her own modest means for the poor and sick (1228), and many other stories concerning Elizabeth's saintly generosity were well known to Agnes. Elizabeth was canonized by Gregory IX on May 25, 1235.[48]

In 1233, Agnes followed Elizabeth's example by establishing a hospital. The building of hospitals for the merciful care of the poor, abandoned, and ill, especially the incurable lepers, was common to the penitential spirit. Agnes placed the care of this hospital in the hands of a pious lay brotherhood, the Crosiers of the Red Star, who organized themselves with the help of the Friars Minor. This

Introduction

brotherhood was the first religious Order native to Bohemia and already in Agnes's lifetime extended its network of social outreach beyond the borders of Bohemia.[49]

Agnes also built a monastery for women and a convent for the friars who would serve as its chaplains. She sent messengers to Rome asking for papal approval for her monastery and requested sisters who followed the form of life of the Poor Sisters of San Damiano. With Gregory IX's approval, Clare sent Agnes five sisters from Trent.[50] Since Trent was part of the Austrian Tyrol, these sisters spoke German, a language commonly understood in Prague.[51]

On June 11, 1234, at the age of twenty-three, Agnes entered the Monastery of the Most Holy Redeemer. Seven bishops officiated and Agnes's brother, King Wenceslas I, and the queen were present for the historic event.[52]

Her role as abbess of this monastery brought her early difficulties with Gregory IX over the question of poverty. With *Cum relicta saeculi* (May 18, 1235),[53] Gregory IX established Agnes's monastery as the beneficiary of the revenues that Agnes had handed over to the Hospital of Saint Francis. This violated the Franciscan ideal of living without property that was so dear to the hearts of the earliest Franciscans. After Agnes leveled a series of protests, the pope retracted[54] and entrusted the direction and revenue of the hospital to the Crosiers of the Red Star.[55]

Correspondence surrounding Agnes illustrates that she was truly captivated by the Franciscan ideal. Clare's tender affection for Agnes, whom she had met only through letters and through the description of messengers, united Clare with the missionary zeal of the brothers. Having been caught in the currents of noble politicking and intrigue, Agnes knew the emptiness of the propertied life, and desired to embrace with all her heart a Rule that would soundly preserve Francis and Clare's ideal of living without property. Both she and Clare received their wish when Innocent IV approved Clare's Rule[56] on August 9, 1253, just two days before Clare's death. Clare's

Clare's Letters to Agnes

Rule, the first ever to be approved that was written by a woman, solved for a time ecclesiastical interference concerning the practice of poverty that both Clare and Agnes had promised to follow.

Agnes outlived Clare by thirty years. As Agnes grew older, the political situation in her beloved Bohemia became more and more precarious. Ecclesiastics repeatedly attempted to persuade Agnes to accept property and revenues in order to protect her from the destitution that falls to the poor during times of war and famine. Knowing well the consequences, Agnes and her sisters steadfastly rejected these privileges.[57]

Although Agnes repeatedly used her influence to try to insure peace and stability for her beloved Bohemia, her nephew King Otakar II's hunger for power and possessions, and his propensity to achieve these ends by means of despotic cruelty, eventually undermined political discretion. Despite warnings from his aunt, and despite a lack of solid allegiance from the Bohemian nobility, Otakar decided to make war against Rudolph of Hapsburg and died in battle on August 26, 1278.[58] Rudolph entrusted Otto, the margrave of Brandenburg, with Bohemia. Otto, a grandnephew of Agnes, misused his power, destroying and plundering royal and ecclesiastical property. He kept the king's widow, Cunegunda, and her three children imprisoned in a castle in northern Bohemia.[59]

Famine, epidemics, and incessant warfare followed in Bohemia, and Agnes's convent became a refuge for the sick and hungry as well as a stronghold of Bohemian pride. There were floods that, along with bringing hardship and disease to an already stressed population, prohibited the mills from operating. Inflation soared. Meat, fish, cheese, eggs, and grain products were difficult to find. Some reports speak about robberies, armed assaults, murders, blood feuds, terrible hunger, mass graves, and even cannibalism. Agnes, who had chosen to live without property against the wishes of those who wanted to protect her nobility from the plight of the poor, now shared in the plight of the destitute and oppressed.[60]

Introduction

On March 2, 1282, Agnes died in her convent in Prague exhausted by hunger, like so many other Bohemians.[61] Bonagracia Tielci, the minister general of the Friars Minor, said her funeral and was accompanied by a great multitude of the poor, diseased, and hungry.[62] She was beatified by Pope Pius IX in 1874.[63]

It was not until November 12, 1989, that Agnes was canonized by Pope John Paul II.[64] John Paul II had asked to come to Czechoslovakia in order to canonize the thirteenth century Bohemian princess, but the government refused permission. Although the canonization was held in Rome, the ramifications were felt in Prague. The people of Prague took to the streets praying before the statue of Agnes in Wenceslas Square and singing hymns. The Communist government resigned on the last day of the novena to Saint Agnes. Seven hundred years after her death, Agnes, the peacemaker, who had once been the royal hope for Bohemians under foreign domination, now seemed to come to the aid of her people again.[65]

Method of This Text

Clare's medieval Franciscan culture permeates her letters. In order to understand more fully Clare's use of scripture passages, her improvisations on *The Legend of Saint Agnes of Rome*, and her references to Agnes of Prague's concerns, Clare's letters need to be studied in context. The reader of these letters wonders why Clare used particular scripture passages, what her source was for *The Legend of Saint Agnes of Rome*, and what the issues were that she alludes to in her letters to Agnes of Prague.

Although no source analysis will satisfactorily answer all contemporary questions, rushing into a hermeneutic on Clare's letters without pondering the clues she leaves in regard to their context invites misinterpretation. To render Clare's letters as purely spiritual documents devoid of history would be to reduce the early Poor Ladies to the realms of rarified, albeit blessed, obscurity. Studying Clare's letters to Agnes within the context of other contemporary historical documents reveals new perspectives on Clare, Agnes, and their sisters that command respect, admiration, and discipleship.

Given the above conviction, I spoke with Brother Edward Coughlin, OFM, of The Franciscan Institute regarding the pursuit of such a contextual study. In devising a process for the study, we both agreed that it needed to begin with a translation of the letters. This translation attempts both to make Clare's letters relevant to moderns, and to invite moderns into Clare's world. It is believed that, respecting Clare's culture and context will provide the reader with richer resources for a contemporary hermeneutic.

The translations being done, the next step of part one was to research an extensive commentary on each of Clare's letters in the form of notes. This research was intended to discern what avenues of contextual study might offer further possibilities, and what avenues might provide only peripheral wanderings.

With the translation of the texts and an extensive commentary in hand, a number of theses were identified that seemed to have the potential of offering insight into Clare's sources. After researching the merits of these theses, three substantial sources of Clare's letters were positively identified, and essays regarding these sources comprise part two of this text.

The first of these essays entitled, "*The Legend of Saint Agnes of Rome* as Source," studies Clare's use of *The Legend of Saint Agnes of Rome*. While doing this research, it became obvious that Clare's reference to *The Legend of Saint Agnes* could not be fully traced through a knowledge of the antiphons and responsories of the January 21, Office of Saint Agnes alone. A few scholars had suggested the liturgy of the consecration of virgins as Clare's source of the Agnes legend,[66]

Introduction

but further study did not substantiate this thesis. It seems that Clare improvised on *The Legend of Saint Agnes* itself, which she surely knew through popular sources and perhaps also through the Regula breviary which included the entire text of *The Legend of Saint Agnes*.

The spirit of Clare's letters is obviously comparable to the spirit of the early Franciscan brothers. There is evidence that suggests that Clare used scriptural word groups in the same way that these same word groups were used in the writings of the early brothers. In other words, it seems as though the early Franciscan movement had its own slogans or jargon that might be partially identified through a careful study of Clare's letters. Using Boccali's apparatus in the 1995 edition of *Fontes Franciscani*[67] as a tool for researching this possibility, the second essay, "The Primitive Franciscan Climate As Source: Clare's Letters and the Early Brothers," examines this thesis. Father Theodore Zweerman's careful reading of my first draft of this essay provided additions to Boccali's work of which I am most grateful. Although not claiming to be exhaustive of all possible texts, aspects of this comparative study between Clare's letters and the writings of the early brothers provide essential insights into Clare's theology and context.

The third essay, "The Privilege of Poverty as Source: Clare's Letters Amid Papal and Royal Correspondence," places Clare's letters within the context of other relevant correspondence. Although study has been done to place these letters within the context of papal bulls especially those found in the *Bullarium Franciscanum*,[68] Czech documents have been largely ignored. Through the expert translation skills of Medieval Latinist Paige McDonald, who translated hundreds of pages of difficult juridical texts, the interactive papal and royal context is becoming clearer.

Part three contains an English translation of *The Legend of Saint Agnes of Rome* translated by my colleague Julia Fleming, Ph.D., of Creighton University. The text of this translation is presented in lessons just as it is divided in Regula breviary manuscript, Assisi, Sacro Convento, 694.

From the beginning, this project strove to be international, reviewing literature and working with scholars in Italian, German, Czech, English, Catalon, Spanish, Dutch, French, and Latin. From this literature and these conversations, I extracted what I felt could be tested and substantiated. I have been heartened by the dedication and generosity of those in the international community of Clare scholars that I have had the privilege to meet through this project.

There are numerous colleagues who assisted me with the preparation of this manuscript. As mentioned above, Dr. Julia Fleming and Paige McDonald were valuable, patient, and competent colleagues. Providing consultation with various language projects were Dr. Andreas Gommermann, Yvonne Reher, Sr. Dolorosa Kremlacek, ND, Sr. Suzanne Noffke, OP, Sr. Ludmila Pospíšilová, OSF, Fr. Richard McGloin, S.J., Dr. Thomas Coffey, Dr. Geoffrey Bakewell, Fr. Reginald Foster, OCD, Maria Teresa Vanderboegh, Jean François Godet, and Vanda Bočanová.

Dr. Carol Lanham of Rhetorica, Inc., offered her expertise in the difficult task of translating Clare's salutations, and Holly Coty of Stanford University was particularly helpful with the final editing of Clare's letters. Despite all this expert assistance, any deficiencies in translation or interpretation are my own.

I am grateful to the librarians who aided my research. The entire library staff at Creighton University is a scholar's dream, but particularly helpful to my project were Lynn Schneiderman who assisted tirelessly in obtaining interlibrary loan materials. Also helpful were Gayle Crawford, Gerry Chase, Gail Risch, Marina Smyth of the University of Notre Dame, Brother Anthony LoGalbo of Saint Bonaventure University, and Jack Marler of Saint Louis University. Gratitude is also owed to English graduate assistant Jennifer Eimers who competently proofread the text.

Introduction

The staff of the Klementinum, particularly PhDr. Miroslava Hejnová, was most kind in providing me with manuscripts and microfilms during and after my stay in Prague. In the same way, I am grateful to Padre Pasquale Magro and Stefano Cannelli of the Biblioteca Sacro Convento in Assisi who provided me with similar hospitality, to Br. Timothy Arthur, OFM, of the Old Mission in Santa Barbara, CA, and to the Newberry Library in Chicago for providing me with access and copies of manuscripts.

Scholarly critique and support is essential in the undertaking of a project such as this one. In this regard, I am deeply grateful to Sr. Edith Van den Goorbergh, OSC, Fr. Theodore Zweerman, OFM, and to Sr. Frances Teresa, OSC, who provided scholarly critique, dialogue, and personal support. I am also grateful to Dr. Ray Hobbs who generously provided me with ground transportation and professional encouragement and advice while I did research in Prague.

This project was made possible through grants given by the Graduate School of Creighton University; the College of Arts and Sciences, Creighton University; and the Chicago Poor Clare's Endowment Fund.

Clare's Letters to Agnes

Notes

[1]crebrius suis graciosis literis materne reverenter ac affectuosissime consolans, studiose in sancto proposito confortavit. *LegAg* 4:3. The *Legend of Saint Agnes of Prague*, like other medieval legends, was written to promote and inspire the Agnes cult, not as a modern historical account. This being recognized, it is also true that the author of the legend was concerned with the veracity of his project. He was a friar of the Bohemian province living in Prague probably in the friary attached to Agnes's own monastery who relied on eyewitnesses that he refers to by name in the legend. He wrote the legend shortly after the death of Agnes. Many of the details found in the legend are substantiated by other historical sources. In the prologue of the legend, the author promises to write only about those things that he learned from credible witnesses. For a critical evaluation of the historical value of *The Legend of Saint Agnes of Prague* see Jan Kapistrán Vyskočil, *Legenda Blahoslavené Anežky a čtyri listy Sv. Kláry* (Prague: Nakladatelství Universum, 1932), 90-93.

All Latin references to the legend in this text rely on Vyskočil's critical edition. Divisions of the legend follow the *Canonizationis Beatae Agnetis de Bohemia* (Rome: Sacra Congregatio Pro Causis Sanctorum, 1987), 214-46.

[2]See "Un codice pragense a Milano con testo inedito della vita di S. Agnese di Praga," *Rendiconti dell'Istituto Lombardo di Scienze e Lettere* (1896): 392-96.

[3]*AASS*, Mart. I:505-7.

[4]*AF* III (1897): 184-86.

[5](Aberdeen: The University Press, 1915).

[6]Walter Seton, "The Letters from Saint Clare to Blessed Agnes of Bohemia," *AFH* 17 (1924): 509-10.

[7]Walter Seton, "Some New Sources for the Life of Blessed Agnes of Bohemia," *British Society of Franciscan Studies* 7 (1915): 17-18.

[8]Seton, "The Letters," 510.

[9]Ibid., 511.

[10]See Krsto Stošič, "Naš stari rukopis o bl. Janji iz Praga," in *Bogoslovska smotra* XIX (1931): 223-29.

[11]*Legenda Blahoslavené.*

[12]Ibid., 39-40.

[13]"Para las *Cartas* nos hemos servido del texto crítico, cuidadosamente fijado por el P. Giovanni Boccali, que ha confrontado de nuevo las

Introduction

---

ediciones conocidas con el manuscrito original de la Biblioteca del Cabildo de la Basílica Ambrosiana y con el de la Biblioteca Ambrosiana de Milán," 22-23.

[14]"Comme nous l'avons déjà signalé dans l'Introduction, le texte original des *Lettres à Agnès de Prague* est celui de l'édition critique de J. K. Vyskočil," 79.

[15]Perhaps the best biography is Marco Bartoli's, *Chiara d'Assisi* (Roma: Institut Storico dei Cappuccini, 1989). This text is translated into English as *Clare of Assisi*, trans. Frances Teresa, OSC (Quincy, IL: Franciscan Press, 1993). See also Ingrid J. Peterson, OSF, *Clare of Assisi: A Biographical Study* (Quincy, IL: Franciscan Press, 1993).

[16]See Arnaldo Fortini, "Nuove Notizie Intorno a S. Chiara di Assisi," *AFH* 46 (1952): 3-43; translated by M. Jane Frances, PCC, under the title "New Information about Saint Clare of Assisi," *GR* 7 (1993): 27-69.

[17]*Proc* 12:2; 17:3.

[18]See the witness of Lady Bona, *Proc* 17:5. See also Luigi Padovese, "La 'Tonsura' di Chiara: Gesto di Consacrazione o Segno di Penitenza?," *Laurentianum* 31 (1990): 389-404; translated by Madonna Balestrieri, OSF, under the title "Clare's Tonsure: Act of Consecration or Sign of Penance?," *GR* 6 (1992): 67-80.

[19]For information regarding this monastery see Arnaldo Fortini, *Nova Vita di San Francesco*, vol. 1 (Santa Maria degli Angeli: Edizioni Assisi, 1959), 425-30. For an edited English translation see, Arnaldo Fortini, *Francis of Assisi*, trans. Helen Moak (New York: Crossroad: 1992), 341-45.

[20]*Proc* 12:4; 18:3; 20:6.

[21]*Proc* 12:5. For information concerning this monastery see Francesco Santucci, "S. Angelo di Panzo presso Assisi," in *Atti Accademia Properziana del Subasio in Assisi* 13 (1986): 83-112; translated by Lori Pieper, SFO, under the title "Sant'Angelo di Panzo Near Assisi," *GR* 8 (1994): 219-38.

[22]*LegCl* 24-26.

[23]See *Sicut manifestum est, BF* I:771.

[24]For further details on the Privilege of Poverty see the essay, "The Privilege of Poverty as Source: Clare's Letters Amid Papal and Royal Correspondence," pages 207-49 of this volume.

[25]For the text of Clare's Rule see the August 9, 1253 papal bull, *Solet annuere, BF* I:671-78. Clare's placement of poverty as the center of her Rule is the thesis of Margaret Carney's study, *The First Franciscan Woman: Clare of Assisi and Her Form of Life* (Quincy, IL: Franciscan Press, 1993).

[26]The following are helpful sources for the life of Agnes of Prague: Jaroslav Polc, *Agnes von Böhmen 1211-1282: Königstochter—Äbtissin—*

Clare's Letters to Agnes

Heilige (München: R. Oldenbourg Verlag, 1989); Alfonso Marini, *Agnese di Boemia* (Roma: Istituto Storico dei Cappuccini, 1991); Jaroslav Nemec, *Agnese di Boemia: La Vita, Il Culto, La 'Legenda'* (Padova: Edizioni Messaggero, 1987). For background information in English see Peter Demetz, *Prague in Black and Gold: Scenes from the Life of a European City* (New York: Hill and Wang, 1997): 48-52; Petr Pitha, "Agnes of Prague—A New Bohemian Saint," *FranzStud* 72 (1990): 325-40; and Poor Clare Colettine Community, *Aneska: Princess of the House of Premysl* (Wales: Tŷ Mam Duw, 1996).

[27] The date of Agnes's birth is not known for certain. Various sources suggest dates from 1205-1211. Because the legend consistently refers to Agnes's age, rather than to dates, this uncertainty about Agnes's birth date makes it difficult for historians to pinpoint other important dates of her early life. Concerning the date of Agnes's birth, Jan Kapistrán Vyskočil says the following: "The year and date of her birth are not mentioned in the legend, but the Bollandists give the date as January 20, 1205. For that reason, they say, she was given the name 'Agnes.' She was baptized by Bishop Daniel on the feast of Saint Agnes, January 21. This, however, is an addition to the legend made by Crugerius, perhaps to provide an explanation for her name. The legend does not give any further particulars concerning her birth, but it does give other information about her life, important for determining the date of her birth. For example, the legend says that she was fourteen years of age when she returned from Austria, and this happened in the year 1225; thus she must have been born in the year 1211. Pulkava places the birth of Agnes's older brother Wenceslas I in the year 1207 (*FRB*, V:121, 290); on the basis of this Beda Franziskus Dudík, *Dějiny Moravy*, vol. V (Praha: B. Tempský, 1875), 167, claims that Agnes was born in 1208. This same date is listed by Jiří Palacký, *Dejiny Národu Českého*, vol. I (Praha: Stráz, 1968), 2, 346, in his genealogy of the Přemysl family. Walter W. Seton in *Some New Sources*, 45, gives the date 1205, following the Bollandists, saying that this date is unanimously accepted; but he does not offer any proof of his own. Therefore, the most probable date of Blessed Agnes's birth is the year 1211." *Legenda Blahoslavené*, note 18, 152. The English translations of Vyskočil's footnotes used in this text are the work of Vitus Buresh, OSB.

[28] *LegAg* 1:2.

[29] For further information regarding Agnes's family see Polc, *Agnes von Böhmen*, 11-18.

[30] Kamil Krofta, "Bohemia to the Extinction of the Přemyslids," in *The Cambridge Medieval History*, vol. VI (New York: The Macmillan Company, 1929), 434-36; J. F. N. Bradley, *Czechoslovakia* (Edinburgh: Edinburgh University Press, 1971), 16-18.

Introduction

[31]Agnes had a third sister, Blažena (known as Guglielma Boema in Italian sources). She and her son settled in Milan and were eventually given a home in the Cistercian abbey of Chiaravalle. There Blažena attracted a group of followers who marveled at her piety, humility, and virtue, and who credited her with miraculous healings. Blažena died on August 24, 1282, only a few months after the death of her younger sister Agnes. The Chiaravalle abbey built an altar and a chapel above her grave. Soon after, her cult became convinced that Blažena was the female incarnation of the Holy Spirit. The Inquisition could not tolerate such claims and eventually discredited Blažena disinterring her body and burning her corpse. Three of her followers also went to the stake. The Czechs, proud of their saintly dynasty and Hussite martyrs, have all but forgotten her. See Demetz, *Prague*, 52-53; and Polc, *Agnes von Böhmen*, 15-16.

[32]Vyskočil notes: "This was probably in the year 1214. About the year 1216, her older sister Anna was espoused to Henry of Silesia." *Legenda Blahoslavené*, note 20, 152.

[33]*LegAg* 1:4.

[34]Vyskočil speculates that following Anna's marriage in 1216, Agnes returned to Bohemia: "This ended the education of Agnes's older sister Anna in the convent of Trebnitz; and Agnes, who was there to be educated with Anna, was returned to her parents." *Legenda Blahoslavené*, note 23, 153.

[35]*LegAg* 1:5.

[36]Meta Harrsen postulates that a manuscript at the Pierpont Morgan Library was a gift sent to Agnes when Agnes was at the Doxany convent. See *Cursus Sanctae Mariae: A Thirteenth-Century Manuscript, Now M. 739 in The Pierpont Morgan Library* (New York: The Pierpont Morgan Library, 1937), 8.

[37]*LegAg* 1:7-8.

[38]*Cronica Reinhardsbrunnensis*, MGH SS 30/1, 606-7. A few years after his marriage, Henry, unhappy with a wife ten years older than he and still not in possession of the dowry promised by Duke Leopold, dissolved his marriage with Margaret of Austria claiming it invalid because of his former engagement to Agnes of Prague. Because Frederick wanted to win the favor of Austria, he found his son's behavior politically unnerving. Seeing Henry's future as precarious, Agnes's brother, Wenceslas I, remained loyal to Frederick. Frederick II eventually took Henry, his wife Margaret, and their two sons as prisoners to Apulia. After some time, he freed Margaret and her sons, but Henry died a prisoner of his father in 1242. See Polc, *Agnes von Böhmen*, 36-37.

[39]*LegAg* 1:10.

[40]See Bradley, *Czechoslovakia*, 18-19.

Clare's Letters to Agnes

---

[41]John B. Freed, *The Friars and German Society in the Thirteenth Century* (Cambridge: The Mediaeval Academy of America, 1977), 59-60, states: "The Ascanians' patronage of the Franciscans can be explained in part by Otto III's marriage to Beatrice of Bohemia, the niece of the Bl. Agnes of Prague, the foundress and abbess of the Prague Poor Clares. Through her influence the Premyslids and their relatives became particularly devoted to the Poor Clares and the Franciscans. Margrave Henry the Illustrious of Meissen (1221-1288) established the nunnery of the Poor Clares in Seusslitz in 1268 in memory of his wife Agnes, another niece of the Prague abbess. Agnes of Prague's influence was especially strong among the Silesian Piasts. Her sister, Anna of Bohemia, founded in 1257 the nunnery of the Breslau Poor Clares, where she was subsequently buried. Anna's husband, Duke Henry II of Silesia (1238-1241), who had been killed by the Mongols at Liegnitz in 1241, was interred in the convent of the Breslau Franciscans. Herbord, a Breslau Franciscan, apparently served as the confessor of Henry's and Anna's sons, Bogusław II of Liegnitz (1241-1278), Henry III of Breslau (1241-1266), Conrad of Glogau (1251-1273), and Archbishop Władysław of Salzburg (1265-1270). Their sister belonged to the nunnery of the Poor Clares in Breslau."

[42]The exact date of the friars' arrival in Prague is not known. Vyskočil proposes the following: "The Minorites, Agnes could have come to know as early as her stay at the Austrian court, and she certainly would have met them at her father's court, for they came there from the Thuringian court, where they were trusted counselors and confessors to Saint Elizabeth and her husband, Ludwig. The chronicle of Fr. Jordan of Giano specifically mentions a certain Fr. Rodeger, who later became guardian in Halberstadt, identifying him as Saint Elizabeth's teacher and adviser, from whom she learned how to observe chastity, humility, patience, vigils in prayer, and diligence in works of mercy. It can be presupposed almost with certainty that the Minorites made such a visit when Landgrave Ludwig came in 1226, to placate Přemysl and to reconcile him with Leopold of Austria. Their advice during such a mission was certainly needed." *Legenda Blahoslavené*, note 49, 157.

[43]Vyskočil describes Henry III's proposal to Agnes as an "anti-French, political scheme." *Legenda Blahoslavené*, note 32, 155.

[44]*LegAg* 1:10.

[45]Vyskočil speculates in this manner: "Why, then, did not anything come of these negotiations which had been opened, when in the letter of the English king there is expressed a desire that the negotiations be completed—when from his last letter it can be concluded that even Přemysl, who opened negotiations, lost interest; rather one can imagine Agnes's opposition. Precisely because Přemysl was not as much interested

Introduction

---

now in an English marriage as in an imperial one, he would more readily delay any further negotiations. Here the legend elaborates by recording a miracle, but it does not invent the incident; for the author could have been well-informed concerning this matter." *Legenda Blahoslavené*, note 32, 155.

[46]There are numerous documents attesting to Frederick's proposal. Gregory IX refers to it in his letter to Beatrice of Castille, *BF* I:164-67; as does Clare herself in *1LAg* 5. See also *Annales Stadenses* in *MGH SS*, 16, 363.

[47]Et ut in suo proposito, quod deo inspirante conceperat, securius permaneret, manum mittens ad forcia, nobili Cristi vicario domino pape Gregorio nono per honestos nuncios et discretos suum ocultum intentum patefecit. Qui felix antistes tam generose virginis devocioni congaudens, per eosdem nuncios ipsam graciosis litteris in domino confortavit, propositum eius sanctum commendans pariter et confirmans, adoptatamque in filiam multis spiritualibus donis invisit, cunctis diebus suis eam prosequens pii patris affectu. At Cristi famula de hiis, que a summo pontifice receperat, in responsis multa spiritus consolacione repleta, statim propositum suum germano suo domino regi Wencesslao intrepide propalavit. Quo rex audito non sine magna turbacione ad se ut decuit excusandum sororisque propositum detegendum imperatori nuncios destinavit. Ad quorum legacionem imperator fertur taliter respondise: "Si a quocumque homine nobis hec iniuria illata fuisset, tante despeccionis obprobrium vindicare nullatenus cessaremus. Sed quia nobis maiorem dominum perelegit, hoc despectui nostro nequaquam asscribimus, cum instinctu divino istud factum credamus." Unde intencionem bonam virginis magnis extollens laudum preconiis, preciosa ei munera et reliquias multas transmisit, hortans per litteras et inducens, ut quod salubriter cepit feliciter consumaret.

[48]See the canonization bull, *Gloriosus in Majestate*, *BF* I:162-64.

[49]For the history of this Order see Milan M. Buben, *Rytířský Řád Křižovníků S Červenou Hvězdou* (Praha: L. P., 1996), and V. Bělohlávek, *Dějiny českých křižovníků s červenou hvězdou* (Prague: Nákl. rádu Ceských krizovníku, 1930).

[50]*LegAg* 3:3.

[51]Poor Clare Colettine Community, *Aneska*, 7.

[52]*LegAg* 3:3-4. Concerning the date of Agnes's entrance, Vyskočil suggests that "perhaps the best solution to this question can be made by using the papal letters as a guide. According to the pope's letter of August 30, 1234 (*Sincerum animi tui*), Agnes was already then in the convent, for the pope instructed her in that letter to recite the Office according to the Gallican Psalter and received her convent and hospital under his protection.

Clare's Letters to Agnes

On the next day, he issued a letter (*Sincerum animi carissimae*) in which he instructed John, the provincial of Saxony, and Thomas, the custodian in Bohemia, to make Agnes the abbess of the convent of Saint Francis. Before this date, there was no mention of Agnes in the pope's letters, but in 1234 suddenly four letters in succession were written concerning Agnes. From this it can be concluded that in that year, at Pentecost, Agnes entered the convent." *Legenda Blahoslavené*, note 61, 158.

[53]*BF* I:156.

[54]This retraction can be seen by examining the differences between *Prudentibus Virginibus* issued on July 25, 1235 (*BF* I:171-72) and *Prudentibus Virginibus* issued on April 14, 1237 (*BF* I:215-16).

[55]See *Omnipotens Deus*, *CDB* III:195-98. On the juridical dealings concerning Agnes's royal dowry see Joan Mueller, "Agnes of Prague and the Juridical Implications of the Privilege of Poverty," *FS* (2000): 261-87.

[56]*Solet annuere*, *BF* I:671-78.

[57]*LegAg* 5:1.

[58]See Krofta, *The Cambridge Medieval History*, "Bohemia to the Extinction of the Přemyslids," 439-40.

[59]Polc, *Agnes von Böhmen*, 136-39.

[60]*LegAg* 5:3-4. See also Polc, *Agnes von Böhmen*, 139-41.

[61]*LegAg* 11:1. From 1281 until the middle of 1282 there was a severe famine in Bohemia. *LegAg* 15:5 states that more than three hundred thousand people died. Vyskočil, *Legenda Blahoslavené*, note 282, 176, writes: "Really there was a famine followed by a pestilence in Bohemia as a result of revolts and civil wars, but this famine came in 1281 and lasted until the middle of 1282. This date was established by Palacký on the basis of the consensus of chroniclers; all the ancient chroniclers speak of the horrors of famine and pestilence in those years."

[62]*LegAg* 12:1-4.

[63]The official documents regarding Agnes's beatification can be found in *Acta Sanctae Sedis*, VIII (1874): 299, and 406-24.

[64]For a summary of the history of Agnes's cause see *Canonizationis Beatae Agnetis de Bohemia*, Officium Historicum 168 (Rome: Sacra Congregatio pro Causis Sanctorum, 1987), viii-xii, and 19-25.

[65]Poor Clare Colettine Community, *Aneska*, 1. See also Jonathan Luxmoore and Jolanta Babiuch, *The Vatican and the Red Flag: The Struggle for the Soul of Eastern Europe* (New York: Geoffrey Chapman, 1999), 291-92.

[66]See for example, Regis Armstrong, OFM Cap., ed. and trans., *Clare of Assisi: Early Documents* (Saint Bonaventure, NY: Franciscan Institute Publications, 1993), 33; and Edith Van den Goorbergh, OSC, and Theodore

Introduction

Zweerman, OFM, *Light Shining Through a Veil: On Saint Clare's Letters to Saint Agnes of Prague* (Leuven: Peeters, 2000), 44.
[67](S. Maria degli Angeli—Assisi: Edizioni Porziuncola).
[68]See particularly the work of Maria Pia Alberzoni in *Chiara e Il Papato* (Milano: Edizioni Biblioteca Francescana, 1995); and in "'Nequaquam a Christi sequela in perpetuum absolvi desidero:' Chiara tra Carisma e Istituzione," *Chiara d'Assisi e la Memoria di Francesco*, Atti del convegno per l'VIII centenario della nascità di S. Chiara (Rieti: Petruzzi Editore, 1995): 41-65; translated into English by Nancy Celaschi, OSF as "'Nequaquam a Christi sequela in perpetuum absolvi desidero:' Clare between Charism and Institution," in *GR* 12 (1998): 81-121.

PART ONE

CLARE'S LETTERS TO AGNES

Clare's First Letter
To Agnes of Prague

Clare's first letter was most likely written after Pentecost, June 11, 1234, the day of Agnes's entrance into the monastery at Prague. Elated that Agnes had rejected a marriage to Frederick II in order to embrace the following of the Poor Christ, Clare, who was in her early forties and had entered San Damiano twenty-two years earlier, began her correspondence with the twenty-three year old Agnes.

The decision of the royal Bohemian princess to enter the Franciscan Order tipped the balance of power in Europe. Since her childhood Agnes's father, Otakar I, in the hope of advancing his own political agendas, maneuvered a series of marital contracts for his daughter. Frederick II asked for Agnes's hand in the spring of 1228. Pope Gregory IX opposed this union for political reasons. It seems that sometime after his return from Jerusalem in 1231, most probably during 1233, Frederick issued a second request for a marriage with Agnes. Agnes rejected the emperor's proposal, founded a monastery and the Hospital of Saint Francis in Prague and, according to her legend, asked the Friars Minor to instruct her concerning the form of life of the Monastery of San Damiano.

Clare's letter is a hymn to the "sacred exchange," the giving of all of one's goods to the poor in the hope of obtaining both earthly necessities as well as eschatological rewards. Reflecting on The Legend of Saint Agnes of Rome, Clare focuses not so much on Agnes of Rome's bravery in the face of martyrdom as on her fidelity to her bridegroom, the Poor Christ.

(1) Venerabili et sanctissimae virgini, dominae Agneti, filiae excellentissimi ac illustrissimi regis Bohemiae, (2) Clara, indigna famula Iesu Christi et ancilla *inutilis*[1] dominarum inclusarum monasterii Sancti Damiani, sua ubique subdita et ancilla, recommendationem sui omnimodam cum reverentia speciali aeternae felicitatis *gloriam adipisci.*[2]

(3) Vestrae sanctae conversationis et vitae honestissimam famam audiens, quae non solum mihi, sed fere in toto est orbe terrarum egregie divulgata, *gaudeo* plurimum *in Domino et exsulto;*[3] (4) de quo non tantum ego singularis valeo exsultare, sed universi qui faciunt et facere desiderant servitium Iesu Christi.

(5) Hinc est quod, cum perfrui potuissetis prae ceteris pompis et honoribus et saeculi dignitate, cum gloria excellenti valentes inclito Caesari legitime desponsari, sicut vestrae ac eius excellentiae decuisset, (6) quae omnia respuentes, toto animo et cordis affectu magis sanctissimam paupertatem et corporis penuriam elegistis, (7) sponsum *nobilioris generis*[4] accipientes, Dominum Iesum Christum, qui vestram virginitatem semper immaculatam custodiet et illaesam.

---

[1]Cf., Lc 17:10.
[2]Cf., Sir 50:5.
[3]Hab 3:18.
[4]Cf., Regula breviary, January 21, Saint Agnes of Rome, Matins: 1st nocturn, 2nd lesson.

The First Letter

(1) To the venerable[1] and most holy virgin, the Lady Agnes, daughter of the most renowned[2] and illustrious[3] king of Bohemia,[4] (2) Clare, unworthy servant[5] of Jesus Christ[6] and useless[7] handmaid[8] of the enclosed ladies[9] of the Monastery of San Damiano,[10] her subject and handmaid in all circumstances,[11] commends herself in every way and sends,[12] with special respect, the prayer that Agnes attain the glory of everlasting happiness.[13]

(3) Hearing the account,[14] one that brings you the highest honor, of your[15] holy conversion and manner of life,[16] an account that has been reputably disseminated not only to me but to nearly every region of the world, I rejoice and exalt exceedingly in the Lord. (4) Concerning this news, I am not the only one able to rejoice, but also all those who serve and desire to serve Jesus Christ.[17]

(5) I rejoice because you, more than others, could have enjoyed public ostentation, honors, and worldly status having had the opportunity to become, with eminent[18] glory, legitimately married to the illustrious[19] emperor,[20] as would befit your and his pre-eminence. (6) Spurning all these things with your whole heart and mind, you have chosen instead holiest poverty[21] and physical want,[22] (7) accepting a nobler[23] spouse, the Lord Jesus Christ,[24] who will keep your virginity[25] always immaculate[26] and inviolate.[27]

(8)   *Quem cum amaveritis casta estis,*
       cum tetigeritis mundior efficiemini,[5]
       cum acceperitis virgo estis.[6]

(9)   *Cuius possibilitas fortior, generositas celsior,*
       cuius aspectus pulchrior, amor suavior
       et omnis gratia elegantior.[7]

(10)   Cuius *estis iam amplexibus astricta,*[8]
       qui pectus *vestrum*
       ornavit lapidibus pretiosis
       et *vestris auribus*
       tradidit inaestimabiles margaritas.[9]

(11)   *Et* totam *circumdedit vernantibus*
       atque coruscantibus gemmis[10]
       atque vos coronavit *aurea corona*
       signo[11] *sanctitatis expressa.*[12]

---

[5]Regula breviaries, Assisi, Sacro Convento, 694, and Chicago, Newberry Library 23 (OFM Perugia), as well as *The Breviary of St. Francis* and *The Breviary of St. Clare* use "sum" here. The verb *effecio* seems to be original to Clare.

[6]Regula breviary, January 21, Saint Agnes of Rome, Matins: 1st nocturn, 3rd lesson, 3rd responsory.

[7]Regula breviary, January 21, Saint Agnes of Rome, Matins: 1st nocturn, 2nd lesson.

[8]Regula breviary, January 21, Saint Agnes of Rome, Matins: 1st nocturn, 2nd lesson.

[9]Regula breviary, January 21, Saint Agnes of Rome, Matins: 1st nocturn, 2nd antiphon, 2nd lesson, 2nd responsory; 2nd nocturn 4th responsory; 3rd nocturn, 7th responsory.

[10]Regula breviary, January 21, Saint Agnes of Rome, Matins: 1st nocturn, 2nd lesson, 2nd responsory; 2nd nocturn, 4th responsory; 3rd nocturn, 8th antiphon.

[11]Clare uses the word *signum* from *The Legend of Saint Agnes* as a pivot to transition into Sir 45:14. Cf., Regula breviary, January 21, Saint Agnes of Rome, Matins: 1st nocturn, 2nd lesson, 3rd antiphon, 2nd responsory.

[12]Sir 45:14.

(8)   Having[28] loved him, you are chaste;
        having touched him, you will be made
        more pure;
        having received him, you are a virgin.[29]

(9)   His power[30] is stronger,
        his nobility[31] higher,
        his appearance lovelier,
        his love sweeter,[32]
        and his every grace more elegant.[33]

(10)   You are now held fast in the embraces of the
        one who has adorned[34] your breast with precious
        stones and has hung[35] priceless pearls[36] from
        your ears.

(11)   He has completely surrounded you with
        glittering[37] and sparkling gems,[38] and has
        placed on your head a golden crown[39] engraved
        with the seal[40] of holiness.

(12) Ergo, soror carissima—immo domina veneranda nimium, quia *sponsa* et *mater* estis et *soror*[13] Domini mei Iesu Christi, (13) virginitatis inviolabilis et paupertatis sanctissimae vexillo resplendentissime insignita—in sancto servitio confortamini pauperis Crucifixi ardenti desiderio inchoato. (14) Qui pro nobis omnibus *crucis sustinuit*[14] passionem, *eruens nos de potestate* principis *tenebrarum*[15]—qua ob transgressionem primi parentis vincti vinculis tenebamur—et *nos reconcilians*[16] Deo Patri.[17]

(15) O beata paupertas
quae diligentibus et amplexantibus eam
divitias praestat aeternas!

(16) O sancta paupertas,
quam habentibus et desiderantibus,
a Deo *caelorum regnum*[18] promittitur
et aeterna gloria vitaque beata
procul dubio exhibetur!

(17) O pia paupertas
quam Dominus Iesus Christus,
qui caelum terramque regebat et regit,
qui *dixit* etiam *et sunt facta*,[19]
dignatus est prae ceteris amplexari!

---

[13]Cf., Mt 12:50; 2 Cor 11:2.
[14]Hbr 12:2.
[15]Col 1:13.
[16]2 Cor 5:18.
[17]Cf., Rm 5:10; 2 Cor 5:19-20.
[18]Cf., Mt 5:3.
[19]Ps 32:9; 148:5.

The First Letter

(12) Therefore, dearest sister[41]—or should I say, most venerable lady,[42] because you are spouse and mother[43] and sister[44] of my Lord Jesus Christ,[45] (13) and are most resplendently distinguished by the banner[46] of inviolable virginity and holiest poverty[47]—be strengthened[48] in the holy service begun in you[49] out of a burning desire for the Poor Crucified. (14) For all of us he endured the passion of the cross, rescuing us from the power of the prince of darkness— by whose power we were kept in chains because of the transgression of our first parent[50]—and reconciling us to God the Father.[51]

(15) O blessed poverty
that provides eternal riches to those who love[52] and embrace it!

(16) O holy poverty,
to those who possess and desire it, God promises the kingdom of heaven[53] and, of course, gives eternal glory and a happy life!

(17) O pious[54] poverty[55]
that the Lord Jesus Christ,[56] who ruled and is ruling heaven and earth, and who spoke and all things were made, deigned to embrace before anything else!

(18) *Vulpes* enim *foveas,* inquit, *habent et volucres caeli nidos, Filius autem hominis,* id est Christus, *non habet ubi caput reclinet,*[20] sed, *inclinato capite, tradidit spiritum.*[21]

(19) Si, ergo, tantus et talis Dominus in uterum veniens virginalem, despectus, egenus, et pauper in mundo voluit apparere (20) ut homines, qui erant pauperrimi et egeni, caelestis pabuli sufferentes nimiam egestatem, efficerentur in illo divites regna caelestia possidendo,[22] (21) *exsultate* plurimum et *gaudete,*[23] repletae ingenti gaudio et laetitia spiritali. (22) Quia—cum vobis magis placuisset contemptus saeculi quam honores; paupertas quam divitiae temporales; et magis *thesauros in caelo* recondere quam in terra (23) *ubi nec rubigo consumit, nec tinea demolitur, et fures non effodiunt nec furantur*[24]*—merces vestra copiosissima est in caelis,*[25] (24) et fere digne meruistis *soror, sponsa,* et *mater*[26] altissimi Patris Filii et gloriosae Virginis nuncupari.

(25) Credo enim firmiter vos novisse quod *regnum caelorum* nonnisi *pauperibus*[27] a Domino promittitur et donatur, quia dum res diligitur temporalis fructus amittitur caritatis; (26) *Deo et mammonae deservire non posse,* quoniam *aut unus diligitur et alter odio habetur,* et *aut uni* serviet *alterum contemnet;*[28] (27) et *vestitum cum nudo* certare non posse, *quia citius ad terram deicitur qui habet unde teneatur;*[29]

---

[20]Lc 9:58
[21]Io 19:30.
[22]Cf., 2 Cor 8:9.
[23]Cf., Hab 3:18.
[24]Mt 6:20.
[25]Mt 5:12.
[26]Cf., Mt 12:50; 2 Cor 11:2.
[27]Cf., Mt 5:3.
[28]Cf., Mt 6:24.
[29]Gregory the Great, *Homilia in Evangelia* II,32,2 (*PL* 76, 1233b).

(18) For foxes have dens, he says, and the birds of the sky have nests, but the Son of Man, who is Christ, has nowhere to lay his head; instead, bowing his head, he handed over his spirit.[57]

(19) If, then, so great as such a Lord who, coming into the virgin's womb, chose to appear contemptible, needy, and poor[58] in this world[59] (20) so that human beings, who were utterly poor and needy, suffering from an extremely grave lack of heavenly food, might be made rich in him by means of the kingdom of heaven that they will indeed possess, (21) exalt exceedingly and rejoice,[60] filled with great joy and spiritual happiness. (22) Because—since contempt of the world[61] has pleased you more than its honors; poverty more than temporal riches;[62] and storing up treasures in heaven rather than on earth (23) where neither rust consumes them, nor moth[63] destroys them, and thieves do not dig them up and steal them[64]—your most abundant[65] reward is in heaven,[66] (24) and you have quite fittingly deserved to be called[67] sister, spouse, and mother[68] of the Son of the most high Father and the glorious Virgin.

(25) For, I am sure that you know that the kingdom of heaven is promised[69] and given by the Lord only to the poor,[70] because as long as something temporal is the object of love, the fruit of charity is lost. (26) You know, too, that one cannot serve God and material wealth, since either the one is loved and the other hated, or a person will serve one and despise the other. (27) You also know that a person wearing clothing cannot fight with another who is naked, because the one who has something that might be grasped is more quickly thrown to the ground.[71] (28) You know, too, that it is

(28) et gloriosum manere in saeculo et illic regnare cum Christo; et quoniam ante *foramen acus* poterit *transire camelus* scandere *quam dives* caelica *regna*.[30] (29) Ideo abiecistis vestimenta, videlicet divitias temporales, ne luctanti succumbere penitus valeretis, ut per *arctam viam* et *angustam portam*[31] possitis regna caelestia introire.

(30)   Magnum quippe ac laudabile commercium:
relinquere temporalia pro aeternis,
promereri caelestia pro terrenis,
centuplum pro uno *recipere*,
ac beatam *vitam* perpetuam *possidere*.[32]

(31) Quapropter vestram excellentiam et sanctitatem duxi, prout possum, humilibus precibus *in Christi visceribus*[33] supplicandam, quatenus in eius sancto servitio confortari velitis, (32) crescentes de bono in melius, *de virtutibus in virtutes*,[34] ut cui toto mentis desiderio deservitis, dignetur vobis optata praemia elargiri.

(33) Obsecro etiam vos in Domino, sicut possum, ut me vestram famulam, licet *inutilem*,[35] et sorores ceteras vobis devotas mecum in monasterio commorantes habere velitis in sanctissimis *vestris orationibus*[36] commendatas, (34) quibus subvenientibus mereri possumus misericordiam Iesu Christi, ut pariter una vobiscum sempiterna mereamur perfrui visione.

(35) Valete in Domino et *oretis pro*[37] me.

---

[30]Cf., Mt 19:24.
[31]Cf., Mt 7:13-14.
[32]Cf., Mt 19:29.
[33]Cf., Phil 1:8.
[34]Cf., Ps 83:8.
[35]Cf., Lc 17:10.
[36]Cf., Rm 15:30.
[37]Cf., 1Th 5:25.

not possible for a person to remain glorious in the world and to reign with Christ in heaven; and that a camel will be able to pass through the eye of a needle before a rich person ascends into the kingdom of heaven. (29) These are the reasons why you disposed of your clothing, I mean your worldly wealth,[72] so that you might have the strength not to succumb completely to the one struggling against you, so that you may enter the kingdom of heaven by the narrow road and constricted gate.

(30)　It is indeed a great and praiseworthy exchange:[73]
to give up the temporal for the everlasting,
to merit the heavenly rather than the earthly,[74]
to receive a hundredfold[75] instead of one,
to have a happy, eternal life.

(31) I thought, therefore, that I should do all I can to implore Your Excellency and Holiness with humble prayers in the innermost heart[76] of Christ,[77] given that you want to be strengthened in his holy service,[78] (32) growing from good to better, from virtue to virtue, so that the one to whose service you devote yourself with every desire of your mind may deign to bestow freely upon you the rewards you have desired.

(33) I also beseech you in the Lord, as best as I can, to be so kind as to include in your most holy prayers me, your servant, although useless,[79] and the other sisters[80] who are devoted to you who live with me in the monastery.[81] (34) By the help of your prayers, may we be able to merit[82] the mercy of Jesus Christ so that we, together with you, may deserve to enjoy the everlasting vision.

(35) Farewell in the Lord and please pray for me.

Notes

[1]*Venerabilis* is a common title found in Latin letters and can properly be used to address a lay woman of higher rank. See Sister Mary Bridget O'Brien, "Titles of Address in Christian Latin Epistolography to 543 A.D." (Ph.D. diss., The Catholic University of America, 1930), 122.

[2]An address appropriate both to laymen and ecclesiastics. Ibid., 131 and 166.

[3]A title appropriate to civil officials. Ibid., 166.

[4]The king referred to is King Přemysl Otakar I. In *3LAg* 1, Clare uses this same title to refer to Agnes's brother, Wenceslas I.

[5]O'Brien, "Titles of Address," 83. Clare follows Francis in describing herself as servant. For examples see *LtMin* 9; *LtR* 1; *2LtF* 1-2.

[6]Regis Armstrong, OFM Cap., notes that "the person of Jesus is at the very heart of this letter: Clare mentions his name nine times (vs. 2, 4, 12, 17, 18, 28, 31, and 34), more than in any of her other writings." "Starting Points: Images of Women in the Letters of Clare," *GR* 7 (1993): 353.

[7]The correct tone of the description of the sender, the *intitulatio,* was self-deprecation. See *SF*, 25.

[8]*Clara. . .ancilla*: cf., *RCl* 1:3. Cross-references to Franciscan sources will be limited in these notes to Clare's letters and Rule, and to selected early Franciscan sources. A full list of cross-references can be found in *Fontes Franciscani,* ed. Enrico Menestò and Stefano Brufani, with apparati by Giovanni M. Boccali (S. Maria degli Angeli—Assisi: Edizioni Porziuncola, 1995). For a study concerning the cross-referencing of other Franciscan sources with Clare's letters see the essay, "The Primitive Franciscanism Climate as Source: Clare's Letters and the Early Brothers," pages 149-205 in this volume.

The term *ancilla* refers to a household servant and is commonly used to describe holy Italian thirteenth-century women who were employed as domestic servants, i.e., Zita of Lucca (1218?-72), Margaret of Città di Castello (ca., 1286/7-1320), Veridiana Attavanti of Castelfiorentino (d. 1247?), Oringa or Christiana of Santa Croce sull'Arno (1240-1310), and Jane of Orvieto (ca. 1264-1306). In a monastery, the term *ancilla* was used as a proper and formal description of the religious nun: *ancilla Dei* or *ancilla Christi.* The term was frequently used specifically to describe nuns whose role was to perform domestic duties. Since we know that Clare literally performed the role of the common *ancilla* in her monastery, i.e., washing the

The First Letter

feet of the sisters (*Proc* 2:3), cleaning the mattresses of the sick sisters (*Proc* 2:1), bringing the sisters water (*Proc* 3:9), Clare's meaning, in referring to herself as *ancilla*, goes beyond the formal sense and describes her literally as the servant of her sisters. See Michael Goodich, "*Ancilla Dei*: The Servant as Saint in the Late Middle Ages," *Women of the Medieval World: Essays in Honor of John H. Mundy*, eds. Julius Kirshner and Suzanne F. Wemple (Oxford: Basil Blackwell, 1985), 119-36. In *RCl* 10:4-5, Clare outlines her concept of abbess as the *ancilla* of the sisters.

[9]*Clara. . .dominarum, 2LAg* 2; *3LAg* 2.

[10]*monasterii. . .Damiani*: cf., *4LAg* 2. The Church of San Damiano is dedicated to Saints Cosmos and Damian.

[11]In the salutation, "the modifiers themselves should be such as offer honour and respect, appropriate to the position of the recipient and conforming to his rank. But the modifiers describing the sender should touch a note of humility, suggest devotion, swear fidelity, or breathe forth the odour of charity." Transmundus, *Introductiones dictandi*, ed. and trans. Ann Dalzell (Toronto: Pontifical Institute of Mediaeval Studies, 1995), 63.

[12]"The verbs used in the salutation are 'sends,' 'directs,' 'asks,' and 'desires.' These, however, will not be written in the formula of the salutation but will be understood from the context." Ibid.

[13]Clare's salutation follows the classical formula for the salutation of a Latin letter: "the *intitulatio* (the sender's name, with his attributes), the *inscriptio*, (the name of the addressee with his attributes), and the *salutatio* (the initial greeting)." *SF*, 7.

[14]Reputation played an important role in medieval society. See Raoul Manselli's description of *fama publica* in *St. Francis of Assisi* (Chicago: Franciscan Herald Press, 1988), 26-27. Both Francis and Clare highly valued a reputation of integrity, which was built upon the solid foundation of a religious lifestyle without pretense or veneer, serving as a Christian example within the church. This notion of reputation grounded in truthful integrity is delightfully illustrated in a saying attributed to Francis in the *AC* 81: "I want to live before God, in hermitages and other places where I stay, just as the people see and know me. If they believe that I am a holy man and I do not lead a life becoming a holy man, I would be a hypocrite" [Taliter volo vivere apud Deum in heremis et aliis locis ubi maneo, qualiter homines scirent et me viderent; quoniam si credunt me sanctum hominem et non facerem vitam quam convenit facere sancto homini, essem ipocrita]." One remembers the story of Francis publicly confessing that he had eaten food prepared with lard because of his infirmity (*2C* 131; *AC* 81); or the story of Francis not allowing a fox skin to be sewn into his habit to protect his spleen

and stomach from the cold unless a skin would also be sewn on the outside of his habit for all to see (*2C* 130; *AC* 81).

Clare appropriated the spirituality of an "honest repute" already in her life before her "conversion" and deepened this spirituality through the preaching of Francis. Clare's *honestissima fama* is affirmed repeatedly in her *Process of Canonization*. Sr. Pacifica states that Clare "was considered by all those who knew her [to be a person] of great honesty [*grande honestà*] and of very good life" (*Proc* 1:1). Sister Benvenuta of Perugia says that Clare was "held in much veneration by all who knew her even before she entered religion. This was because of her great honesty [*molta honestà*], kindness, and humility" (*Proc* 2:2). Sister Beatrice confirms that "her good reputation [*bona fama*] was spread about among all who knew her," and that Francis went to preach to her after he "heard of the reputation of her holiness [*audita la fama de la sua sanctità*]" (*Proc* 12:1-2). Lord Ugolino de Pietro Girardone, a knight of Assisi, testified that Clare was "a virgin of a very upright manner of life [*honestissima conversatione*] in her father's house" (*Proc* 16:2).

[15]Clare formally addresses Agnes throughout this first letter using the polite forms of the second person pronoun coupled with the plural verb. In the following letters, she uses the familiar address. In English, the translator either has to chose between the archaic "thee" pronoun or a capitalized pronoun to illustrate this formality. This causes complications with the pronouns for Jesus Christ, which would then require an additional degree of formality. Since Clare's pronouns are numerous and the above solutions still fail to bring precise clarity, I am choosing to make the reader aware of the formality Clare uses, and here said, will reserve the use of capitals in these letters for proper titles and names.

[16]At first glance, Clare's use of *conversatio* and *vita* may seem redundant. Marco Bartoli in his *Clare of Assisi* (Quincy, IL: Franciscan Press, 1993), trans. Sister Frances Teresa, OSC, addresses this problem in his reflections on the structure of *The Process of Canonization of Saint Clare*. Bartoli explains: "Pope Innocent IV wanted to proceed as quickly as possible to the canonisation of Clare and he wrote to this effect to Bartolomeo, the archbishop of Spoleto, inviting him to institute a true and proper process to interrogate the witnesses about the *life, conversion, conversation, and miracles* of the lady of Assisi. The first term, *life* meant that period which Clare had spent living in her father's house, in other words her youth. The second term, *conversion*, meant her passage from life 'in the world' to life 'in religion.' *Conversation* covered the period she spent at San Damiano and the last term *miracles*, covered the proofs of holiness both before and after her

death. In this way the sanctity of Clare was to be studied in four distinct sections, each with its own ideal point of reference" (36).

Timothy Fry's translation of the *Rule of St. Benedict* (Collegeville, MN: The Liturgical Press, 1981), 458-66, distinguishes *conversio* from *conversatio* suggesting a translation of *conversatio* as a manner of living particular to monastic life. John E. Lawyer, "*Conversatio* in *RB*: The Making of a Christian," *Cistercian Studies Quarterly* 27 (1992): 13-27, suggests that *conversatio* is a commitment to an entire way of life lived in common with others. It is a promise to be continually converted with a community of people who are also committed to continual personal and communal conversion.

Possibilities for the translation of *conversatio* include conversion, commencement of monastic life, monastic life, taking monastic vows, conduct, or way of life. Marco Bartoli in *Santa Chiara d'Assisi: Scritti e Documenti* (Assisi: Editrici Francescane, 1994), 81, chooses the Italian word *conversazione* meaning "manner of life—especially a monastic manner of life." The Becker/Godet/Matura translation, *Claire d'Assise: Écrits* (Paris: Les Éditions du Cerf, 1985), 83, chooses the French term *conduite* meaning "conduct" or "behavior." Regis Armstrong, OFM Cap., *Clare of Assisi: Early Documents* (St. Bonaventure, NY: Franciscan Institute Publications, 193), 34, and Sr. Frances Teresa, OSC, whose translation is published in Edith Van den Goorbergh, OSC and Theodore Zweerman, OFM, *Light Shining Through a Veil: On Saint Clare's Letters to Saint Agnes of Prague* (Leuven: Peeters, 2000), 37, also translate the word as "conduct."

Clare is expressing two realities in her use of *conversatio* and *vita*. Given the context of the letter, Clare seems to be distinguishing between Agnes's embrace of the Franciscan life and her admirable living of it within her monastery.

[17]Clare describes the form of life that Agnes has chosen three times in this letter as the "service" of Christ (*1LAg* 4, 13, 31). The expression was commonly used for describing a consecrated lifestyle.

[18]*Excellens* is a difficult word to translate into modern English. Its apparent cognate is "excellent" which works to some degree here. However, the word in Medieval Latin also carries an element of royalty or station as is carried over in the sense of "Your Excellency." I choose the word "eminent" to try to capture both the sense of a glory that is "high" and "lofty" with the sense of a glory that is of "high station" or "rank."

[19]*Inclitus* is an attribute proper to an emperor. O'Brien, *Titles of Address*, 135.

[20]Jean Leclercq in "St. Clare and Nuptial Spirituality," trans. Edward Hagman, OFM Cap., *GR* 10 (1996): 171-78, originally published as "Sainte Claire et la spiritualité nuptiale," *Hagiographica* I (1994): 227-34, comments: "If we replace the Latin word *Caesar* at the end of this phrase with the name Frederick II, we can see how relevant the message was at the time and judge to what an extent (it) was part of the culture of the era" (178).

[21]*sanctissimam. . .paupertatem: 1LAg* 13; *2LAg* 7; *RCl* 6:6, 8; *1C* 39:5.

[22]Clare's words are *corporis penuriam,* literally bodily scarcity, dearth, shortage, or want. Sister Frances Teresa, OSC translates the phrase as "physical hardship." Armstrong and Becker/Godet/Matura translate the word as "destitution." Medieval Latin had the word *destitutio* that Clare could have chosen. Although the stories of Clare and her sisters do illustrate situations of grave need at the San Damiano monastery, "destitution" may be a shade more extreme than Clare intended. It also leaves little vocabulary for those whose lot in life is not voluntary poverty, but true destitution, a distinction noted by the early companions of Francis (*L3C* 10:39). Francis and Clare, although they did not always exercise it themselves, advocated discretion regarding the degree of *corporis penuriam* followed by their disciples (*AC* 50; *3LAg* 38-41). Those who are destitute do not always have the luxury of this discretion.

[23]The language *nobilioris generis*, refers to the Roman *Legend of Saint Agnes* [*AASS*, 21 Jan]. For Clare's use of the Agnes legend in her letters see the essay, "*The Legend of Saint Agnes of Rome* as Source" on pages 107-48 in this volume. For an English translation of the entire Agnes legend see *Clare's Sources in Translation: The Legend of Saint Agnes of Rome*, pages 253-65 in this volume.

[24]*sponsum. . .Christum: 1LAg* 12; *2LtF* 50. Jean Leclercq sees Clare's use of the *sponsa Christi* tradition in her first letter as building on the tendency of women mystics of the twelfth and early thirteenth-century to contemplate the poverty of the divine spouse. Such tendencies were also represented in the monastic tradition by St. Lutgarde (d. 1246) and St. Ida of Nivelles (d. 1231). "Agnes could either marry a powerful, rich and noble husband, or she could choose Christ, the eternal King, who became poor and humble out of love. Love is the key to her spirituality. Love means joyfully embracing poverty and suffering with faith in the Poor Crucified [*pauper crucifixus*]. In *The Passion of Saint Agnes of Rome*, virginity is associated with martyrdom; in St. Clare it is linked with poverty." "St. Clare and Nuptial Spirituality," 174.

[25]Note the repeated connection between poverty and virginity (see *1LAg* 6-7, 13, and 15-19). The foundations of Agnes's commitment are poverty

and virginity. See Van den Goorbergh and Zweerman, *Light Shining Through a Veil*, 60-62.

[26]An obvious Marian reference.

[27]The idea of a virginity that is kept always immaculate and inviolate introduces the following section taken from the Roman *Legend of Saint Agnes*. Agnes is celebrated as a faithful, woman martyr whose virginity was kept miraculously inviolate. In the Agnes legend, the Roman prefect, angered by Agnes's rejection of his son's advances, has Agnes stripped nude and subjected to the wiles of a brothel. God's fidelity is seen in that Agnes's hair miraculously grows so long that it covers her body better than clothing. God's radiance also forms a brilliant light around her that frightens those who were tempted to do her harm. See *The Legend of Saint Agnes*: cf., Office of Saint Agnes, [Regula breviary, Assisi, Sacro Convento, 694, fols., 269r-273r], Matins: 2nd nocturn, 5th-7th lessons.

[28]The *cum* clauses here are circumstantial rather than temporal. In the context of the legend, Agnes of Rome states that she has already been joined to her lover—"Already his body has been united with my body [Iam corpus eius corpori meo sociatum est]." The love-making, therefore, between Agnes and her spouse has already occurred. It is under the circumstances of having loved her spouse that Agnes is chaste, pure, and virginal. Since Agnes of Prague's entrance has already occurred, this circumstantial reading also fits the context of Clare's letter. Clare is simply paraphrasing the Agnes legend.

[29]Verses 8-11 are modeled after the Roman *Legend of Saint Agnes*. For verse 8, cf., Office of Saint Agnes, Matins: 1st nocturn, 3rd lesson, and 3rd responsory. The legend text reads: "Having loved him, I am chaste; having touched him, I am pure; having received him, I am a virgin [Quem cum amavero, casta sum; cum tetigero, munda sum; cum accepero, virgo sum]."

[30]Meanings of *possibilitas* include health, bodily strength, possibility, power, resources, means, and landed estate. In the classical and medieval world, one's possibility and power were directly connected to one's resources and land.

[31]In classical and Medieval Latin, *generositas* means birth, native status of a person, prestige, influence, lineage, nobility, and good breeding and refers more to the purity of a bloodline than to one's beneficence. Clare has taken this line from *The Legend of Saint Agnes* [cf., Office of Saint Agnes, Matins: 1st nocturn, 2nd lesson]. In the story, the son of the Roman prefect falls in love with Agnes, speaks of his love for her, and sends her precious gifts. Agnes declares that she already has a lover who is "far nobler than the prefect's son in both birth and position [longe te nobilior et genere et

dignitate]." *Generositas* captures both a sense of nobility and a sense of liberality associated with those who are of true noble stock and upbringing.

[32]*Suavior* suggests meanings such as sweet, gentle, good, pleasant, gracious, kind, suave, and agreeable. The English word "suave" portrays the sense of being well-mannered, a meaning Clare would have probably agreed with, but also carries a negative sense of being blandly polite or of portraying oneself as a smooth talker or operator which is not Clare's meaning. In short, even though "suave" is an English cognate, the English language does not have a word that adequately portrays the idea here. Christ's love is polite, kind, tender, gracious, pleasant, sweet, gentle, and courteous.

[33]Verse 9 is modeled after *The Legend of Saint Agnes*: cf., Office of Saint Agnes, Matins: 1st nocturn, 2nd lesson. The text that Clare uses in verse 9 is not repeated as either an antiphon or responsory in the Agnes Office. The Latin text of the legend reads, "whose nobility is higher, his power stronger, his appearance lovelier, his love sweeter, and his every grace more elegant [cuius est generositas celsior, possibilitas fortior, adspectus pulchrior, amor suavior, et omni gratia elegantior]."

[34]The verb *orno* means adorned but also has connotations such as to furnish, provide with money and supplies.

[35]*Trado* has connotations of handing down, handing over, giving as an inheritance, bequeathing.

[36]The pearl is an early Christian symbol of virginity referred to by Clement of Alexandria, Gregory Nazianzus, Gregory of Nyssa, Athanasius and others. See Sister M. Rosamond Nugent, OSF, "Portrait of the Consecrated Woman in Greek Christian Literature of the First Four Centuries" (Ph.D. diss., Catholic University of America, 1941), 90-91. The Genoese Dominican, Jacobus de Voragine, in the first volume of *The Golden Legend*, trans. William Ryan (Princeton, NJ: Princeton University Press, 1993), develops in medieval style this symbolism of the pearl in his description of Saint Margaret of Antioch. He writes: "The name Margaret is also the name of a precious jewel called *margarita*, pearl, which is shining white, small, and powerful. So Saint Margaret was shining white by her virginity, small by humility, and powerful in the performance of miracles" (368).

[37]See *Souter*, s.v. "vernans."

[38]Verses 10-11a are modeled after *The Legend of Saint Agnes*. The legend reads: "He adorned my right hand with a precious bracelet, and encircled my neck with precious stones. He hung priceless pearls from my ears, and surrounded me with glittering and sparkling gems [dexteram

meam, et collum meum cinxit lapidibus pretiosis. Tradidit auribus meis inaestimabiles margaritas, et circumdedit me vernantibus atque coruscantibus gemmis]." Cf., Office of Saint Agnes, Matins: 1st nocturn, 2nd antiphon, 2nd lesson, 2nd responsory; 2nd nocturn, 4th responsory; 3rd nocturn, 8th antiphon, 7th responsory.

[39]Van den Goorbergh and Zweerman in *Light Shining Through a Veil*, 56, note that "precious stones," "pearls," "jewels," and a "crown," are signs of royalty. Agnes now derives her royalty from Christ rather than from her Bohemian lineage.

[40]A reference to the "seal" can be seen in *The Legend of Saint Agnes*: "Posuit signum in faciem meam [He placed a seal on my face]:" cf., Office of Saint Agnes, Matins: 1st nocturn, 3rd antiphon, 2nd lesson, 2nd responsory. The image the "seal" evoked in the Agnes legend transitions into Sirach 45:14, the primary source for verse 11b; "Upon his turban a crown of gold, its plate wrought with the seal of holiness [Corona aurea super mitram eius, lamina cum signo sanctitatis]."

[41]Clare refers to Agnes as "sister," thus recognizing her as part of the Franciscan family. While she is "sister" to Clare, Agnes's primary relationship stemming from her *conversio* are her royalty as "spouse and mother and sister of my Lord Jesus Christ."

[42]*soror. . .domina*: cf., *2LAg* 24. Note that Clare rhetorically corrects herself addressing Agnes as "most venerable lady" because she is "spouse and mother and sister of my Lord Jesus Christ."

[43]In *LMj* 7:6:5, Francis calls the privilege of poverty "his mother, his spouse and his lady:" "Nonetheless, he (Francis) had chosen to glory above all in the privilege of poverty which he was accustomed to call his mother, his bride, and his lady [licet gloriari praeelegerit in privilegio paupertatis, quam modo matrem, modo sponsam, modo dominam nominare solebat]."

[44]Clare, following Francis, repeatedly uses these three terms, i.e., spouse, mother, sister/brother, to depict the relationship of "the ladies" with Christ. See Marianne Schlosser, "Mother, Sister, Bride: The Spirituality of St. Clare," trans. Ignatius McCormick, OFM Cap., *GR* 5 (1991): 233-49, originally published as "Mutter, Schwester, Braut: Zur Spiritualität der hl. Klara," *Laurentianum* 31 (1990): 176-97.

[45]*sponsa. . .Christi*: cf., *1LAg* 7, 24; *1LtF* 1:7; *2LtF* 50; *Ant OfP*. Note Francis's use of this expression in *1LtF* 1:7. According to Francis, those who persevere in doing penance are "spouses, brothers, and mothers of our Lord Jesus Christ [sponsi, fratres et matres Domini nostri Jesu Christi]." This expression is repeated by Francis in *2LtF* 50.

Note also that in the antiphon, "Holy Virgin Mary" repeated throughout *The Office of the Passion*, Mary is referred to as "daughter and handmaid of the most high and supreme King and Father in heaven, mother of our most holy Lord Jesus Christ, spouse of the Holy Spirit [filia et ancilla altissimi summi Regis Patris caelestis, mater sanctissimi Domini nostri Jesu Christi, sponsa Spiritus Sancti]."

[46]A *vexillum* is a military standard usually consisting of a piece of cloth suspended from a cross-piece at the head of a pole. *Niermeyer* defines *vexillum* as the sign of the cross; a standard symbolizing military commandership, a banner symbolizing the fief and handed over by the lord to the lay vassal during the ceremony of investiture; or a banner symbolizing the regalian rights and revenues conceded by the emperor to towns, especially to the Italian towns.

[47]*paupertatis sanctissimae*: cf., *1LAg* 6; *RCl* 6:6; *1C* 39:5.

[48]*in. . .confortamini*: cf., *1LAg* 31. *Confortamini* means to be comforted, strengthened, encouraged, to be inspired with courage, to be invigorated. Any of these meanings could be applied here.

[49]Clare, like Francis (*Test* 1-3), understands the moment of *conversio* to be a particularly important moment of grace. The beginning of Agnes's service is characterized by "a burning desire for the Poor Crucified." In *2LAg* 11, Clare again invites Agnes "to be mindful, like a second Rachel, of your founding purpose always seeing your beginning;" while in *4LAg* 19, Clare exhorts Agnes to, "Look closely, I say, to the beginning of the life of this admired one, indeed at the poverty of him who was wrapped in swaddling clothes and placed in a manger." The beginning of the Franciscan vocation for Clare and for Francis demands that one sell what one has and give it to the poor. Practically this means, in imitation of the Poor Christ, being content with poor housing and poor clothing.

[50]Note Clare's use of the singular reference here.

[51]For Clare, salvation through the passion of Jesus Christ occurs in two movements: First, Jesus' rescuing us from the power of the prince of darkness, and second, his reconciling us to God the Father.

[52]*Diligens* means to be fond of, devoted to, careful, attentive, diligent, conscientious. Clare is referring to those whose love is characterized by a selfless diligence or loving solicitude for the loved one. One is reminded of the kind of love characterized in the diligence of the prudent virgins of Mt 25:1-13.

[53]*a Deo. . .promittitur*: cf., *1LAg* 25.

[54]In speaking about *pius* as a title applied to emperors, Sr. Mary Bridget O'Brien defines *pius* as kind, see *Titles of Address*, 137. Medieval

interpretations include holy, pious, just, merciful, loving, conscientious, devoted, virtuous, faithful to one's duties owed to God and parents. The sense seems to be that of a good medieval lord who is rightfully merciful toward his subjects and who shows his care for them by justly and generously providing for their needs. For an excellent essay on the etymological development of "piety" and "pious" see James D. Garrison, *Pietas from Vergil to Dryden* (University Park, PA: Pennsylvania State University Press, 1992).

St. Bernard in "Sermon 12" on *The Song of Songs* describes *pietas* in this fashion: "But there is another ointment, far excelling these two [contrition and devotion], to which I give the name loving-kindness (*pietas*), because the elements that go to its making are the needs of the poor, the anxieties of the oppressed, the worries of those who are sad, the sins of wrong-doers, and finally, the manifold misfortunes of people of all classes who endure affliction, even if they are our enemies. These elements may seem rather depressing, but the ointment made from them is more fragrant than all other spices (Song 4:10). It bears the power to heal, for 'Happy the merciful; they shall have mercy shown them (Mt 5:7).' A collection therefore of manifold miseries on which the eye rests with loving-kindness, represents the ingredients from which the best ointments are made, ointments that are worthy of the breasts of the bride and capable of winning the Bridegroom's attention. . . . Who in your opinion, is the good person who takes pity and lends (Ps 111:5), who is disposed to compassion, quick to render assistance, who believes that there is more happiness in giving than in receiving (Acts 20:35), who easily forgives but is not easily angered, who will never seek to be avenged, and will in all things take thought for his neighbor's needs as if they were his own?" Bernard of Clairvaux, *On the Song of Songs I*, trans. Kilian Walsh OCSO, Cistercian Fathers Series (Shannon, Ireland: Cistercian Publications, Inc., 1971), 77.

[55]In the spirit of this hymn to poverty, in *4LAg* 20, Clare exclaims, "*o stupenda paupertas!* [O astonishing poverty!]."

[56]*paupertas/Dominus. . .Christus*: cf., *RCl* 6:7; *ER* 9:1.

[57]*Vulpes. . .reclinet*: cf. *ScEx* 19. Numbering for the *Sacred Exchange* in this text follows *Sacrum commercium sancti Francisci cum Domina Paupertate* (Quaracchi: PP. Collegii S. Bonaventurae, Ad Claras Aquas, 1929).

Van den Goorbergh and Zweerman, *Light Shining Through a Veil*, 29, suggest *1LAg* 15-18 as the core of a chiasmically structured letter. They diagram the structure of the letter as follows:

|Verses 3-4: Serving Christ
| |Verses 5-7: Agnes's commerce/exchange
| | |Verses 8-11: The Bridegroom
| | | |Verses 12-13a: Bride, mother, and sister
| | | |Verse 13b: Be strong
| | | | | |Verses 13c-14: The cross
| | | | | | |Verses 15-18: *Praise of Poverty*
| | | | | |Verses 19-20: The incarnation
| | | | |Verse 21: Be joyful
| | | |Verses 22-24: Sister, mother, and bride
| | |Verses 25-29: The adversary
| |Verse 30: The commerce
|Verse 31-34: Perseverance in serving

[58]*egenus. . .pauper*: cf., *OfP* 8:6.

[59]*pauper in mundo*: cf., *RCl* 8:3; *LR* 6:4; *1C* 76:9; *LJS* 45:7.

[60]*exsultate. . .gaudete*: cf., *1LAg* 3.

[61]*contemptus saeculi*: cf., *RCl* 6:2.

[62]*divitiae temporales*: cf., *1LAg* 29, 30.

[63]In his sermon for the Sixth Sunday after Easter, Saint Anthony of Padua, commenting on Exodus, compares the moth to avarice. "Raamses signifies avarice, which like a gnawing moth eats away at the fabric of the spirit. 'This gnawing moth is called *tinea* because it is so tenacious, and because it worms its way in, where it can bite and bite (Isid., *Etym.* XII, 5, 11, cf., *PL* 82, 449).' Thus avarice gnaws at the spirit of the avaricious man to make him increase his abundance, but the poor wretch just gets hungrier the more he has." '*Sermones*' *for the Easter Cycle*, ed. George Marcil, OFM (St. Bonaventure, NY: The Franciscan Institute, 1994), 209.

[64]*thesauros. . .furantur*: cf., *ScEx* 31.

[65]Mt 5:12 reads: "Rejoice and exult, for your reward is great in heaven [Gaudete et exsultate, quoniam merces vestra copiosa est in caelis]." Note that while the Vulgate uses *copiosa*, Clare renders the word superlative, *copiosissima*.

[66]*merces. . .caelis*: cf., *ER* 16:16.

[67]*Nuncupo* means to name, call, consecrate, vow, give official notice of, or appoint.

[68]*soror. . .mater*: cf., *1LAg* 12; *1LtF* 1:7; *2LtF* 50; *OfP Ant*: 2.

[69]*regnum. . .promittitur*: cf., *1LAg* 16.

[70]Referring to the Beatitude (Mt 5:3): "Blessed are the poor in spirit, for theirs is the kingdom of heaven [Beati pauperes spiritu, quoniam ipsorum est regnum caelorum]." See also *ScEx* 2.

The First Letter

[71]This statement, a favorite of the thirteenth-century poverty movement, is taken from Gregory the Great, *Homilia in Evangelia* II, 32,2 (*PL* 76,1233b) which says: "Therefore, we ought to wrestle with the nude, in the nude. For if a clothed person wrestles with a nude opponent, the clothed person is thrown to the ground more quickly, because he has (a place) from where he may be caught [Nudi ergo cum nudis luctari debemus. Nam si vestitus quisquam cum nudo luctatur, citius ad terram dejicitur quia habet unde teneatur]." Gregory advocates nakedness as the best protection for Christians wrestling with evil spirits who possess nothing of their own in this world. Liturgically this passage was used in Matins, 12th lesson for the Common of a Martyr. It is also referred to in *1C* 6:15, "Look! Now he wrestles naked with the naked. After putting aside all that is of the world, he is mindful only of divine justice [Ecce iam nudus cum nudo luctatur, et depositis omnibus quae sunt mundi, solius divinae iustitiae memoratur]."

Nakedness, as a symbol of poverty, carries differing vulnerabilities for Franciscan women and Franciscan men. When Clare refers to Gregory's sermon in the context of her first letter, one is reminded of Saint Agnes's nakedness before the Roman prefect as recorded in *The Legend of Saint Agnes*. Because the Roman virgin, Agnes, is true to her spousal promises to Christ, God's providence covers her nakedness protecting her virginity, but not shielding her from ultimate martyrdom. For Clare, virginity (feminine vulnerability), poverty (nakedness), martyrdom (the ultimate *imitatio Christi*), and providence are related theological themes.

[72]*divitias temporales*: cf., *1LAg* 22, 30.

[73]The theme of the "holy exchange" is a frequent one in the history of spirituality and in the early Franciscan movement. Van den Goorbergh and Zweerman suggest that the *commercium* is the theme of the first letter and outline a number of convincing theological similarities between Clare's letters and *The Sacred Exchange* namely: *1LAg* 11 and *ScEx* 21; *1LAg* 15-17 and *ScEx* Prologue and 19; *1LAg* 18 and *ScEx* 19; *1LAg* 21 and *ScEx* 23 and 64; *1LAg* 23 and *ScEx* 31; *1LAg* 29 and *ScEx* 13; the theme of nuptial mysticism and *ScEx* 64. See *Light Shining Through a Veil*, 48, note 8.

The theme of "the holy exchange" is found in the Roman liturgy both in the Divine Office and in Eucharistic texts. For a summary of the development of *commercium* in Christian theology and liturgical practice see *LTK*, 1957 ed., s.v. "commercium."

Of particular liturgical interest, is the antiphon, "O admirable exchange! The Creator of humankind assuming a living body, deigned to be born of a Virgin; and, becoming human without seed, lavished on us his deity [O admirabile commercium! creator generis humani, animatum corpus sumens, de virgine nasci dignatus est; et, procedens homo sine semine, largitus est nobis suam deitatem]." Echoing early Greek patristic theologies of exchange, this antiphon expresses the deification of humanity through the incarnation of Christ. The Regula breviary uses this antiphon for the feast of the Purification of the Blessed Virgin Mary, February 2, Vespers: 1st antiphon (cf., Assisi, Sacro Convento, 694, fol. 275v). The antiphon was also used for the Office of the Blessed Virgin, Christmas Season, Lauds: 1st antiphon; Prime: antiphon; Vespers: 1st antiphon (cf., Assisi, Sacro Convento, 694, fol. 386r).

[74]*caelestia pro terrenis*: cf., *2LAg* 23.

[75]*centuplum. . .recipere*: cf., *ER* 1:5.

[76]Medieval meanings of the term *viscera* include the internal organs—heart, lungs, womb, and liver as well as stomach entrails. *Viscera* refers to one's innermost recesses or one's innermost being.

[77]A stained glass window in the Basilica of San Francesco in Assisi illustrates Clare's image perfectly. On one side the Christ Child is being held on the breast/lap/womb of his mother, Mary, who is standing. On the other side, one sees Saint Francis held in the same way within the figure of Christ. One can perhaps appreciate more fully the impact of this image on thirteenth-century Umbrian women if one ponders the pilgrimage of Saint Angela of Foligno (ca 1248-1309). For Angela, the image of Christ and Francis represented in this stained glass window became the focal point of her mystical betrothal to Christ: "Then, on this second time, as soon as I had genuflected at the entrance of the church and when I saw a stained-glass window depicting St. Francis being closely held by Christ, I heard him telling me: 'Thus I will hold you closely to me and much more closely than can be observed with the eyes of the body.'" See "The Book of Blessed Angela: The Memorial," in *Angela of Foligno: Complete Works*, trans. Paul Lachance, OFM (New York: Paulist Press, 1993), 141-42. For a synthesis of various perspectives of the *viscera* as portrayed in this famous window in the Basilica of San Francesco see Jerôme Poulenc, OFM, "Saint François dans le 'vitrail des anges' de l'église supérieure de la basilique d'Assise," *AFH* 76 (1983): 701-13.

[78]*in eius. . .confortari*: cf., *1LAg* 13.

[79]*famulam. . .inutilem*: cf., *4LAg* 2.

[80]*me. . .sorores*: cf., *2LAg* 25. Clare consistently uses the word sisters [*sorores*] rather than nuns [*monachae*]. In the title of her Rule she speaks of "The Form of Life of the Order of Poor Sisters [forma vitae ordinis sororum pauperum]." Although written by Clare and addressed to Agnes, Clare's letters were most probably written to all the sisters at the monastery of Prague and read aloud to the entire community.

The First Letter

---

[81] *in monasterio commorantes*: cf., *4LAg* 2.

[82]"Merit" for Clare is connected not to Pelagian ideals, but to poverty and to "the mercy of Jesus Christ." Clare has already told Agnes that "the kingdom of heaven is promised and given by the Lord only to the poor (*1LAg* 25)." Clare and Agnes can hope to merit the everlasting vision because their choice of poverty beckons the mercy of Jesus Christ. In typical Christian dialectic, their very lack of merit is their merit. Clare and Agnes's poverty calls out to the mercy of Jesus Christ who himself became poor so that human beings might be reconciled to God the Father (*1LAg* 14). Christ's mercy is attracted to those who understand and live the truth (humility) of their poverty before God.

Clare's Second Letter
To Agnes of Prague

Clare's second letter was probably written between spring of 1235 and winter of 1238. Agnes had established her monastery in Prague as an institution financially separate from the Hospital of Saint Francis. Insuring the stability of its mission of caring for the poor and the sick, the royal Přemyslid family richly endowed the hospital. Agnes's monastery, on the other hand, was founded on the Franciscan ideal of living without property and its accompanying privileges.

On May 18, 1235, in the bull "Cum relicta seculi," Gregory IX, nervous about the Roman church accepting responsibility for a monastery of women without guaranteed revenue, overturned Agnes's careful planning by conceding the hospital with all its revenues to the monastery. Agnes wrote to Clare begging for advice and comfort. In her second letter, Clare appeals to the words and the authority of Francis himself and encourages Agnes to remain steadfast even under papal pressure in her vocational decision to follow the Poor Christ. Confident that Brother Elias could help negotiate the matter, Clare recommends that Agnes seek his advice.

Agnes also appealed to her brother, King Wenceslas I, for help and on February 5, 1237, Wenceslas wrote the letter, "Primum quidem excellentissime," to Gregory IX begging him to reconsider his position. Needing the political support of the Bohemian king, Gregory IX reluctantly issued "Pia credulitate tenentes" on April 15, 1238, granting Agnes's monastery the Privilege of Poverty.

Clare's Letters to Agnes

(1) Filiae *Regis regum*, ancillae *Domini dominantium,*[1] sponsae dignissimae Iesu Christi et ideo reginae praenobili dominae Agneti, (2) Clara, pauperum dominarum ancilla *inutilis*[2] et indigna, salutem et semper in summa vivere paupertate.

(3) Gratias ago gratiae largitori, a quo *omne datum optimum et omne donum perfectum*[3] creditur emanare, quod te tantis virtutum titulis decoravit et tantae perfectionis insigniis illustravit, (4) ut, *perfecti Patris*[4] effecta diligens imitatrix, perfecta fieri merearis, ne *oculi* sui aliquid in te *videant imperfectum.*[5]

(5) Haec est illa perfectio, qua te sibi *Rex* ipse in *aethereo thalamo* sociabit, ubi *sedet stellato solio*[6] gloriosus, (6) quod terreni regni fastigia vilipendens et oblationes imperialis coniugii parum dignas, (7) aemula sanctissimae paupertatis effecta in spiritu magnae humilitatis et ardentissimae caritatis *eius* adhaesisti *vestigiis,*[7] cuius meruisti connubio copulari.

---

[1] Cf., Apc 19:16; 1 Tim 6:15.
[2] Cf., Lc 17:10.
[3] Iac 1:17.
[4] Cf., Mt 5:48.
[5] Cf., Ps 138:16.
[6] Regula breviary, August 15, Assumption of the Blessed Virgin Mary, Matins: 3rd nocturn, 1st reponsory; Lauds, 2nd antiphon.
[7] Cf., 1 Pt 2:21.

The Second Letter

(1) To the daughter of the King of kings, handmaid[1] of the Lord of lords, most worthy spouse[2] of Jesus Christ[3] and therefore,[4] very distinguished queen, the Lady Agnes, (2) Clare, useless and unworthy handmaid[5] of the Poor Ladies,[6] sends her greetings[7] and the prayer that Agnes may always live in the utmost poverty.[8]

(3) I thank the one who liberally bestows grace, from whom every best and perfect gift is believed to come, because he has adorned you[9] with such a good reputation founded upon your virtues and has made you shine[10] with the honors of so much perfection.[11] (4) He did this so that once you have been made a diligent[12] imitator[13] of the Father who is perfect, you may deserve[14] to be made perfect, so that his eyes may not see anything imperfect in you.

(5) This is that perfection with which the King will unite you to himself in marriage in heaven's bridal chamber[15] where he sits in glory upon his starry throne,[16] (6) because despising the heights of an earthly kingdom and the less than worthy offers of an imperial marriage, (7) you have been made an imitator[17] of the holiest poverty,[18] and in a spirit of great humility and the most ardent charity, you have clung[19] to the footsteps of him with whom you have been worthy to be united in marriage.

(8) Cum vero noverim te virtutibus oneratam, parcens prolixitati verborum nolo verbis superfluis onerare, (9) licet tibi nihil superflui videatur ex illis de quibus posset tibi aliqua consolatio provenire. (10) Sed quia *unum est necessarium,*[8] hoc unum obtestor et moneo per amoren illius, cui te *sanctam* et beneplacentem *hostiam*[9] obtulisti, (11) ut tui memor propositi velut altera *Rachel* tuum semper *videns principium,*[10]

> quod tenes teneas,
> quod facis facias *nec dimittas,*[11]

(12)   sed cursu concito, gradu levi,
        pedibus inoffensis
        ut etiam gressus tui pulverem non admittant,

(13)   secura gaudens et alacris
        per tramitem caute beatitudinis gradiaris,

(14)   nulli credens, nulli consentiens,
        quod te vellet ab hoc proposito revocare,
        quod tibi *poneret* in via *scandalum,*[12]
        ne in illa perfectione,
        qua Spiritus Domini te vocavit,
        redderes Altissimo vota tua.[13]

---

[8]Lc 10:42.
[9]Cf., Rm 12:1.
[10]Cf., St. Jerome, *Liber de Nominibus Hebraicis* 15 (*PL* 23:783).
[11]Cf., Ct 3:4.
[12]Cf., Rm 14:13.
[13]Ps 49:14.

The Second Letter

(8) Moreover, since I know that you are laden with virtues,[20] I shall refrain from saying too much as I do not wish to laden[21] you with superfluous words, (9) even though to you no word seems superfluous of those that could be the source of some consolation for you. (10) But because one thing is necessary, I invoke this one thing and advise[22] you, by the love of him to whom you have offered yourself as a holy and pleasing sacrifice, (11) to be mindful, like a second Rachel, of your founding purpose[23] always seeing your beginning.[24]

What you hold, may you continue to hold,
what you do, may you keep doing and not
stop,

(12)   but with swift pace, nimble step, and feet that
do not stumble so that even your walking
does not raise any dust,[25]

(13)   may you go forward tranquilly,[26] joyfully,
briskly, and cautiously[27] along the path of
happiness,[28]

(14)   trusting in no one[29] and agreeing with no one
insofar as he might want to dissuade you from
pursuing your founding purpose or might
place a stumbling block[30] in your way,
preventing you, in that perfection with which
the Spirit of the Lord has called you, from
fulfilling your vows to the Most High.

(15) In hoc autem, ut *mandatorum* Domini securius *viam*[14] perambules, venerabilis patris nostri fratris nostri Heliae, generalis ministri, consilium imitare; (16) quod praepone consiliis ceterorum et reputa tibi carius omni dono.

(17)   Si quis vero aliud tibi dixerit,
        aliud tibi suggesserit,
        quod perfectionem tuam impediat,
        quod vocationi divinae contrarium videatur,
        etsi debeas venerari,
        noli tamen eius consilium imitari,

(18)   sed pauperem Christum,
        virgo pauper, amplectere.

(19) Vide contemptibilem pro te factum et sequere, facta pro ipso contemptibilis in hoc mundo. (20) Sponsum tuum *prae filiis hominum speciosum*,[15] pro salute tua factum virorum vilissimum, *despectum*,[16] *percussum*[17] et toto corpore multipliciter *flagellatum*,[18] inter ipsas crucis angustias morientem, regina praenobilis, intuere, considera, contemplare, desiderans imitari.

(21)   Cui si *compateris conregnabis*,
        condolens congaudebis,
        in cruce tribulationis *commoriens*[19]
        cum ipso *in sanctorum splendoribus*[20]
        mansiones aethereas possidebis,

---

[14]Cf., Ps 118:32.
[15]Ps 44:3.
[16]Cf., Is 53:3; Ps 21:7-8.
[17]Cf., Is 53:4.
[18]Cf., Mt 27:26.
[19]Cf., Rm 8:17; 2 Tim 2:11-12.
[20]Ps 109:3.

The Second Letter

(15) Now concerning this, so that you may walk more tranquilly along the way of the Lord's commands,[31] follow the advice of our venerable father, our Brother Elias,[32] minister[33] general. (16) Prefer his advice to the advice of others and consider it more precious to you than any gift.

(17)   Indeed, if someone tells you something else
or suggests anything to you that may hinder
your perfection and that seems contrary to
your divine vocation, even though you must
respect him, still, do not follow his advice;[34]

(18)   instead, poor virgin,
embrace the Poor Christ.[35]

(19) Now that you have made yourself contemptible[36] in this world for his sake, look upon and follow the one who made himself contemptible for your sake. (20) Gaze upon, examine, contemplate,[37] most noble queen,[38] desiring to follow your spouse, who is more beautiful than the sons of humankind, and who for your salvation became the vilest[39] of men, despised, struck, and flogged repeatedly over his entire body,[40] dying while suffering the excruciating torments of the cross.

(21)   If you suffer with him, with him[41] you will reign,
grieving with him, with him you will rejoice,
dying with him on the cross of tribulation,
with him you will possess[42] mansions[43] in
heaven among the splendors of the saints,

(22)   et *nomen* tuum in *libro vitae*[21] notabitur futurum inter homines gloriosum.

(23) Propter quod in aeternum et in saeculum saeculi regni caelestis gloriam pro terrenis et transitoriis, aeterna bona pro perituris participes et vives in saecula saeculorum.

(24) Vale, carissima soror et domina, propter Dominum tuum sponsum; (25) et me cum sororibus meis, quae gaudemus de bonis Domini, quae in te per suam gratiam operatur,[22] stude tuis devotis orationibus *Domino commendare.*[23] (26) Sororibus etiam tuis nos plurimum recommenda.

---

[21]Phil 4:3; Apc 3:5.
[22]Cf., 1 Cor 15:10.
[23]Cf., Act 14:22.

(22)   and your name will be recorded in the *Book
of Life* and will bring you glory among men
and women.

(23) This is why you may forever in eternity share the
glory of the heavenly kingdom rather than[44] what is earthly[45]
and transitory, eternal goods instead of those that perish, and
why you will live forever and ever.

(24) Farewell,[46] dearest sister and lady,[47] for the sake of
the Lord, your spouse;[48] (25) and constantly remember me,
as well as my sisters—for we rejoice in the good things of
the Lord that he is accomplishing in you through his
grace—in your devout prayers[49] to the Lord. (26) Also, as
often as possible, please remind your sisters to pray for us.[50]

Clare's Letter's to Agnes

Notes

[1]Clare's address to Agnes echoes the terminology of daughter and handmaid found in the form of life Francis gave to the Damianites preserved in *RCl* 6:3: "Because by divine inspiration, you have made yourselves daughters and handmaids of the most high and supreme King, the Father of heaven, and have taken the Holy Spirit as your spouse, choosing to live according to the perfection of the holy Gospel. [Quia divina inspiratione fecistis vos *filias* et *ancillas* altissimi summi Regis, Patris caelestis, et Spiritui Sancto vos desponsastis eligendo vivere secundum perfectionem sancti Evangelii]." Because of this echoing, one can postulate that the King of kings referred to here is God the Father, not Christ. The same words and relationship with the Father are used in the *OfP* Ant:2, "You are the daughter (*filia*) and handmaid (*ancilla*) of the most high and supreme King, the Father of heaven."

[2]*Filiae/ancillae/sponsae*: cf., *RCl* 6:3; *OfP* Ant:2.

[3]*sponsae. . .Christi*: cf., *1LAg* 12. If Clare's relational model for this greeting is the form of life that Francis gave to the Damianites, it is interesting that Clare changes the model here. While Francis speaks of the sisters as spouses of the Holy Spirit, Clare consistently refers to Agnes as the spouse of Jesus Christ.

[4]Clare calls Agnes "very distinguished queen, the Lady Agnes" not for her royal breeding but because of her espousal to Jesus Christ.

[5]*Clara. . .ancilla*: cf., *1LAg* 2; *3LAg* 2; *4LAg* 2; *RCl* 1:3.

[6]*pauperum dominarum*: cf., *3LAg* 2; *1C* 18:4; 116:4; *LJS* 13:3; 23:9; 72:4; *L3C* 24:7; *dominarum. . .inutilis*: cf. *1LAg* 2.

[7]*Clara. . .salutem*: cf., *3LAg* 2; *4LAg* 2.

[8] This greeting to "always live in the utmost poverty" is the theme of Clare's second letter and is prominent in the entire Clare corpus. Regis Armstrong, OFM Cap., notes, "While Francis only uses the word *paupertas* sixteen times in his writings, Clare does so forty-one times throughout hers and most frequently with the adjectives: *sancta* or *sanctissima* (16 times), *summa* or *altissima* (5), *beata* (3), *pia* (1), and *stupenda*" (1). See *Clare of Assisi: Early Documents* (St. Bonaventure, NY: Franciscan Institute Publications, 1993), 40, note a.

[9]Clare discontinues the use of formal address (*vos* and its forms) that she had used in her first letter, and adopts the familiar (*tu* and its forms).

She begins to use the familiar pronoun here and continues this familiarity throughout the rest of her correspondence with Agnes.

[10]Clare's use of *illustravit* here seems to have both outer and inner implications. On the one hand, Agnes is renowned in the world because of her royal station. *Illustris* is an attribute of rank and is used for both men and women of nobility. See Sister Mary Bridget O'Brien, "Titles of Address in Christian Latin Epistolography to 543 A.D." (Ph.D. diss., The Catholic University of America, 1930), 147. On the other hand, *illustrare* means to enlighten by the light of religious truth, see *Niermeyer*, s.v. "illustrare." Clare attributes Agnes's reputation for virtue, honors of perfection, and illumination not to the possession of worldly goods and to the advantages of nobility, but to her choice of following Jesus Christ.

[11]In this letter, Clare is addressing Agnes's concerns regarding her ability to be allowed to persevere not in the traditional monastic rendering of religious poverty—holding all goods in common, but in Clare's *propositum* of religious poverty, namely having "no possessions whatsoever [nullas omnino possessiones habere proponitis]," (*Sicut manifestum est*: *BF* I: 771). Since the time of Pachomius (ca., 290-ca., 347), monastic religious life was referred to as the "life of perfection." This concept of monastic perfection was closely associated with virginity, although it also included renouncing individual possessions in lieu of possessing resources in common, and obedience to one's superiors. See Guerric Couilleau, "Perfection: II Pères et Premiers Moines," in *DS*, cols., 1104-18.

"Perfection" in the 12th century poverty movements denoted the imitation of the Poor Christ. Religious perfection as the following of the Poor Christ inspired the foundations of Robert of Arbrissel (d., 1117), Bernard of Thiron (d., 1117), Vitalis of Savigny (d., 1122), and Norbert of Xanten (ca., 1082-1134). See Karl Suso Frank, "Perfection: III Moyen Âge," in *DS*, cols. 1121-25. For biographies of the above preachers see Raffaele Pazzelli, *St. Francis and the Third Order* (Chicago: Franciscan Herald Press, 1989), 47-49.

Clare, culturally situated at the climax of the *vita apostolica* of the 12th and early 13th centuries, understands the religious state of Franciscan perfection not only as the practice of virginity and the pooling of common property, but also as the *imitatio Christi pauperis*. Clare specifically and vehemently rejects the imposition of a Benedictine practice of poverty, insisting that the very foundation of the Franciscan *propositum*, which is the way of perfection for her sisters, is to follow the Poor Christ without property. Any agreement to relinquish this *propositum* would undermine the very nature of Clare's life of perfection. Clare, who usually tends to evoke spirit rather than prescription in her Rule, precisely outlines her concept of poverty for her sisters (*RCl* 6:10-15): "And just as I, together with my sisters, have always been solicitous to safeguard the holy poverty that we promised to the Lord God and to Blessed Francis, in the same way, the abbesses who succeed me in office and all the sisters are bound to observe it inviolably until the end: that is, by not receiving or having possession or ownership either by themselves or through an intermediary, or even anything that might reasonably be called property, except as much land as necessity requires for the integrity and proper seclusion of the monastery, and this land may not be cultivated except as a garden in accordance with the needs of the sisters [Et sicut ego semper sollicita fui una cum sororibus meis sanctam paupertatem quam Domino Deo et beato Francisco promisimus custodire: sic teneantur abbatissae quae in officio mihi succedent et omnes sorores usque in finem inviolabiliter observare, videlicet in non recipiendo vel habendo possessionem vel proprietatem per se neque per interpositam personam, seu etiam aliquid quod rationabiliter proprietas dici possit, nisi quantum terrae pro honestate et remotione monasterii necessitas requirit; et illa terra non laboretur nisi pro horto ad necessitatem ipsarum]."

Although Clare is willing to negotiate with ecclesiastical authorities regarding many of the details of her religious life, this Privilege of Poverty cannot be negotiated. She insists upon the Privilege of Poverty and eventually writes her Rule, going against a mandate of the 1215 Lateran Council which decreed: "Lest too great a variety of religious orders leads to grave confusion in God's church, we strictly forbid anyone henceforth to found a new religious order. Whoever wants to become a religious should enter one of the already approved orders. Likewise, whoever wishes to found a new religious house should take the rule and institutes from already approved religious orders [Ne nimia religionum diversitas gravem in ecclesia Dei confusionem inducat, firmiter prohibemus, ne quis de caetero novam religionem inveniat, sed quicumque voluerit ad religionem converti, unam de approbatis assumat. Similiter qui voluerit religiosam domum fundare de novo, regulam et institutionem accipiat de religionibus approbatis]." Text and translation taken from *Decrees of the Ecumenical Councils*, vol. 1, ed. Norman P. Tanner, S.J. (London: Sheed and Ward, 1990), 242.

The Privilege of Poverty was obviously so identified with Clare's religious way of perfection, which was the following of the Poor Christ, that no one, not even the pope himself, nor the conciliar authority of the official church could persuade her to mitigate her *propositum*. Her way of perfection required Clare to respect those in authority who wished to impose Benedictine poverty upon the monasteries of Poor Ladies, but not to obey them.

According to Francis's form of life that he gave to Clare and her sisters, perfection is the consequent choice of the daughter/handmaid relationship: "Because by divine inspiration, you have made yourselves daughters and handmaids of the most high and supreme King, the Father of heaven, and have taken the Holy Spirit as your spouse, choosing to live according to the perfection of the holy Gospel [Quia divina inspiratione fecistis vos filias et ancillas altissimi summi Regis, Patris caelestis, et Spiritui Sancto vos desponsastis eligendo vivere secundum perfectionem sancti Evangelii]" (*RCl* 6:3). This Franciscan "perfection" is the challenge spoken by Christ in the Holy Gospel, "If you wish to be perfect, go, sell your possessions, and give the money to the poor, and you will have treasure in heaven; then come, follow me" (Mt 19:21).

[12]See note 52 of Clare's first letter.

[13]The word *imitatrix* means a feminine imitator or follower. I am choosing the word "imitator" here even though in verse 15 of this letter, Clare uses the word *imitare* in reference to Brother Elias where her meaning seems better translated as "follow" rather than "imitate." I am also choosing to use "follow" for the translation of *imitari* in verse 20. Although generally "following in the footsteps of Jesus Christ" seems to be a more faithful rendering in early Franciscan sources than the concept of "the imitation of Christ," Clare is speaking here of her relationship to God the Father referring to Mt 5:48: "Be perfect as your heavenly Father is perfect." The pericope of Mt 5:43-48 concerns loving and praying for one's enemies. Clare asks Agnes to imitate the love of the Father whose sun rises on the bad and good, and whose rain falls on the just and unjust.

This context is interesting because rather than speaking of the *imitatio Christi*, Clare develops here the *imitatio perfecti Patris*. Regis Armstrong, in *Clare of Assisi*, 40, note c, notes that this is the only time this image of the "Father who is perfect" is used in the writings of either Clare or Francis.

[14]Note that Agnes's merit here is not in her own deeds, other than her steadfast choice of Jesus Christ, but in the liberal graciousness and gifts of God.

[15]*Thalamus* is a bedroom or apartment occupied by a married couple and used for conjugal relations.

[16]A reference to the antiphon: "The Virgin Mary has been taken up into the heavenly bridal chamber where the King of kings sits upon his starry throne [Maria Virgo assumpta est ad aethereum thalamum, in quo Rex regum stellato sedet solio]." The antiphon is found in the Divine Office of

Clare's Letter's to Agnes

the Assumption of the Blessed Virgin Mary, August 15, Matins: 1st responsory; Lauds: 2nd antiphon; Sext: antiphon; and None: responsory. The antiphon is also found in the Office of the Blessed Virgin, Lauds: 2nd antiphon; and Terce: antiphon.

[17]An *aemula* is defined as a peer rival, a competitor, emulator, a rival in love, a diligent imitator, and an assiduous follower. Agnes is certainly a diligent follower of most holy poverty.

[18]*sanctissimae paupertatis*: cf., *RCl* 6:6, 8; *1LAg* 6, 13; *1C* 39:5; *L3C* 39:8.

[19]Sr. Frances Teresa, OSC, notes in *This Living Mirror: Reflections on Clare of Assisi* (Maryknoll, NY: Orbis Books, 1995), 15, that the word Clare uses here is *adhaerere*, "the word used in Genesis 2:24 about a man cleaving to his wife." The word is also used in Psalm 119, a psalm that Clare cites in verse 15 of this same letter. Psalm 119:32 reads: "I have clung to your commands, O Lord, let me not put to shame. I have run the way of your commandments for you have enlarged my heart [Adhaesi testimoniis tuis, Domine; noli me confundere. Viam mandatorum tuorum curram, quia dilatasti cor meum]."

[20]This respect for and dependence upon the fruits of Agnes's virtue is characteristic of Clare. See for example, *1LAg* 33-34, and *3LAg* 4.

[21]Clare's playful use of *onero* is interesting. The burden of virtues is certainly a different type of burden than the burden of superfluous words. The suffering caused by Agnes's insistence on fidelity to the Franciscan ideal of the Privilege of Poverty (her virtue) is experienced by Agnes as a true burden. Of course, it is this very perseverance amid suffering that makes virtue virtuous. Clare proceeds in the letter gradually suggesting a joyful approach toward the acceptance of the burden of ecclesial misunderstanding, but not before she recognizes Agnes's pain and acknowledges her own need for Agnes's example.

[22]While Paul in Romans 12:1 uses the verb *obsecro* (I urge, beseech, entreat, implore, beg, appeal), Clare advises Agnes to be mindful of her founding purpose. One once again notices in this variant Clare's deep respect for her sister, Agnes.

[23]A *propositum* is not the rule of an official, canonically approved Order. It is rather a first attempt of a religious association to gain initial ecclesiastical approval without adopting one of the older, canonically recognized rules. A *propositum* does not deal with questions of leadership, the composition of a community, and the reception of new members. These structures take years to discern. A *propositum* is rather a short summary of the religious, ethical, and inspirational founding ideals embraced by a new community. It is short and unpretentious, mirroring the

fledgling form of the community itself. See Herbert Grundmann, *Religious Movements in the Middle Ages*, trans. Steven Rowan (Notre Dame, IN: University of Notre Dame Press, 1995): 34-47.

[24]For historical background on the problem of the image of Rachel in this letter see Regis Armstrong, OFM Cap., "Starting Points: Images of Women in the Letters of Clare," *CF* 62 (1992): 63-100. Armstrong notes that Saint Jerome states that the name Rachel is derived from two Hebrew words, *ra'ah* meaning "to see" and *halel* meaning "to begin." Jerome suggests that the word Rachel might be interpreted as *videns principium*, "seeing the beginning." Rachel is contrasted with Leah whose name means "laborious or wearisome" (79). Gregory the Great interprets Rachel as a penitent: "To sit is to seek the humility of penance, as it is written: Stand up after you have been seated (Ps 116:2). Rachel, therefore, hid the idols because the holy Church, following Christ, hides the vices of earthly desires by doing penance. . . . The Psalmist says about this joint effort: Blessed are those whose iniquities are forgiven and whose sins have been taken away (Ps 30:1). Rachel, then, signifies us who, if we condemn the faults of avarice by doing penance, hide the idols by sitting on them" (84). Armstrong continues: "Gregory repeats this passage in the second part of his *Homilies on Ezechiel* suggesting that the image of the penitent Rachel was uppermost in his mind. Later Rabanus Maurus quotes this passage in his *Commentary on Genesis* 17 (*PL* 107: 607), which indicates its firm place in the literature of the Middle Ages" (84).

Anthony of Padua provides an example of Rachel as penitent from the culture of primitive Franciscanism. In his Sermon for Easter Sunday, Anthony writes: "'Rachel,' i.e., the simple penitent soul—note, the name Rachel means sheep—'weeps over her children,' i.e., her deeds, which having been created in sin were dead. 'And she refused to be consoled because they were no more' (Mt 2:18); they were so enjoyable alive, but now they are gone. Oh, it is so easy to sink down low, but so hard to ascend again. 'What took so long to be born slips away so quickly.' 'As she wept, she stooped down, and looked into the monument.' Here is the humility of a real penitent. Note the three phrases: she wept, she stooped, she looked into. To weep is to show contrition; to stoop is to go to confession; to look into is to make amends."

The task of "seeing your beginning" as a penitent is addressed by Anthony in the same sermon: "'and she saw two angels.' These two angels, the word means messengers, signify, in the moral sense, our pitiable entrance into and sad departure from earthly life. We who are the body of Jesus Christ should indeed have an angel 'at the head,' and another 'at the feet,' attending the pitiable beginning and end of our life. They, properly named angels, give a message about the frailty of our body and the vanity of worldly existence. These are the two angels who, as Genesis says, 'brought Lot out of Sodom and said to him: 'Save yourself; do not look back and do not stay anywhere in this region; flee into the mountain, lest you perish in the same manner" (19:17). Whoever intends to examine carefully the beginning and the end of his life, should get out of 'Sodom,' i.e., the world and the stinking circumstances of sin, in order to save his soul. He should not 'look back,' i.e., return to his past sins."

Anthony continues connecting also the metaphor of "dirt" to the penitent Rachel image. "She has a good companion in Mary mother of James, 'whose name means supplanter.' She bespeaks contempt for the world; such contempt treads underfoot all transitory things as though they were dirt and, thus, gets rid of the leaven of the old way of life." *Sermones for the Easter Cycle*, ed. George Marcil, OFM (St. Bonaventure, NY: The Franciscan Institute, 1994), 70-71.

Van den Goorbergh and Zweerman, *Light Shining Through a Veil*, 115, propose that "undoubtedly Clare was influenced by Innocent III's homily *Intravit Ihesus in quoddam castellum*" (*PL* 217, col. 575-82). This sermon was inserted into matins for the feast of the Assumption, cf., Stephen J. P. Van Dijk, OFM and Joan Hazelden Walker, *The Ordinal of the Papal Court From Innocent III to Boniface VIII and Related Documents*, 430. Innocent's sermons were meant to serve as alternatives to the traditional readings of the Fathers, cf. Stephen Van Dijk, *The Origins of the Modern Roman Litrugy*, 104. The Regula breviary, which Jordan of Giano records was distributed to the friars in 1230, does not include the texts of Innocent's sermons. For the feast of the Assumption, *Intravit Ihesus in quoddam castellum* is simply listed as an optional text. Certainly, even if by chance Clare did possess a folio of Innocent's lessons, she most likely could not have assumed that Agnes possessed them.

It seems more probable that Clare's use of the image of Rachel in this letter was derived from popular culture, perhaps transmitted through the sermons of the Franciscan friars who preached at San Damiano, than from the direct influence of Innocent III's sermon. Clare's image is of Rachel, the penitent, who perseveres without ceasing to follow the *propositum* of a penitential lifestyle refusing to stir up the dust of worldly vanities.

[25]Anthony of Padua suggests that the term "dust" denotes "the vanity of the world." See '*Sermones*' *for the Easter Cycle*, 86 and 206. In the sermon for the Sixth Sunday after Easter, Anthony expands this image further: "Jabbok means torrent of dust and it signifies the temporal pleasures which flow by like a torrent; such pleasures are sterile and they blind the eyes like dust." '*Sermones*' *for the Easter Cycle*, 213.

The Second Letter

The image of dust is also used in *1C* 9, to describe money, and in *1C* 71 to refer to "all things that are in the world." See also, Gregory the Great, *Dialogues*, I:Prologue, (*PL* 77, col. 152).

[26]*Secura* means being free from fears and anxieties, untroubled in mind, marked by a freedom from care, peaceful, undisturbed, free from danger, assured. Clare's sense is that one is both secure and safe, and therefore, also tranquil and peaceful.

[27]Note that even within the security and liveliness of the stepping, Clare does not neglect the importance of discretion. Even on the path of joy, Clare advises Agnes to proceed *caute* meaning circumspectly, carefully, without risk or danger, cautiously.

[28]*Beatitudo* means salvation, happiness, blessedness. The way of beatitude is clear for Clare: "Blessed are the poor in spirit, for theirs is the kingdom of heaven" (Mt 5:3).

[29]The translation of *nulli* seems to be "no one," rather than "nothing" for two reasons. First, the genitive singular of *nullus* is commonly used instead of the corresponding case of *nemo*. See Allen and Greenough, *New Latin Grammar* (New Rochelle, NY: Aristide D. Caratzas, 1931, 1998), §314,2a. Second, the verb that follows, *vellet*, demands a personal subject. Clare is most probably referring to Pope Gregory IX.

[30]*Niermeyer* defines *scandulum* as a stone of stumbling, trap, an enticement into sin, quarrel, strife, struggle, discord, hatred, embitterment, fight, battle, act of violence, outrage, evil design, machination, scandal, discredit.

[31]*mandatorum. . .viam perambules*: cf., *1C* 55:1.

[32]For commentary on the relationship between Elias and Clare at the time of this second letter, see Michael Cusato, OFM, "Elias and Clare: An Enigmatic Relationship," *Clare of Assisi: Investigations*, Clare Centenary Series (St. Bonaventure, NY: The Franciscan Institute, 1993), 95-115. See also the analysis of Maria Pia Alberzoni in *Chiara e Il Papato* (Milano: Edizioni Biblioteca Francescana, 1995), 69-96; and Alberzoni's summary of similar material in "'Nequaquam a Christi sequela in perpetuum absolvi desidero:' Chiara tra carisma e istituzione," *Chiara d'Assisi e La Memoria di Francesco*, Atti del convegno per l'VIII centenario della nascita di S. Chiara (Rieti: Petruzzi Editore, 1995): 41-65; translated into English by Nancy Celaschi, OSF, as "'Nequaquam a Christi sequela in perpetuum absolvi desidero:' Clare between Charism and Institution," in *GR* 12 (1998): 81-121.

[33]*fratris. . .ministri*: cf., *LtOrd* 2, 38.

[34]*eius consilium*: cf., *RCl* 6:9. In her Rule 6:7-9, Clare quotes directly from Francis's last will to the Poor Ladies, which he wrote shortly before

his death: "I, Brother Francis, little one, wish to follow the life and poverty of our most high Lord Jesus Christ and his most holy mother and to persevere in this until the end. And I ask and give counsel to you, my ladies, so that you might always live in this most holy life and poverty. And guard yourselves assiduously so that you may never stray from this in any respect whatsoever neither because of the teaching nor because of the counsel of anyone [Ego frater Franciscus parvulus volo sequi vitam et paupertatem altissimi Domini nostri Iesu Christi et eius sanctissimae matris, et perseverare in ea usque in finem. Et rogo vos, dominas meas, et consilium do vobis, ut in ista sanctissima vita et paupertate semper vivatis. Et custodite vos multum ne doctrina vel consilio alicuius ab ipsa in perpetuum ullatenus recedatis]." In advising Agnes to respect, but not to follow papal advice, Clare is calling upon the authority and mandate that Saint Francis himself gave to her and her sisters.

[35]*pauperem Christum*: cf., *3LAg* 4. Notice the spousal union explicit in the Latin construction: "*pauperem Christum, virgo pauper.*" The Latin *sed*/instead, reveals that the point of the *advice* referred to three times (15, 16, 17), is poverty. Elias supported the Poor Ladies in their determination to preserve the Privilege of Poverty. It is clear from Pope Gregory IX's correspondence with Agnes of Prague that the pope was hoping to mitigate Clare and Agnes's position. Not only was the Privilege of Poverty at stake, but also the friar's relationship with the Damianites. See the essay, "The Privilege of Poverty as Source: Clare's Letters Amid Papal and Royal Correspondence," on pages 207-49 in this volume.

[36]Or "worthless." Notice that Clare's choice of poverty includes not only the renunciation of personal and communal property, but also the acceptance of human contempt. The mention of contempt is particularly salient here since perseverance in the Privilege of Poverty is placing both Clare and Agnes at odds with both the pope and a growing number of Franciscan brothers.

[37]See Timothy J. Johnson, "Image and Vision: Contemplation as Visual Perception in Clare of Assisi's Epistolary Writings," *CF* 64 (1994): 195-213.

[38]Here Agnes, the queen, is invited to follow Mary, queen of heaven and lady of sorrows, as she weeps and stays with her son hanging upon the cross.

[39]As Agnes held cheaply or despised "the heights of an earthly kingdom," (*2LAg* 6), so Agnes's spouse is held cheaply or vilely among humankind.

The Second Letter

[40]Clare is referring to the parallel passion narratives of Mark and Matthew who mention flogging, mocking, and striking Jesus with a reed. See Mt 27:26-31 and Mk 15:15-20.

[41]The Latin text emphasizes the spousal union between Agnes and Christ through the use of the *com/con* prefix.

[42]*Possidere* mean to have land in one's control, own, hold, occupy, inhabit a place, appropriate, possess. In Clare's idea of the *sacrum commercium*, one sacrifices property and housing, but in return one will possess a mansion and other riches in the kingdom of heaven.

[43]Note Clare's use of *mansio* also in *3LAg* 22, 23.

[44]With the meaning of "in exchange for." Clare again reminds Agnes of the *sacrum commercium*.

[45]*caelestis. . .terrenis*: cf., *1LAg* 30.

[46]*Vale* is a typical closing formula meaning to have strength, or to be in good health. This Latin formula is taken from the Greek ἔρρωσο and remained the standard closing formula used in early Medieval Latin letters. Although seldom reflected upon, to wish another health as a closing formula is still in common usage. "Farewell" or "take care of yourself" accomplishes this same purpose in English. See *SF*, 69-75.

[47]*carissima. . .domina*: cf., *1LAg* 12.

[48]Again Clare is clear that Agnes is "dearest sister and lady" not because of her noble genealogy, but "for the sake of the Lord, your spouse." The title of lady is particularly poignant here. Agnes's choice of poverty is having an effect upon her ability to influence as a royal lady. Clare reminds her that she is a lady and queen not because of her birthright, but because of her chosen relationship with Christ. This choice has also made her Clare's "dearest sister."

[49]*orationibus. . .commendare*: cf., *1LAg* 33.

[50]*sororibus. . .recommenda*: cf., *3LAg* 42.

Clare's Third Letter
To Agnes of Prague

Clare probably wrote this letter in the summer of 1238. Rejoicing in Gregory IX's gift of the Privilege of Poverty to Agnes, Clare commends Agnes for her progress and refers to her as "God's own helper."

Successfully negotiating the Privilege of Poverty did not fully allay all of Agnes's rightful concerns. Wanting to unify the women's monasteries in central and northern Italy under a Rule that he himself had composed, Gregory IX attempted other strategies to temper Agnes's commitment to poverty. Along with "Pia credulitate tenentes," the papal office issued a fasting mitigation that had the potential to overwhelm the abilities of the Franciscan brothers to beg for the needs of the sisters. Agnes, concerned that the new directives for fasting were not in conformity with those that Saint Francis himself had given to the Monastery of San Damiano, wrote to Clare for clarification.

Clare's third letter is a masterpiece of early Franciscan literature. In it, Clare exhorts Agnes to contemplate the glory of God; a glory that she already possesses because of her uncompromising and faithful embrace of the Poor Christ. Because fasting is not poverty, "the one thing necessary," Clare encourages Agnes to rejoice that she now possesses the Privilege of Poverty and to practice eschatological living.

Towards the end of her letter, Clare responds to Agnes's questions, passing on the instructions concerning fasting given to her and her sisters by Saint Francis himself. Clare also begs Agnes to undertake her fasting disciplines with discretion. The cold and damp conditions of the Bohemian climate and the unavailability of Italian "fasting foods" will require prudent adjustments.

Clare's Letters to Agnes

(1) In Christo sibi reverendissimae dominae ac prae cunctis mortalibus diligendae sorori Agneti, illustris regis Bohemiae germanae, sed iam summo caelorum Regi *sorori* et *sponsae,*[1] (2) Clara, humillima et indigna Christi ancilla et dominarum pauperum serva, salutis gaudia in *auctore salutis*[2] et quidquid melius desiderari potest.

(3) De sospitate tua, felici statu et successibus prosperis quibus te in incepto cursu ad obtinendum caeleste *bravium*[3] vigere intelligo tanto repleor gaudio (4) tantaque in Domino exultatione respiro, quanto te novi et arbitror vestigiorum pauperis et humilis Iesu Christi tam in me quam in aliis ceteris sororibus imitationibus mirifice supplere defectum.

(5) Vere gaudere possum nec me aliquis posset a tanto gaudio facere alienam, (6) cum, *quod* sub caelo *cuncupivi iam tenens,*[4] callidi hostis astutias et perditricem humanae naturae superbiam et vanitatem humana corda infatuantem te quadam mirabili ipsius Dei oris sapientiae praerogativa suffultam terribiliter ac inopinabiliter videam supplantare (7) *absconsumque in agro* mundi et cordium humanorum *thesaurum incomparabilem,*[5] quo illud *emitur*[6] a quo cuncta de nihilo *facta sunt,*[7] humilitate, virtute fidei, ac paupertatis brachiis amplexari; (8) et, ut proprie ipsius apostoli verbis utar, ipsius *Dei* te iudico *adiutricem*[8] et ineffabilis corporis eius cadentium membrorum sublevatricem.

---

[1]Cf., Mt 12:50; 2 Cor 11:2.
[2]Cf., Hbr 2:10.
[3]Cf., 1 Cor 9:24; Phil 3:14.
[4]Cf., Regula breviary, January 21, Saint Agnes of Rome, Matins: 3rd nocturn, 9th lesson; Lauds: Benedictus antiphon.
[5]Regula breviary, January 21, Saint Agnes of Rome, Matins: 1st nocturn, 2nd lesson; 2nd nocturn, 5th responsory.
[6]Cf., Mt 13:44; 2 Cor 4:7.
[7]Cf., Io 1:3.
[8]Cf., 1 Cor 3:9; Rm 16:3.

The Third Letter

(1) To Agnes, most venerable lady and sister[1] in Christ, deserving of love before all other mortals, blood-sister of the illustrious king of Bohemia,[2] but now sister[3] and spouse of the most high King[4] of the heavens, (2) Clare, most humble and unworthy handmaid[5] of Christ and servant of the Poor Ladies,[6] sends her prayer[7] for the joys of salvation[8] in him who is the Author of Salvation[9] and for everything better that can be desired.

(3) I am filled with such great joy about your well-being,[10] your happiness, and your favorable successes through which, I understand, you are thriving on the journey you have begun to obtain the reward of heaven; (4) and I breathe again in the Lord with elation equal to my knowledge and belief that you are supplying in wonderful ways what is lacking both in me and in the other sisters who are following in the footsteps of the poor and humble Jesus Christ.[11]

(5) I am indeed able to rejoice, and there is no one who could separate me from such great joy, (6) since I already possess what under heaven I have yearned for, and I see that you, supported by some kind of wonderful claim on the wisdom that comes from God's own mouth,[12] are formidably and extraordinarily undermining the stratagems of the cunning enemy, the pride that destroys human nature, and the vanity[13] that beguiles human hearts. (7) I see, too, that you are embracing with humility, the virtue of faith, and the arms of poverty the incomparable treasure[14] that lies hidden in the field of the world and the hearts of human beings, where it is purchased by the One by whom all things were made from nothing. (8) And, to use as my own the words of the apostle himself, I consider you someone who is God's own helper and who supports the drooping limbs of his ineffable body.

(9) Quis ergo de tantis mirandis gaudiis dicat me non gaudere? (10) *Gaudeas* igitur et tu *in Domino semper*,[9] carissima, (11) nec te involvat amaritudo et nebula, o in Christo dilectissima domina, angelorum *gaudium et corona*[10] sororum; (12) pone mentem tuam in speculo aeternitatis, pone animam tuam in *splendore gloriae*,[11] (13) pone cor tuum in *figura* divinae *substantiae*[12] et *transforma* te ipsam totam per contemplationem *in imagine*[13] divinitatis ipsius, (14) ut et ipsa sentias quod sentiunt amici gustando *absconditam dulcedinem*,[14] quam ipse Deus ab initio suis amatoribus reservavit.[15]

(15) Et omnibus qui in fallaci mundo perturbabili suos caecos amatores illaqueant penitus praetermissis, illum totaliter diligas, qui se totum pro tua dilectione donavit,[16] (16) *cuius pulchritudinem sol et luna mirantur*,[17] cuius praemiorum et eorum pretiositatis et *magnitudinis non est finis*;[18] (17) illum dico Altissimi Filium, *quem Virgo peperit et post* cuius *partum virgo permansit*.[19] (18) Ipsius dulcissimae matri adhaereas, quae talem genuit Filium, *quem caeli capere non poterant*,[20]

---

[9]Cf., Phil 4:4.
[10]Cf., Phil 4:1.
[11]Cf., Hbr 1:3.
[12]Cf., Hbr 1:3.
[13]Cf., 2 Cor 3:18; Col 1:15.
[14]Cf., Ps 30:20.
[15]Cf., 1 Cor 2:9.
[16]Cf., Gal 2:20.
[17]Regula breviary, January 21, Saint Agnes of Rome, Matins: 1st nocturn, 3rd lesson; 2nd nocturn, 6th responsory; 3rd nocturn, 7th antiphon, 9th antiphon, 7th responsory.
[18]Ps 144:3.
[19]Regula breviary, February 2, Purification of the Blessed Virgin Mary, Vespers: Magnificat antiphon.
[20]*Regula Breviary*, March 25, Feast of the Annunciation, Matins: 2nd nocturn, 3rd responsory; and Office of the Blessed Virgin, Matins: 1st nocturn, 1st responsory. Cf. 3 Re 8:27.

The Third Letter

(9) Who, then, would tell me not to rejoice about such great and marvelous joys? (10) That is why you, too, dearest, must always rejoice in the Lord,[15] (11) and not let bitterness and confusion[16] envelop you, O Lady most beloved in Christ, joy of the angels, and crown of your sisters. (12) Place[17] your mind[18] in the mirror[19] of eternity; place your soul in the splendor of glory;[20] (13) place your heart in the figure of the divine substance;[21] and, through contemplation, transform your entire being into the image of the Divine One himself,[22] (14) so that you, yourself, may also experience what his friends experience when they taste the hidden sweetness that God alone has kept from the beginning for those who love him.

(15) And completely ignoring[23] all those who in this deceitful and turbulent world ensnare their blind lovers, you might totally love him who gave himself totally out of love for you,[24] (16) whose beauty the sun and moon admire,[25] and whose rewards, in both their preciousness and magnitude, are without end. (17) I am speaking about the Son of the Most High, to whom the Virgin gave birth and, after whose birth, she remained a virgin.[26] (18) May you cling to his most sweet Mother, who gave birth to the kind of Son whom the heavens could not contain,[27] (19) and yet, she carried him in

(19) et tamen ipsa parvulo claustro sacri uteri *contulit* et *gremio*[20] puellari gestavit.

(20) Quis non abhorreat humani hostis insidias, qui per fastum momentaneorum et fallacium gloriarum ad nihilum redigere cogit quod maius est caelo? (21) Ecce iam liquet per Dei gratiam dignissimam creaturarum fidelis hominis animam maiorem esse quam caelum, (22) cum *caeli* cum creaturis ceteris *capere nequeant*[21] Creatorem, et sola fidelis anima ipsius mansio sit et sedes, et hoc solum per caritatem qua carent impii, (23) Veritate dicente: *Qui diligit me diligetur a Patre meo, et ego diligam eum,*[22] *et ad eum veniemus, et mansionem apud eum faciemus.*[23]

(24) Sicut ergo Virgo virginum gloriosa materialiter, (25) sic et tu, *sequens eius vestigia,*[24] humilitatis praesertim et paupertatis, casto et virgineo corpore spiritualiter semper sine dubietate omni portare potes, (26) illum *continens* a quo tu et *omnia continentur,*[25] illud possidens quod et comparate cum ceteris huius mundi possessionibus transeuntibus fortius possidebis. (27) In quo quidam mundani reges et reginae falluntur, (28) quorum *superbiae usque ad caelum* licet *ascenderint, et caput earum nubes tetigerit, quasi sterquillinium in fine perducuntur.*[26]

---

[20]Regula breviary, March 25, Feast of the Annunciation, Matins: 2nd nocturn, 3rd responsory; and Office of the Blessed Virgin, Matins: 1st nocturn, 1st responsory.
[21]Cf., 2 Par 2:6; 3 Rg 8:27.
[22]Io 14:21.
[23]Io 14:23.
[24]Cf., 1 Pt 2:21.
[25]Cf., Sap 1:7; Col 1:17.
[26]Iob 20:6-7.

the tiny enclosure of her sacred womb, and held him on her young girl's lap.[28]

(20) Who would not abhor the treachery of the enemy of humanity who, by means of the pride that results from fleeting and false glories, compels[29] that which is greater than heaven to return to nothingness? (21) See, it is already clear that the soul of a faithful person, the most worthy of God's creations through the grace of God, is greater than heaven, (22) since the heavens and the rest of creation together cannot contain[30] their Creator and only the soul of a faithful person is his dwelling place[31] and throne[32] and this is possible only through the charity that the wicked[33] lack. (23) For the Truth says: The one who loves me, will be loved by my Father, and I shall love him and we shall come to him and make our dwelling place[34] with him.

(24) So, just as the glorious Virgin of virgins carried him physically, (25) so, you too, following in her footsteps especially those of humility and poverty, can without any doubt, always carry him spiritually in your chaste and virginal body, (26) containing him by whom both you and all things are contained, and possessing that which, even when compared with the other transitory possessions of this world, you will possess more securely. (27) Regarding this, some kings and queens of this world are deceived; (28) even though in their pride they have climbed all the way up to the sky, and their heads have touched the clouds, in the end they are destroyed like a pile of dung.

(29) Super his autem quae me iam tibi reserare mandasti, (30) quae scilicet essent festa quae forte, ut te opinor aliquatenus aestimasse, in varietate ciborum gloriosissimus pater noster sanctus Franciscus nos celebrare specialiter monuisset, caritati tuae duxi respondendum. (31) Noverit quidem tua prudentia, quod praeter debiles et infirmas, quibus de quibuscumque cibariis omnem discretionem quam possemus facere nos monuit et mandavit, (32) nulla nostrum sana et valida nisi cibaria quadragesimalia tantum, tam in diebus ferialibus quam festivis, manducare deberet, die quolibet ieiunando, (33) exceptis diebus dominicis et Natalis Domini, in quibus bis in die comedere deberemus. (34) Et in diebus quoque Iovis solitis temporibus pro voluntate cuiuslibet, ut quae scilicet nollet, ieiunare non teneretur. (35) Nos tamen sanae ieiunamus cottidie praeter dies dominicos et Natalis. (36) In omni vero Pascha, ut scriptum beati Francisci dicit, et festivitatibus sanctae Mariae ac sanctorum apostolorum ieiunare etiam non tenemur, nisi haec festa in sexta feria evenirent; (37) et sicut praedictum est, semper quae sanae sumus et validae, cibaria quadragesimalia manducamus.

(38) Verum quia *nec caro nostra caro aenea est nec fortitudo lapidis fortitudo nostra,*[27] (39) immo fragiles et omni corporali sumus debilitati proclivae, (40) a quadam indiscreta et impossibili abstinentiae austeritate quam te aggressam esse cognovi, sapienter, carissima, et discrete te retrahi rogo et in Domino peto, (41) ut *vivens confiteris*[28] Domino, *rationabile* tuum Domino reddas *obsequium*[29] et tuum *sacrificium* semper *sale conditum.*[30]

---

[27]Iob 6:12.
[28]Cf., Is 38:19; Sir 17:27.
[29]Cf., Rm 12:1.
[30]Lv 2:13.

The Third Letter

(29) Now, I thought that I should respond to your charity about the things that you have asked me to clarify for you; (30) namely, what were the feasts—and, I imagine, that you have perhaps figured this out to some extent—that our most glorious father, Saint Francis, urged us to celebrate in a special way with different kinds of foods. (31) Indeed, your prudence knows that, with the exception of the weak and the sick, for whom he advised and authorized us to use every possible discretion with respect to any foods whatsoever, (32) none of us who are healthy and strong ought to eat anything other than Lenten fare,[35] on both ordinary days and feastdays, fasting every day (33) except on Sundays and on the Lord's Nativity, when we ought[36] to eat twice[37] a day. (34) And, on Thursdays in Ordinary Time, fasting should reflect the personal decision of each sister, so that whoever might not wish to fast would not be obligated to do so.[38] (35) All the same, those of us who are healthy fast every day except Sundays and Christmas. (36) Certainly, during the entire Easter week,[39] as Blessed Francis states in what he has written, and on the feasts of holy Mary and the holy apostles, we are also not obliged to fast, unless these feasts should fall on a Friday;[40] (37) and, as has already been said, we who are healthy and strong always eat[41] Lenten fare.

(38) But because neither is our flesh the flesh of bronze, nor our strength the strength of stone, (39) but instead, we are frail and prone to every bodily weakness, (40) I am asking and begging in the Lord that you be restrained wisely, dearest one, and discreetly[42] from the indiscreet and impossibly severe fasting that I know you have imposed upon yourself, (41) so that living, you might profess the Lord, and might return to the Lord your reasonable worship and your sacrifice always seasoned with salt.[43]

(42) Vale semper in Domino, sicut me valere peropto, et tam me quam meas sorores tuis sacris orationibus recommenda.

The Third Letter

(42) Stay well[44] always in the Lord, just as I very much desire to stay well, and be sure to remember both me and my sisters in your holy prayers.[45]

Notes

[1]The word "sister" is repeated three times in this first verse. First, Clare identifies Agnes as her sister in Christ. Second, Agnes is the "blood-sister of the illustrious king of Bohemia." Third, and most importantly, Agnes is the "sister and spouse of the most high King of the heavens."

[2]*illustris. . .Bohemiae*: cf., *1LAg* 1. Agnes's father, Otakar I, had died some years earlier (December 15, 1230). Clare addresses Agnes not as the daughter of the king of Bohemia, but rather as the blood-sister of the king of Bohemia, referring to Agnes's brother, Wenceslas I, who reigned from December 1230 to September 1253.

[3]This relationship of "sister and spouse of the most high King of the heavens" takes precedence over the blood relationship Agnes has with her brother. "But now," (*sed iam*), emphasizes this point.

[4]*summo/Regi*: cf., *4LAg* 17; *RCl* 6:3.

[5]*Clara. . .ancilla*: *1LAg* 2; *2LAg* 2; *4LAg* 2; *RCl* 1:3.

[6]*dominarum pauperum*: cf., *2LAg* 2; *1C* 18:4; 116:4; *LJS* 13:3; 23:9; 72:4; *L3C* 24:7.

[7]*Clara. . .salutem*: *2LAg* 2; *4LAg* 2-3; *RCl* Prologue:2.

[8]For Christians, meanings for *salus* (salvation) include: a wish for a state of health and well-being, greetings in the name of the Lord, and also final salvation in the Lord. Clare's use is consistent with this triple play. See *SF*, 25-26.

[9]Using this same Christological title, the Office of the Blessed Virgin contained a hymn, *Memento salutis auctor*, that was sung at all the little hours and at compline.

[10]*Sospes*, (well-being), means safety, health, welfare. A *sospitator* is a savior, preserver, deliverer, or redeemer. Again Clare is playing on the Christian sense of *salus*.

[11]*pauperis/Christi*: cf., *2LAg* 18.

[12]The "wisdom that comes from God's own mouth" differs from the wisdom of knowing good and evil that was promised to Eve by the "cunning enemy" in Genesis 3:1-6. The fruits of following the false teacher are pride and vanity; the fruit of following the Poor Christ is true wisdom. See Eric Jager, *The Tempter's Voice: Language and the Fall in Medieval Literature* (Ithaca, NY: Cornell University Press, 1993), 45-48.

[13]Clare's juxtaposition of wisdom and vanity reflect her insights on poverty. Clare understands wisdom as the embrace of poverty that sees through the deception of earthly pomp. *The Legend of Clare* 47:9 records that at Clare's funeral, the bishop of Ostia commemorated Clare's life by eulogizing her as "contemptuous of vanity."

[14]The word sequence, *thesaurum incomparabilem*, is taken from the *Legend of Saint Agnes of Rome*, cf., Office of Saint Agnes, Matins: 1st nocturn, 2nd lesson. The expression is not repeated in the antiphons or responsories.

[15]*gaudeas. . .Domino*: cf., *1LAg* 3.

[16]*Nebula*, (confusion), is a mist or fog, a cloud of dust or smoke, a thin film, or veneer, a darkness or obscurity. Personified, a *nebulo* is a worthless person, trifler, scoundrel, loafer, or rascal. In Medieval Latin, cf., *Latham*, a *nebulator* is a fool or jester (1205), and feminized, a *nebulatrix* is a harlot (1221). Obviously, keeping oneself enveloped in the dark cloud has implications for virtue and character.

[17]*Ponere*, (place), means to place, set, or position. It also means to cease holding or carrying, to put down, to lay down one's arms, to rest, to set aside, to deposit in a temple, dedicate, give up, rid oneself of, lay aside, abandon, drop, to yield up life, to weigh carefully, ponder, consider, to calm, quiet. Many of these alternatives would give an interesting variation to Clare's thought. Consider for example: "Quiet your mind in the mirror of eternity."

The perfect passive participle of *ponere* is *positus*, the etymological root of the English word "positive." See Onions, *The Oxford Dictionary of English Etymology* (1995), s.v. *posit*.

[18]The term *mens*, (mind), is a broader concept than the modern word "mind" and holds such definitions as: mind, disposition, heart, soul, conscience, understanding, reason, judgment, discernment, consideration, reflection, plan, purpose, intention, design, boldness, and courage. For further discussion on the translation of *mens* see Ewert Cousins, introduction to *Bonaventure* (New York: Paulist Press, 1978), 21.

[19]*Speculum* is a mirror. The verb, *specto*, means to look at, behold, to gaze at, or to observe. In particular, it means to look to a thing as to an end or as a guide of action. Thus, *speculum* is related to the *imitatio*.

The Third Letter

[20]*splendore gloriae*: cf., *4LAg* 14.

[21]In Heb 1:3, the "figure of the divine substance" refers to Jesus.

[22]Dino Dozzi, "Chiara e lo Specchio," in *Chiara: Francescanesimo al Femminile*, ed. Davide Covi and Dino Dozzi (Roma: Edizioni Dehoniane, 1992), 290-318, outlines verses 12-13 as follows, advocating both horizontal and vertical readings:

a) pone mentem tuam (place your mind)	a) in speculo (in the mirror)	a) aeternitatis (of eternity)
b) pone animam tuam (place your soul)	b) in splendore (in the splendor)	b) gloriae (of glory)
c) pone cor tuum (place your heart)	c) in figura (in the figure)	c) divinae substantiae (of the divine substance)
d) et transforma te ipsam totam per contemplationem (and, through contemplation, transform your entire being)	d) in imagine (into the image)	d) divinitatis ipsius (of the Divine One himself)

Read in this way, one sees that Clare involves the entire person in transforming oneself into the image of the divinity.

[23]*Praetermitto*, (ignore), means to allow or permit to go by, to let pass, to omit, neglect, leave undone, to overlook, or wink at. Clare suggests that Franciscans do not cast out or send away those who ensnare them, but rather they peacefully ignore or merely wink at them.

[24]In *LtOrd* 29, Francis also expresses this theme of exchange: "Hold nothing back of yourselves for yourselves, that he who gives himself totally to you may receive you totally [Nihil ergo de vobis retineatis vobis, ut totos vos recipiat, qui se vobis exhibet totum]."

[25]*cuius. . .mirantur*: cf., *4LAg* 10. The line "whose beauty the sun and moon admire [*cuius pulchritudinem sol et luna mirantur*]," is taken from the Roman *Legend of Saint Agnes*, and was included in the Roman Office for the feast of Saint Agnes, January 21, Matins: 1st nocturn, 3rd lesson; 2nd nocturn, 3rd responsory; 3rd nocturn, 1st and 3rd antiphons, 1st responsory.

[26]A reference to the antiphon: "The old man carried the child, but the child guided the old man: the child to whom the virgin gave birth, and after whose birth she remained a virgin; she adored him whom she brought forth [Senex puerum portabat, puer autem senem regebat: quem virgo peperit, et post partum virgo permansit; ipsum quem genuit, adoravit]." Regula breviary, feast of the Purification of the Blessed Virgin Mary, February 2, Vespers: Magnificat antiphon (cf., Assisi, Sacro Convento, 694, fol. 276r).

[27]*caeli. . .poterant*: cf., *3LAg* 22. The word *continere*, (contain), is related to the word *continentia* meaning continence or self-control. A

medieval religious woman might fast so that she could be emptied of all that was not of God. If she fed upon the Eucharist, she might understand herself holding God as Mary did. Clare warns Agnes that nothing created can make itself worthy of God, who chose to dwell within the young girl, Mary. In *3LAg* 23, Clare reminds Agnes that love, not force, invites the indwelling presence of God. Clare suggests that the way to invite this indwelling presence is not through extreme and self-destructive fasting, but through following the Virgin Mary in humility and poverty, cf., *3LAg* 25.

[28]Verse 18 is a reference to the antiphon: "Holy and immaculate virginity! I do not know how to lift up praises to you. Because he whom the heavens are not able to contain, you held on your lap [Sancta et immaculata virginitas, quibus te laudibus efferam nescio: Quia quem caeli capere non poterant, tuo gremio contulisti]." The antiphon was used in Regula breviary, Office of the Blessed Virgin, Matins: 1st nocturn, 1st responsory (cf., Assisi, Sacro Convento, 694, fol. 386r); and also for the feast of the Annunciation, March 25, Matins: 2rd nocturn, 3rd responsory (cf., Assisi, Sacro Convento, 694, fol. 284r). The Latin word, *gremium*, can refer either to a lap or a bosom.

Clare's ideas here are similar to those in the hymn *Quem terra, pontus, aethera*, that was sung during matins for the Office of the Blessed Virgin. The hymn is also used for matins for the feast of the Annunciation, March 25; Matins: feast of the Assumption, August 15; and Matins: feast of the Nativity of the Virgin Mary, September 8.

[29]*Cogo* means to force or to induce. I have translated the word as "compels." Regis Armstrong, OFM Cap., *Clare of Assisi: Early Documents* (St. Bonaventure, NY: Franciscan Institute Publications), 46, translates *cogo* simply as "attempts." Sr. Frances Teresa, OSC chooses "schemes." Becker/Godet/Matura, *Claire d'Assise: Écrits*, 105, use the French *s'efforce* meaning "to try, or to force," while Marco Bartoli, *Santa Chiara d'Assisi: Scritti e Documenti* (Assisi: Editrici Francescane, 1994), 99, uses the Italian word *spinge* meaning "pushes, thrusts, shoves." I think the idea of force is key to Clare's theology here and needs to be conveyed in some sense. The force might be brute or it might be intelligent, as in the sense of convening or calling together for council. See *OLD*, s.v. *cogo*, 4. This notion of force in terms of intelligent scheming makes Sr. Frances Teresa's choice attractive. I have chosen "compels" to include both the notion of brute force and the concept of malicious scheming.

[30]*caeli. . .nequeant*: cf., *3LAg* 18. *Capio*, (contain), has physical meanings such as to capture, to take hold of, or grasp. It also has intellectual meanings such as to receive, obtain, or understand. Clare, perhaps still meditating on Mary here, permits both meanings

simultaneously. Physically Mary held Jesus in her arms; she also, more than anyone else, understood his mind and heart. The faithful soul is to follow in Mary's footsteps, cf., *3LAg* 24-25.

[31]*Mansio*, (dwelling place), can also refer to the fact of remaining or staying, continuance (in a state or condition), or a day's journey or a stage. The elusiveness of the term *mansio*, dependent upon Jn 14:23, allows the mystic to describe God's indwelling without defining it too precisely.

[32]While *sedes* is a seat or throne, it can also be translated as a dwelling of a god, a temple, or an enclosure. In the Middle Ages, the word could describe both a secular throne as well as an episcopal see, 725, c. 900, c. 1070, 1549; or an abbatial see, c. 1100. The word carried medieval juridical implications: judgment-seat or meeting-place of court, 1202, session of a guild or council, 1227, 1335, place, membership in a guild, 1198, 1260. See *Latham*, s.v. *sedes*; and *Niermeyer*, s.v. *sedes*.

Examples of medieval art still exist that depict the enthroned God within the *visera* of Mary. See Caroline Walker Bynum, *Holy Feast and Holy Fast* (Berkeley: University of California Press, 1987), plate 13.

[33]The *impii*, (wicked), are those who are irreligious, abandoned, ungodly, irreverent, those who are undutiful without reverence or respect for God, one's parents, or one's country.

[34]See note 31 above.

[35]*sana. . .quadragesimalia*: cf., *3LAg* 37.

[36]*Deberemus* implies an obligation to eat twice a day on Sundays and on Christmas day.

[37]*Natalis. . .bis*: cf., *RCl* 3:9.

[38]*ieiunare non teneretur*: cf., *ER* 3:12; *LR* 3:9, 10.

[39]For an analysis of the translation of *omni Pascha* and of Clare's description of fasting in this letter see Gerard Pieter Freeman, "Klarissenfasten im 13. Jahrhundert," *AFH* 87 (1994): 217-85.

[40]*nisi / sexta feria*: cf., *ER* 3:12; *LR* 3:9.

[41]*sanae. . .manducamus*: cf., *3LAg* 32.

[42]For a study on discretion in the writings of Clare see Optatus van Asseldonk, "Chiara, donna di divina discrezione cristiana," *L'Italia Francescana* 62 (1987): 485-94.

[43]Through the use of this scriptural admonition, Clare exhorts Agnes to a more prudent discretion in regard to her fasting practices.

[44]Clare's focus in this closing is on wellness. This wellness is both physical and spiritual, with the weight in this letter, because it addresses Agnes's indiscretions in regard to fasting, being placed perhaps on the physical.

[45]*sorores. . .recommenda*: cf., *2LAg* 26.

Clare's Fourth Letter
To Agnes of Prague

Clare wrote her fourth letter to Agnes on her deathbed in 1253, nearly fifteen years after her third letter. Clare's blood-sister, Agnes of Assisi, is at her side. Assuring Agnes of Prague of her deep care, Clare excuses her lapse in correspondence on the shortage of messengers and the perils of travel.

Both Clare and Agnes have struggled over the years to remain faithful to the form of life given to them by Saint Francis. There has been papal pressure to dilute their commitment to living without property; the Friars Minor themselves have wavered in their commitment to poverty and in their responsibility of caring for the sisters; political upheavals have brought grave hardships to both monasteries. Through all of this, Agnes has proven herself to be a true support and joy to Clare by persevering in her commitment to follow the Poor Christ.

In her fourth letter Clare expresses her love for Agnes of Prague as a daughter dear to her heart. She again freely improvises upon The Legend of Saint Agnes of Rome, demonstrating her familiarity with this text. The eschatological note of the letter is worthy of one who is preparing for death, but it is much more than this. Clare has taken the beatitude, "Blessed are the poor in spirit, for theirs is the kingdom of heaven (Mt 5:3)," literally. She is confident of heaven, because of Christ's promise.

Clare exhorts Agnes to ponder the birth, public life, death, and glory of Jesus Christ, her spouse. In embracing and contemplating the mystery of the Poor Christ, Agnes will share in eschatological glory, and will be united with Clare again before the throne of God.

(1) Animae suae dimidiae et praecordialis amoris armariae singularis, illustri reginae, Agni Regis aeterni sponsae, dominae Agneti, matri suae carissimae ac filiae inter omnes alias speciali, (2) Clara, indigna Christi famula et ancilla *inutilis*[1] ancillarum eius commorantium in monasterio Sancti Damiani de Assisio, (3) salutem et cum reliquis sanctissimis virginibus ante thronum Dei et Agni *novum cantare canticum* et *quocumque ierit Agnum sequi.*[2]

(4) O *mater* et filia, *sponsa*[3] Regis or..nium saeculorum, et si tibi non scripsi frequenter, prout anima tua et mea pariter desiderat et peroptat aliquatenus, non mireris (5) nec credas ullatenus incendium caritatis erga te minus ardere suaviter in visceribus matris tuae. (6) Hoc est impedimentum defectus nuntiorum et viarum pericula manifesta. (7) Nunc vero scribens caritati tuae, congaudeo et exsulto tibi *in gaudio spiritus,*[4] sponsa Christi, (8) quia velut altera virgo sanctissima, sancta Agnes, *Agno immaculato,*[5] *qui tollit peccata mundi,*[6] es mirifice desponsata, sumptis omnibus vanitatibus huius mundi.

---

[1]Cf., Lc 17:10.
[2]Cf., Apc 14:3-4.
[3]Cf., Mt 12:50; 2 Cor 11:2.
[4]Cf., 1 Th 1:6.
[5]Cf., 1 Pt 1:19.
[6]Io 1:29.

The Fourth Letter

(1) To the other half of her[1] soul and repository[2] of the special[3] love of her deepest heart, illustrious queen, spouse of the Lamb of the eternal King,[4] the Lady Agnes, her own dearest mother[5] and, among all the others, her special daughter,[6]   (2) Clare, unworthy servant of Christ and useless[7] handmaid[8] of his handmaids who live in the Monastery[9] of San Damiano[10] in Assisi, (3) sends greetings and her prayer[11] that Agnes, together with the other most holy virgins, will sing a new song before the throne of God and of the Lamb, and will follow the Lamb[12] wherever he goes.

(4) O mother and daughter, spouse of the King of all ages, even if I have not written to you as frequently as both your soul and mine would have desired and longed for, do not for a moment wonder (5) or believe in any way that the fire of my love for you burns any less sweetly in the deepest heart[13] of your mother. (6) The truth is that a shortage of messengers and the obvious perils of travel have hindered me. (7) But now, as I write to your love, I rejoice and exult for you in the joy of the Spirit,[14] spouse of Christ, (8) because like that other most holy virgin, Saint Agnes,[15] you have been in an astonishing way espoused to the immaculate Lamb,[16] who, having assumed responsibility for all the vanities of this world, takes away the sins of the world.

(9)   Felix certe
       cui hoc sacro datur potiri convivio,
       ut ei adhaereatur totis cordis praecordiis,

(10)   *cuius pulchritudinem*
       omnia beata caelorum agmina
       incessabiliter ad*mirantur,*[7]

(11)   cuius affectus afficit,
       cuius contemplatio reficit,
       cuius implet benignitas,

(12)   cuius replet suavitas,
       cuius memoria lucescit suaviter,

(13)   *cuius odore mortui reviviscent,*[8]
       cuiusque visio gloriosa beatificabit
       omnes cives supernae Ierusalem:

(14)   quae *cum sit splendor* aeternae *gloriae,*[9]
       candor lucis aeternae
       et speculum sine macula.[10]

---

[7]A variant on "cuius pulchritudinem sol et luna mirantur," from the *Legend of Saint Agnes of Rome*. Cf., *3LAg* 16.

[8]*Regula Breviary*, January 21, Saint Agnes of Rome, Matins: 1st nocturn, 3rd lesson.

[9]Hbr 1:3.

[10]Sap 7:26.

The Fourth Letter

(9)   Happy, indeed, is the one permitted to share
in this sacred banquet so as to be joined[17]
with all the feelings of her heart to him

(10)   whose beauty all the blessed hosts of the
heavens unceasingly admire,

(11)   whose affection moves,
whose contemplation invigorates,
whose generosity fills,

(12)   whose sweetness replenishes,
whose remembrance pleasantly brings light,

(13)   whose fragrance will revive the dead,[18]
and whose glorious vision will bless
all the citizens of the heavenly Jerusalem,[19]

(14)   because the vision of him[20] is the splendor of
everlasting glory,[21]
the radiance of everlasting light,
and a mirror[22] without tarnish.

(15) Hoc speculum cottidie intuere, o regina, sponsa Iesu Christi, et in eo faciem tuam iugiter speculare, (16) ut sic totam interius et exterius te adornes amictam *circumdatamque varietatibus*,[11] (17) omnium virtutum floribus et vestimentis pariter adornata, sicut decet, filia et sponsa carissima summi Regis. (18) In hoc autem speculo refulget beata paupertas, sancta humilitas et ineffabilis caritas, sicut per totum speculum poteris cum Dei gratia contemplari.

(19) Attende, inquam, principium huius speculi paupertatem *positi* siquidem *in praesepio* et *in panniculis involuti*.[12] (20) O miranda humilitas, o stupenda paupertas! (21) Rex angelorum, *Dominus caeli et terrae*[13] *in praesepio reclinatur*.[14] (22) In medio autem speculi considera humilitatem, saltem beatam paupertatem, labores innumeros ac poenalitates quas sustinuit pro redemptione humani generis. (23) In fine vero eiusdem speculi contemplare ineffabilem caritatem, qua pati voluit in crucis stipite et in eodem mori omni mortis genere turpiori.

---

[11]Cf., Ps 44:10.
[12]Cf., Lc 2:12.
[13]Cf., Mt 11:25.
[14]Cf., Lc 2:7.

The Fourth Letter

(15) Look into this mirror every day, O queen, spouse of Jesus Christ, and continually examine your face in it, (16) so that in this way you may adorn yourself completely, inwardly and outwardly, clothed and covered in multicolored apparel, (17) adorned in the same manner with flowers and garments made of all the virtues as is proper, dearest daughter and spouse of the most high King.[23] (18) Moreover, in this mirror shine blessed poverty, holy humility, and charity beyond words, as you will be able, with God's grace, to contemplate throughout the entire mirror.

(19) Look closely, I say, to the beginning[24] of the life of this admired one,[25] indeed at the poverty of him who was wrapped in swaddling clothes and placed in a manger.[26] (20) O marvelous humility! O astonishing poverty![27] (21) The King of the angels, the Lord of heaven and earth is laid to rest in a manger![28] (22) Consider also the midst[29] of his[30] life, his humility, or at least his blessed poverty, the countless hardships, and the punishments that he endured for the redemption of the human race. (23) Indeed, ponder the final[31] days of this mirrored one, contemplate the ineffable love with which he was willing to suffer on the tree of the cross and to die there a kind of death that is more shameful than any other.

(24) Unde ipsum speculum, in ligno crucis positum, hic consideranda transeuntes monebat dicens: (25) *O vos omnes qui transitis per viam, attendite et videte si est dolor sicut dolor meus;*[15] (26) respondeamus, inquit, ei clamanti et eiulanti una voce, uno spiritu: *Memoria memor ero et tabescet in me anima mea.*[16] (27) Huius igitur caritatis ardore accendaris iugiter fortius, o regina caelestis Regis!

(28) Contemplans insuper indicibiles eius delicias, divitias, et honores perpetuos (29) et suspirando prae nimio cordis desiderio et amore proclames:

(30)   *Trahe me post te,
        curremus in odorem unguentorum tuorum,*[17]
        sponse caelestis!

(31)   Curram nec deficiam,
        donec *introducas me in cellam vinariam,*[18]

(32)   donec *laeva tua* sit *sub capite meo
        et dextera feliciter*[19] *amplexabitur me,*[20]
        osculeris me felicissimo *tui oris osculo.*[21]

---

[15]Lam 1:12.
[16]Lam 3:20.
[17]Ct 1:3.
[18]Ct 2:4.
[19]For Clare's source of this word inserted into this text from the *Song of Songs* see her Privilege of Poverty, Gregory IX, *Sicut manifestum est,* September 17, 1228, *BF* I:771.
[20]Ct 2:6; 8:3.
[21]Ct 1:1.

The Fourth Letter

(24) That mirror[32] suspended upon the wood of the cross from there kept urging those passing by of what must be considered, saying: (25) O all you who pass by this way, look and see if there is any suffering like my suffering. (26) In response let us with one voice and in one spirit answer him who is crying out and lamenting: I will remember this over and over[33] and my soul will sink within me. (27) Therefore, seeing this, O queen of the heavenly King, you must burn ever more strongly with the fervor of charity!

(28) Furthermore, as you contemplate his indescribable delights, riches, and everlasting honors, (29) and heaving a sigh because of your heart's immeasurable desire and love may you exclaim:

(30)　　Draw me after you, Heavenly Spouse, we
　　　　shall run in the fragrance of your perfumes!

(31)　　I shall run and not grow weary until you
　　　　bring me into the wine cellar,

(32)　　until your left hand is under my head[34] and
　　　　your right arm[35] blissfully[36] embraces me;[37]
　　　　and you kiss me with the most blissful kiss
　　　　of your mouth.[38]

(33) In hac contemplatione posita, habeas memoriam pauperculae matris tuae, (34) sciens quod ego tuam felicem memoriam *descripsi* inseparabiliter *in tabulis cordis mei,*[22] habens te prae omnibus cariorem.

(35) Quid plura? Sileat in dilectione tua lingua carnis; hoc inquit, et loquatur lingua spiritus. (36) O filia benedicta, quoniam dilectionem, quam ad te habeo, nullatenus posset exprimere plenius lingua carnis, hoc inquit quae semiplene scripsi. (37) Oro benigne ac devote suscipias attendens in eis saltem affectum maternum, quo circa te ac filias tuas caritatis ardore afficior omni die, quibus me ac filias meas in Christo plurimum recommenda. (38) Ipsae vero filiae meae, sed praecipue virgo prudentissima Agnes, soror nostra, se tibi et filiabus tuis, quantum possunt, in Domino recommendant.

(39) Vale, carissima filia, cum filiabus tuis usque ad thronum *gloriae magni Dei*[23] et optate *pro nobis.*[24]

(40) Latores praesentium carissimos nostros fratrem Amatum, *dilectum Deo et hominibus,*[25] et fratrem Bonaguram caritati tuae, quantum possum, praesentibus recommendo. Amen.

---

[22]Cf., Prv 3:3; 2 Cor 3:3.
[23]Cf., Tit 2:13.
[24]Cf., 1 Th 5:25.
[25]Cf., Sir 45:1.

The Fourth Letter

(33) As you are placed in this contemplation, may you remember your poor little mother, (34) knowing that I have inseparably inscribed the happy memory of you on the tablets of my heart, for I regard you as dearer than all others.

(35) Why say more? Let my physical tongue be silent, as it is said, and let the tongue of the Spirit speak. (36) O blessed daughter, since in no way at all could my bodily tongue express more fully the love that I have for you, (37) that which I have written is certainly inadequate. I beg you to receive these words with kindness and devotion, seeing in them at least the motherly affection, by which every day I am stirred by the fire of love for you and your daughters; please ask them to pray for me and my daughters in Christ. (38) Indeed, inasmuch as they are able, my own daughters, and especially the most prudent virgin, Agnes, our sister, beg you and your daughters to pray for them in the Lord.

(39) Farewell, dearest daughter, together with your own daughters, until we meet at the throne of glory of the great God, and pray for us.

(40) I must now commend[39] to your charity, as fully as possible, our dearest bearers of this letter, Brother Amato, beloved by God[40] and human beings, and Brother Bonaugura.[41] Amen.

Notes

[1]The pronoun "her" refers to Clare.

[2]An *armarium* is a cabinet, cupboard, bookcase, chest, or safe.

[3]Again Clare assures Agnes that her love for her is personal and particular.

[4]In this letter, Clare refers to Agnes as the queen or spouse of Christ or of the King seven times: *4LAg* 1, 4, 7, 8, 15, 17, and 27.

[5]*sponsae. . .matri*: cf., *1LAg* 12. Clare has referred to Agnes as her sister and coworker. In this letter, she also acknowledges Agnes as "her own dearest mother."

[6]*dominae. . .filiae*: cf., *RCl* Prologue:10. A chiastic structure of this opening verse might be suggested. The emphasis is the title "spouse of the Lamb of the eternal King."

⌈Animae suae dimidiae et praecordialis amoris armariae singularis,
|(To half of her own soul and the repository of the singular love of
| her heart),
| ⌈illustri reginae,
| |(the illustrious Queen),
| | ⌈Agni Regis aeterni sponsae,
| | ⌊(spouse of the Lamb of the eternal King),
| |dominae Agneti,
| ⌊(Lady Agnes),
|matri suae carissimae ac filiae inter omnes alias speciali.
⌊(her own dearest mother and daughter special among all
   others).

Note that the first and last phrases describe the relationship between Clare and Agnes. The central phrases describe Agnes's relationship with God. Agnes's title as "spouse of the Lamb" will be repeated throughout this letter. See Van den Goorbergh and Zweerman, *Light Shining Through a Veil*, 221-22.

[7]*famula. . .inutilis*: cf., *1LAg* 33.

[8]*Clara. . .ancilla*: cf., *1LAg* 2; *2LAg* 2; *3LAg* 2; *RCl* 1:3.

[9]*commorantium in monasterio*: cf., *1LAg* 33.

[10]*Clara. . .Damiani*: cf., *1LAg* 2.

[11]*Clara. . .salutem*: cf., *2LAg* 2; *3LAg* 2; *4LAg* 2-3; RCl Prologue:2.

[12]Playing on Agnes's name, Clare asks Agnes, whose name means "lamb" to follow the "Lamb."

The Fourth Letter

---

[13]See *1LAg* 31, note 76.

[14]Although not a direct paraphrase, one recalls here Elizabeth's baby leaping for joy and Mary's rejoicing and exulting in the Lord (Lk 1:44, 47).

[15]Note in the Latin, Clare's wonderful word-play. Agnes is referred to as *sancta Agnes*, while Christ is referred to as *Agno immaculato*. Their spousal bond makes them: *sancta Agnes, Agno immaculato*.

[16]The reason for Clare's joy is Agnes's epousal to the Lamb.

[17]See *2LAg* 7, note 19.

[18]Verses 10-13 are modeled after the *Legend of Saint Agnes of Rome*. There is the clear variation on this legend in verse 10, the threading of the legend's *cuius* construction throughout these verses, and a quotation of the legend in verse 13. For further analysis of Clare's reference to the *Legend of Saint Agnes of Rome* in this letter see the essay, "*The Legend of Saint Agnes of Rome as Source*," on pages 107-48 in this volume.

[19]See Rev 19-21 for a description of the wedding feast of the Lamb.

[20]The reference is Christological.

[21]*splendor. . .gloriae*: cf., *3LAg* 12.

[22]Note that Clare also uses the mirror image in *3LAg* 12.

[23]*filia. . .Regis*: cf., *4LAg* 4; *OfP* Ant:2; *RCl* 6:3. *summi Regis*: cf., *3LAg* 1; *OfP* Ant:2; *RCl* 6:3; *1C* 120:1; *LJS* 71:7.

[24]In this context, *principium* refers to the point of time in which a thing begins, rather than to a dimension of a physical mirror. See *OLD*, s.v. "principium," 1 & 2.

[25]Clare is playing on various meanings of the Latin word *speculum*. She begins by referring to Christ as the "mirror" by which the Poor Sister is able to look upon her face and dress herself (verses 15-17). In verse 18, she cleverly shifts from her concrete image of Christ as "mirror," to the more figurative image of Christ as the "model," also *speculum*, of "blessed poverty, holy humility, and charity beyond words." See *Latham*, s.v. "speculum." Unfortunately, the English language does not have a word like *speculum* that is able to reflect both of Clare's meanings simultaneously. Moving away from the concept of a physical mirror to a model of poverty, humility, and charity, however, is necessary if one wishes to understand Clare's instructions.

[26]*in presepio. . .involuti*: cf., *RCl* 2:25.

[27]*o stupenda paupertas*: cf., *1LAg* 15, 16, 17.

[28]*in. . .reclinatur*: cf,. *RCl* 2:25; *1C* 84:8; *AC* 14:5.

[29]*Medio* here refers to the middle of life rather than to a dimension of a physical mirror. Clare is asking Agnes to contemplate the life of Christ, her model. See *OLD*, s.v. "medius," 5 & 6.

[30]Or "the life of this mirror/model."

[31]Again referring to time (the end of life, death), rather than dimension. *OLD*, s.v. "finis," 10a.

[32]With the sense of "the admired one," or "the one whom one wishes to imitate." See above, note 25.

[33]The redundancy seen in *Memoria meror* suggests the sense of remembering over and over.

[34]According to the Privilege of Poverty, the "left hand" of the Spouse supports the Poor Ladies in their choice of poverty: "The lack of goods from this *propositum* does not frighten you, for the left hand of your heavenly Spouse is under your head to uphold the weaknesses of your body that you have submitted to the law of the soul through your well-ordered love [nec ab huiusmodi proposito vos rerum terret inopia; Nam laeva Sponsi caelestis est sub capite vestro ad sustentandum infirma corporis vestri, quae legi mentis ordinata caritate stravistis]." *BF* I: 771.

[35]In the Privilege of Poverty, the "right arm" symbolizes the eschatological reward given to those who persevere in poverty: "Accordingly, he who feeds the birds of the sky and clothes the lilies of the field will not fail you in matters of food and of clothing until, passing among you, he serves himself to you in eternity, when indeed his right arm will more blissfully embrace you in the greatness of his vision [Denique qui pascit aves Caeli, et lilia vestit agri, vobis non deerit ad victum pariter, et vastitum; donec seipsum vobis transiens in aeternitate ministret; cum scilicet eius dextera vos felicius amplexabitur in suae plenitudine visionis]." *BF* I:771.

The symbol of the left arm as the symbol of the present life, and of the right arm as symbolizing eternal life is also found in Saint Gregory the Great, *Expositio super Cantica Canticorum* II:6, (*PL* 79, col. 496).

[36]The insertion of "blissfully," (*feliciter*), into this text from the Song of Songs is an echo of the Privilege of Poverty where "blissfully," (*felicius*), is also inserted. *BF* I:771.

[37]Both Song 2:6 and 8:3 read: "His left hand is under my head, and his right arm embraces me [Laeva eius sub capite meo, et dextera illius amplexatur me]." Frederic Raurell proposes that Clare's use of the Song of Songs follows the *Exposition on the Song of Songs* of William of Saint Thierry. Since William's commentary only extends to Song 3:4a, Raurell proposes that only Song 2:6 should be noted as a reference. Raurell's arguments are problematic if one includes, as he suggests, Clare's entire epistolary corpus. In doing this, one also cannot account for the reference to Song 3:4b in *2LAg* 11. See Frederic Raurell, "La Lettura del "Cantico dei Cantici" al Tempo di Chiara e la "IV Lettera ad Agnese di Praga," in

The Fourth Letter

Chiara: Francescanesimo al Femminile, Davide Covi and Dino Dozzi, eds. (Roma: Edizioni Dehoniane, 1992), 219, note 84.

[38]Song 1:1 reads: "Let him kiss me with the kiss of his mouth! [Osculetur me osculo oris sui!]."

What is Clare's source for the Song of Songs and what medieval exegete might one follow to uncover Clare's sense of these passages? Although many theories could be proposed, three can be substantiated. First, commentary on the Song of Songs was an essential element of the 13th century popular religious milieu. The Poor Ladies were certainly somewhat familiar with this popular religious culture. Second, the 1st and 3rd lessons for matins of the feast of the Nativity of Mary, September 8, are taken from the Song of Songs and can account for all the verses highlighted by Clare, cf., Assisi, Sacro Convento, 694, fols. 327r and v. Third, Clare's insertion of "blissfully" points to the Privilege of Poverty as a definite source of Clare's reflections. Clare concludes her correspondence with Agnes, alluding to the Privilege of Poverty, which was the very bond of their relationship.

[39]*plurimum recommenda*: cf., *2LAg* 26.

[40]*ad. . .Dei*: cf., *4LAg* 3.

[41]The name *Bonagura* means "good luck," "good wishes" or "farewell."

PART TWO

IDENTIFYING CLARE'S SOURCES

The Legend of Saint Agnes of Rome as Source

The Agnes Legend in the Middle Ages

The Legend of Saint Agnes of Rome dramatizes the story of
a tenacious Christian girl whose fidelity to Christ as her
bridegroom eventually gained for her the crown of martyrdom.
Enjoying extraordinary popularity during the Middle Ages, the
prominence of *The Legend of Saint Agnes* surpassed other
hagiographic legends of women whose historicity is more
solidly substantiated.[1] Even in cursory ambles through
thirteenth century art collections, one commonly discovers
portrayals of the Christian girl who preferred martyrdom rather
than infidelity to her divine bridegroom.

Saint Agnes enjoyed early prominence in the Roman
liturgy. Her name found its way into the Roman Martyrology
and eventually into the Tridentine Canon. Her legend became
part of the early Roman Office of Matins and recovered its
prominence and length after Innocent III's efforts at
abbreviation. The medieval liturgy of the solemn consecration
of virgins, while oddly neglecting references to the Virgin
Mary, placed primacy on the legends of Saints Agnes and
Agatha, borrowing from no other hagiographic source.[2]

There is evidence that the popular *Legend of Saint Agnes*
was already translated into vernacular languages in the twelfth
century. Herbert Grundmann cites one example:

> At approximately the time Waldes was having the Bible
> translated in Lyon, the priest Lambert (d. 1177) was
> translating the *Acts of the Apostles* and *The Legend of
> Saint Agnes* in Liège, not for himself or as the basis for
> an apostolic mission, but for the edification of others.
> Lambert had been seeking to combat the worldly
> doings of urban culture through sermons and example.

Particularly, he had organized communities of pious laity who sought to return a Christian character to the Sunday celebration, instead of desecrating it with minstrels, entertainers, and comedians, through drinking, games, indecent songs, dancing, and shameless carousing. He prepared his translations and pious essays in the vernacular: for women there was a version of *The Legend of Saint Agnes*, and for all of them together there was an edition of the *Acts of the Apostles*, both of them interspersed with his own moral observations and in verse.[3]

Given this popularity, it is not surprising to find references to the Agnes legend in the writings of medieval women. The letters of Saint Clare of Assisi to Saint Agnes of Prague serve as an example.[4] In her four letters to Agnes of Prague, Clare directly quotes, paraphrases, and makes allusions to the Agnes legend.

Although it is neither original nor difficult to identify citings of and allusions to *The Legend of Saint Agnes* within Clare's letters to Agnes of Prague, Clare's source for this legend has not yet been systematically questioned. Given the poverty of the San Damiano monastery and the cost of a medieval manuscript, it is clear that Clare did not have a library of codices at her disposal. Because of this paucity, perhaps the proverbial scholarly exclamation, "If I only knew what was on her bookshelf," could be hypothesized in Clare's case.

Clare's Source of the Agnes Legend

In pondering Clare's source of the Agnes legend, three possibilities come to mind. First, Clare's knowledge of *The Legend of Saint Agnes* sprang from popular sources such as sermons, poems, songs, or plays which depicted the Agnes legend; second, Clare's source was the Roman consecration of virgins liturgy which incorporated elements of the Agnes legend; third, Clare used as her primary source the text of the Divine Office recited at San Damiano.

The Legend of Saint Clare 37 suggests that Clare loved to listen to sermons. It is possible that sermons or other venues of popular culture were Clare's primary source of the Agnes legend. Clare's poetic license in referring to the legend might suggest a poetic or dramatic source. Such a source, however, does not seem to have been preserved. Throughout her letters, Clare uses scriptural sources fluidly, rarely quoting texts literally, often changing verb tenses, combining passages to illustrate her theological purpose more clearly, or weaving scriptural allusions with prose. Given Clare's freedom with scriptural texts, one sees that Clare is quite capable of using poetic license, making a theory that Clare's freedom signals a solely popular source for the Agnes legend unsubstantiated.

Given Clare's sensitivity to Agnes of Prague, and her reverence and respect toward Agnes as a royal woman, an educated woman, and a spouse of Christ, it is unlikely that Clare would have chosen a local vernacular source unfamiliar to Agnes. However, since Agnes of Rome was Agnes of Prague's patron saint, one can certainly speculate that Clare may have rightly assumed that Agnes of Prague knew well *The Legend of Saint Agnes.*

Without doubting popular knowledge of a vernacular source of the Agnes legend, could one also imagine a liturgical source for the legend existing at the Monastery of San Damiano? Following the study by Mary Teresa Tavormina, Regis Armstrong recalls the influence of *The Legend of Saint Agnes* on the Roman liturgy of the consecration of virgins.[5] Edith Van den Goorbergh, OSC, and Theodore Zweerman, OFM, in *Light Shining through a Veil* connect *1LAg* 8-11 to the consecration liturgy itself.[6] If Clare's first letter was written to celebrate the occasion of Agnes's entrance into the monastery, this reasoning becomes all the more enticing. Upon examination, however, one finds that the consecration liturgy was probably not Clare's source.

In examining thirteenth-century sacramentaries, one discovers textual problems with the theory that Clare depended upon the liturgy of the consecration of virgins as her source for the Agnes legend. Michel Andrieu's manuscript synthesis of the thirteenth-century pontifical liturgy includes the *Ordo ad virginem benedicendam*. Andrieu's synthesis shows little variation in this liturgy among thirteenth-century manuscripts. In the pontificals, Andrieu records the following three quotations from the Agnes legend.

> 1) *Induit me dominus ciclade auro texta et immensis monilibus ornavit me.*
> (The Lord clothed me in a robe of state woven with gold, and adorned me with innumerable necklaces).

> 2) *Posuit signum in faciem meam, ut nullum preter eum amatorem admittam.*
> (He placed a seal on my face, so that I will admit no lover except him).

> 3) *Cui angeli serviunt, cuius pulchritudinem sol et luna mirantur.*
> (Angels serve him, whose beauty the sun and moon admire).[7]

Of these three quotations, Clare quotes part of the third in *3LAg* 16: *cuius pulchritudinem sol et luna mirantur.* She alludes to this same source in *4LAg* 10: *cuius pulchritudinem omnia beata caelorum agmina* incessabiliter ad*mirantur.*

Using English consecration ceremonies as her source, Tavormina highlights sections of the Agnes legend transposed into the liturgy.[8] Although she does not include her Latin text,

The Legend of Saint Agnes of Rome as Source

Tavormina cites only one other line from the Agnes legend from her English liturgical sources that is employed by Clare in *1LAg* 8: "Having loved him, I am chaste; having touched him, I am clean; having received him, I am a virgin."

This analysis of the liturgy of the consecration of virgins makes it difficult to account for many of Clare's paraphrases and allusions to the Agnes legend. Given this data, it is necessary to exclude the consecration of virgins liturgy as Clare's primary source for the Agnes legend.

The Divine Office as a Possible Source

With the approved Rule of 1223, the Franciscan Order not only became more disciplined in its recital of the Roman Office, but also set up a scriptorium in Assisi to produce master copies of the Regula breviary, based on the office of the Roman court, to be sent all over Europe.[9] Given papal impetus and Franciscan missionary activity, the papal Office spread rapidly in the years following 1223.[10]

In his synthesis of the Office of Saint Agnes,[11] Van Dijk cites "*Lectiones leguntur de passione eius [Servus Christi Ambrosius]*,"[12] and includes the cues for the antiphons and responsories in three nocturns signaling nine lessons. There is also listed an octave for the feast with three additional lessons. The goal of Innocent III's reform was to curb unwieldy lessons in order to reduce the time needed to say the Office and to make possible a portable breviary.[13] An Office of twelve lessons was exceptional. The Regula Office for the feast of Saint Agnes with its twelve lengthy lessons intact was such an exception.

It does not seem unfair to hypothesize that the early friars, and certainly in the case of Saint Clare, Saint Francis himself, might have seen to it that the monasteries of the Poor Ladies of San Damiano and of Prague each had a copy of the Regula breviary. In 1253, Saint Clare states in her Rule 3:1-2 that her sisters could have these breviaries: "Let the sisters who can read, say the Divine Office according to the custom of the Friars Minor. For this, they may have breviaries, reading them without singing."[14] However, we also know that Francis's companions, Leo, Angelo, and Rufino used *The Breviary of Saint Francis*, a pre-Regula breviary with several Haymonian corrections added by Leo, well after 1230. In 1257-58, these brothers gave this breviary as a gift to the sisters. Clare's sisters continued to use the book after 1257.[15]

At the general chapter of 1230, copies of the breviary produced at the Assisi scriptorium were distributed to the provinces of the Order.[16] While it is possible that both Clare and Agnes might have had copies of this Regula breviary at the time that Clare wrote her letters, it would be just as probable, particularly in the case of the sisters of San Damiano, that Clare and her sisters continued to use an earlier manuscript perhaps donated to them by Bishop Guido or by the canons of San Rufino early in the history of their community. This earlier edition may simply have been corrected in line with liturgical reforms.

Even if the new breviaries were not available to both Clare and Agnes, the Assisi and Prague monasteries would have needed some manuscript to fulfill their religious obligation of reciting the Divine Office. Since the Office of Saint Agnes was an ancient office, it would have been found both in the Regula breviary and in older medieval breviaries.

Further testing of our hypothesis that Clare used the text of the January 21st Office of Matins as a source of the Agnes legend in her letters to Agnes of Prague is required. One needs to search the antiphons, responsories, and the lessons of the Agnes Office to find possible sources for Clare's direct quotes and paraphrases, as well as for the allusions that Clare may have borrowed from the Office.

The Legend of Saint Agnes of Rome as Source

Matins—The Feast of Saint Agnes of Rome

A sort of "holy week" for women, the ancient Office of Saint Agnes of Rome began on January 21, the date commemorating Agnes's trial and the beginning of her passion, and closed on January 28, the celebrated date of her death.[17] The author, who names himself as "Ambrose," openly suggests that the example of Agnes described in the legend should be imitated by other virgins: "to the honor of so great a martyr, I have written down her deeds as I have come to know them. I thought that the account of her passion had been destined for your imitation, oh virgins of Christ, and I pray to the Holy Spirit that our labors find fruit before the Lord in the similarity of your lives."[18]

To attempt to identify the text of the Office of Saint Agnes that may have been prayed by Clare and her sisters in 1234, seven 13th century manuscripts were consulted. The first manuscript, *The Breviary of Saint Francis*, is perhaps the most ancient extant rubricated portable breviary. On the first folio there is a note written by Brother Leo attesting that the book belonged to Francis, Leo, and Angelo. Along with Brother Rufino, Brothers Leo and Angelo gave the precious relic to Sister Benedicta (d. 1260), Clare's successor as abbess, for safekeeping in about 1257-58, when the sisters moved their monastery within the walls of Assisi.[19]

The rendering of the January 21st Office of Saint Agnes in *The Breviary of Saint Francis* is interesting and typical to the style of this particular manuscript.[20] The feast and its octave contain nine lessons each, but these lessons are considerably shortened from those found in all but one of the other manuscripts studied. In this breviary the eighteen lessons for the feast of Saint Agnes and its octave do not cover the same amount of text that others cover in nine lessons for the feast and three lessons for the octave. Although interesting for the study of the life of Saint Francis, this breviary was not the one used by Clare and her sisters during the years that Clare was writing to Agnes of Prague.

Leo made several corrections to the text of Francis's breviary in 1244, shortly after the publication of Haymo's Ordo.[21] This observation is helpful to this study, since it points to the fact that Franciscans used breviaries other than those produced in the Assisi scriptorium after the promulgation of the Rule of 1223. Saint Francis, in his eagerness to promptly follow the mandate of the 1223 Rule, probably obtained this breviary from a chaplain of the papal court before the Assisi scriptorium could be established and a Regula breviary produced.[22]

The reader may wonder why the so-called *Breviary of Saint Clare*, housed at the Monastery of San Damiano, was not considered as the only manuscript upon which to base this study. Van Dijk's analysis of this breviary, which is in reality both a breviary and a missal, proposes that it was written between 1231-41 at the direction of the bishop of Assisi who wished to reform the liturgy of San Rufino.[23] A note on the last leaf supposedly written by Leo says, "of (for) Clare of the city of Assisi," created a tradition, which can be traced to the early part of the 17th century, that Brother Leo copied the manuscript for Clare and her sisters. Van Dijk proposes that this tradition "must be dismissed on historical as well as palaeographical grounds."[24]

According to Van Dijk, the sanctorale of *The Breviary of Saint Clare* is likely to have been copied from a Franciscan breviary, perhaps after Easter of 1234.[25] After studying the Office of Saint Agnes, this thesis raises some questions. The lessons for the feast of Saint Agnes are greatly abbreviated in *The Breviary of Saint Clare*, while the Regula manuscripts, even though their overall agenda was abbreviation, contain the entire *Legend of Saint Agnes*. Given this observation, one might imagine that the sanctorale could have been commissioned by the local ordinary of Assisi who was perhaps eager to honor the Franciscan saints of his diocese. In any case, *The Breviary of Saint Clare* was not a manuscript used in 1234 by Clare and her sisters.

Two examples of Franciscan, pre-Haymonian breviaries were also studied: Assisi, Sacro Convento, 694[26] and Chicago, Newberry Library, 24 (23817).[27] The Assisi manuscript, which was most likely produced in the Assisi scriptorium, was used as a model for the copying of other breviaries. Since there were twenty provinces at the time of the 1230 chapter, twenty copies of the *breviaria-antiphonaria*, (or perhaps the original was really a *breviaria-missalia*), were possibly distributed at the chapter. The superior of each province was to insure that adequate copies of these manuscripts were made to provide for the friaries in his province.[28] However, in saying this one must remember that Brothers Leo, Angelo, and Rufino were probably using Francis's breviary, a pre-Regula breviary, well into the 1240s. Because of their poverty, the friars used what they had, accepting books that had been discarded by others and updating them as they could.

In regard to the Office of Saint Agnes, the text of the nine lessons as well as the antiphons and responsories for the January 21st feast in the Assisi and Newberry manuscripts are essentially the same—a simple division of the entire Roman *Legend of Saint Agnes* ending with the account of Agnes's death and burial on the feastday, and completing the legend, in three lessons, during the octave. Although the agenda of the Regula breviary was abbreviation, the feast of Saint Agnes and its legend were left untouched.

Two Prague manuscripts were also studied.[29] The first, the so-called *Franciscan Breviary* housed in the Prague Museum of Decorative Arts, does not contain lessons for the Agnes feast. *The Osek Lectionary* (circa 1270), preserved in the National Library in Prague, is known for its splendid illuminated representation of Agnes of Prague with Agnes of Rome. The illumination is found at the beginning of the readings for the January 21st feast of Saint Agnes of Rome. Written in a wonderfully clear script, unlike that of the Regula breviaries, *The Osek Lectionary* for the feast of Saint Agnes contains the full text of the first and second lessons of Regula breviary, Sacro Convento, 694. The second *Osek* lesson, continues without a break into the third Sacro Convento, 694 lesson. It ends in the middle of a sentence and then continues with a small portion of the second Sacro Convento, 694 lesson for the octave. The third lesson of *The Osek Lectionary* continues with the text of the Regula octave's second lesson and goes to the end of the Roman legend. It is obvious that *The Osek Lectionary* is based on an entirely different model for the divisions and use of the Agnes lessons than the Regula model.

Can one find any clues that Clare may have relied on the lessons for matins of the Office of Saint Agnes from the text of her letters? Upon examination of the manuscripts, it was noted that Clare's use of the legend in *1LAg* 10-11, seems to prohibit a source similar to *The Breviary of Saint Francis*, since this breviary divides Clare's text between two lessons. Of lesser importance is the observation that the text of the legend seemingly alluded to by Clare in *1LAg* 7, is excluded from the abbreviated lessons found in *The Breviary of Saint Francis*, *The Breviary of Saint Clare*, and *The Osek Lectionary*. If one wants to examine the hypothesis of a breviary source, one must do this by means of a breviary manuscript that contains all the text from the Agnes legend alluded to by Clare. Hence, in our analysis, the Assisi Regula breviary, Sacro Convento, 694, will be used, although this in no way espouses the belief that one can be certain that Clare and/or Agnes had the use of a Regula breviary.

There is also the possibility that Clare is not using the text of *The Legend of Saint Agnes* at all, but is relying on antiphons and responsories from the Agnes office. This hypothesis, which some scholars seem to have espoused,[30] also needs to be tested.

There are a variety of ways to proceed. One could merely extract from Clare's letters all quotes, paraphrases, and allusions to the Office of Saint Agnes and demonstrate these parallels to the reader. This method is advantageous in that it could succinctly provide evidence of Clare's possible dependence on the Office of Matins for the feast of Saint Agnes in her letters to Agnes of Prague. However, the very terseness of this method would deprive the reader of any familiarity with the experience Clare and Agnes had of the Agnes Office. Alternatively, one might reproduce the Agnes Office in its entirety. The disadvantage of this method is that the length and enticement of this Office might divert the reader from the task of comparing Clare's letters with the text of the Office. Therefore, I will proceed by way of a compromise route, giving an abbreviated form of the Agnes Office followed by a comparison of relevant passages from the letters of Clare. By using this method, I hope to (1) offer readers an abbreviated sense of the Poor Ladies' possible experience of the Agnes Office, and (2) focus readers on the examination of Clare's use of the Agnes legend in her letters.

Below is an outline of the Office of Matins for the feast of Saint Agnes of Rome taken from the Regula breviary with special emphasis on the lessons of the Office that Clare quoted, paraphrased, or alluded to in her letters to Saint Agnes of Prague.[31] Matins for the January 21st feast contained nine psalms with antiphons and nine readings with responsories divided into three nocturns. In this rendering, neither the author nor the translator wish to provide a paleographical transcription of the Office. For those interested in the history of the Office of Saint Agnes, a more technical study would be needed. The interest of this study is simply to explore Clare's use of the Agnes legend in comparison with its use in the Regula breviary.

Matins for the Office
of the Feast of Saint Agnes of Rome

First Nocturn

First Antiphon

Discede a me, pabulum mortis, quia iam ab alio amatore praeventa sum.	Depart from me, food of death, because I have already been taken by another lover.

Psalm 1: Beatus vir   Happy is the one.

Second Antiphon

Dexteram meam, et collum meum cinxit lapidibus pretiosis: tradidit auribus meis inaestimabiles margaritas.	My right hand and my neck he encircled with precious stones; he hung priceless pearls from my ears.

Psalm 2: Quare fremuerunt   Why do they rage?

Third Antiphon

Posuit signum in faciem meam, ut nullum praeter eum amatorem admittam.	He placed a seal on my face, so that I will admit no lover except him.

Psalm 3: Domine quid multiplicati Lord, how many.

The Legend of Saint Agnes of Rome as Source

First Lesson[32]

Servus Christi Ambrosius Virginibus sacris. Diem festum sanctissimae virginis celebremus. Hinc psalmi resonent, inde concrepent lectiones. Hinc populorum turbae laetentur, inde subleventur pauperes Christi. Omnes ergo gratulemur in domino, et ad aedificationem virginum, qualiter passa sit beatissima Agnes, ad memoriam revocemus. Tertiodecimo aetatis suae anno mortem perdidit, et vitam invenit, quia solum vitae dilexit auctorem. Infantia computabatur in annis, sed erat senectus mentis immensa: corpore quidem juvencula, sed animo cana; pulchra facie, sed pulchrior fide.

Dum a scholis reverteretur, urbis filio adamatur. Cuius parentes cum requisisset coepit offerre plurima et plura promittere. Denique detulerat secum pretiosissima ornamenta, quae a beata Agne veluti

Ambrose, the servant of Christ, to the holy virgins. Let us celebrate the feastday of a most holy virgin. On one side, let the psalms echo; on the other, let the readings sound. On one side, let the crowds of people rejoice; on the other, let Christ's poor be encouraged. Let us all, therefore, give solemn thanks to the Lord, and for the edification of the virgins, recall in how excellent a manner the most blessed Agnes suffered! In the thirteenth year of her youth, she lost death and found life, because she loved the sole Author of Life. She was reckoned an infant in years, but had the wisdom of an elder; youthful indeed in body, but white-haired in spirit; lovely in form, but lovelier in faith.

While she was returning from school, the son of the urban prefect fell in love with her. When he had inquired about her parents, he began to offer many things and to make many promises. Finally, he brought with him extremely

quaedam sunt stercora recusata. Unde factum est, ut juvenis majori perurgeretur amoris stimulo.

Et putans eam meliora velle accipere ornamenta, omnem lapidum pretiosorum secum defert gloriam: et per seipsum, et per amicos et notos et affines coepit aures virginis appellare; divitias, domos, possessiones, familias, atque omnes mundi delicias promittere, si consensum suum eius coniugio non negaret.

precious ornaments, which were refused by the Blessed Agnes as if they were dung. As a result, the young man was spurred by a more intense goad of love.

Thinking that she wished to receive better ornaments, he brought with him every status symbol [including] the most precious stones, and on his own behalf, and through his friends, acquaintances, and relatives, began to accost the virgin's ears to promise riches, houses, possessions, estates, and indeed all the world's delights, if she would not refuse her consent to marry him.

First Responsory

ℝ) Diem festum sacratissimae virginis celebremus: qualiter passa sit beata Agnes, ad memoriam revocemus: tertiodecimo aetatis suae anno mortem perdidit, et vitam invenit: *Quia solum vitae dilexit auctorem. 𝒱) Infantia quidem computabatur in annis; sed erat senectus mentis immensa. // Quia solum vitae dilexit auctorem.

ℝ) Let us celebrate the feastday of a most holy virgin! Let us recall in how excellent a manner the blessed Agnes suffered! In the thirteenth year of her youth, she lost death and found life, *because she loved the sole Author of Life. 𝒱) She was reckoned an infant in years, but had the wisdom of an elder. // Because she loved the sole Author of Life.

The Legend of Saint Agnes of Rome as Source

Second Lesson

Beata Agnes tale juveni fertur dedisse responsum: Discede a me fomes peccati, nutrimentum facinoris, pabulum mortis: discede a me, quia iam ab alio amatore praeventa sum, qui mihi satis meliora obtulit ornamenta, et annulo, fidei suae subarrhavit me, longe te nobilior et genere et dignitate. Ornavit inaestimabili dextrochirio dexteram meam, et collum meum cinxit lapidibus pretiosis. Tradidit auribus meis inaestimabiles margaritas, et circumdedit me vernantibus atque coruscantibus gemmis.

To these things, Blessed Agnes is said to have given the young man this kind of response: "Depart from me, kindling of sin, nourishment of villainy, food of death. Depart from me, because I have already been taken by another lover, who presented me with even better ornaments than you have, and put me under a pledge with the ring of his fidelity, [who is] far nobler than you in birth and position. He adorned my right hand with a priceless bracelet, and encircled my neck with precious stones. He hung priceless pearls from my ears, and surrounded me with glittering and sparkling gems.

Posuit signum in faciem meam, ut nullum praeter amatorem admittam. Induit me cyclade auro texta, et immensis monilibus ornavit me. Ostendit mihi thesauros incomparabiles, quos mihi se donaturum si ei perseveravero repromisit.

He placed a seal on my face, so that I will admit no lover except him. He clothed me in a robe of state woven with gold, and adorned me with innumerable necklaces. He showed me incomparable treasures, which he promised to give to me if I persevere with him.

Non ergo potero ad contumeliam prioris amatoris vel adspicere alium, et illum derelinquere, cum quo sum caritate devincta: cuius est generositas celsior, possibilitas fortior, adspectus pulchrior, amor suavior, et omni gratia elegantior: a quo mihi iam thalamus collocatus est, cuius mihi organa modulatis vocibus resonant, cuius mihi virgines iustissimis vocibus cantant. Iam mel et lac ex eius ore suscepi iam amplexibus eius castis adstricta sum.

Therefore, I am unable to consider another, to the insult of my prior lover, or to desert him, with whom I have been bound by love: whose nobility is higher, his power stronger, his appearance lovelier, his love sweeter, and his every grace more elegant—by whom a marriage bed has already been prepared for me; his instruments echo for me in measured tones; whose virgins sing for me with the most perfect voices. Already, I have received milk and honey from his mouth; already, I have been held fast in his chaste embraces."

Second Responsory

℟) Dexteram meam, et collum meum cinxit lapidibus pretiosis, tradidit auribus meis inaestimabiles margaritas: *Et circumdedit me vernantibus, atque coruscantibus gemmis. 𝒱) Posuit signum in faciem meam, ut nullum praeter eum amatorem admittam. // Et circumdedit me vernantibus.

℟) My right hand and my neck he encircled with precious stones. He hung priceless pearls from my ears, *and surrounded me with glittering and sparkling gems. 𝒱) He placed a seal on my face, so that I will admit no lover except him. // And surrounded me with glittering.

Third Lesson

Iam corpus eius corpori meo sociatum est, et sanguis eius ornavit genas meas. Cuius mater virgo est, cuius pater feminam nescit. Cui angeli serviunt, cuius pulchritudinem sol et luna mirantur. Cuius odore reviviscunt mortui, cuius tacta foventur infirmi. Cuius opes numquam deficiunt, cuius divitiae non decrescunt. Ipsi soli servo fidem. Ipsi me tota devotione committo.

Quem cum amavero, casta sum; cum tetigero, munda sum; cum accepero, virgo sum. Nec deerunt post nuptias filii, ubi partus sine dolore succedit, et foecunditas quotidiana cumulatur.

Audiens haec insanus iuvenis, amore carpitur caeco, et inter angustias animi et corporis, anhelo cruciatur spiritu. Inter haec lecto prosternitur, et per alta suspiria amor a medicis aperitur. Fiunt nota patri; quae fuerant inventa a medicis; et eadem paterna

"Already, his body has been united with my body, and his blood has adorned my cheeks. His mother is a virgin; his father has never known a woman. Angels serve him, whose beauty the sun and moon admire; by whose fragrance the dead revive, by whose touch the sick are relieved, whose wealth never fails, whose riches do not diminish. I keep faith with him alone. To him, I commit myself with complete devotion.

Having loved him, I am chaste; having touched him, I am pure; having received him, I am a virgin. Nor will children be lacking after marriage, when birth advances without sadness, and fruitfulness is increased every day."

Hearing these things, the crazed young man, harassed by blind love, and in the midst of mental and physical difficulties, was tortured by wheezing. Meanwhile, he prostrated himself on his bed, and through his deep sighs, love became visible to the doctors. What the

voce, quae fuerant iam dicta a filio, ad petitionem virginis revolvuntur.

Abnegat Agnes beatissima, et se nullo pacto asserit prioris sponsi foedera violare. Cumque pater diceret, in fascibus constitutum se praefecturam agere, et idcirco sibi, quamvis illustrissimum, minime debere praeferre; coepit tamen vehementer inquirere, quis esset sponsus, de cuius se Agnes potestate iactaret.

Extitit quidam ex parasitis eius, qui diceret hanc Christianam esse ab infantia, et magicis artibus ita occupatam, ut dicat Christum suum sponsum esse.

doctors found became known to his father; and in order to petition the virgin, the father's voice reiterated the same things already said by the son.

The most blessed Agnes refused, and asserted that she would not violate the covenant with her prior spouse by any agreement. Although the father said that he had been established in magisterial authority to discharge the prefecture, and for that reason, ought by no means to give precedence [to another], however distinguished, over himself; nevertheless, he began to inquire energetically, who the husband might be, about whose power Agnes was bragging.

Then one of his toadies arose, who said she had been a Christian from infancy, and was so possessed by magic arts that she said that Christ was her husband.

Third Responsory

℟) Amo Christum, in cuius thalamum introibo, cuius mater virgo est, cuius pater

℟) I love Christ, into whose marriage bed I will enter. His mother is a virgin; his

feminam nescit, cuius mihi organa modulatis vocibus cantant: *Quem cum amavero, casta sum; cum tetigero, munda sum; cum accepero, virgo sum.
𝒱) Annulo fidei suae subarrhavit me, et immensis monilibus ornavit me.
// Quem.

father has never known a woman. His instruments sing for me in measured tones. *Having loved him, I am chaste; having touched him, I am pure; having received him, I am a virgin.
𝒱) He put me under a pledge with the ring of his fidelity, and adorned me with innumerable necklaces.
// Having.

Second Nocturn

Fourth Antiphon

Induit me dominus cyclade auro texta, et immensis monilibus ornavit me.

The Lord clothed me in a robe of state woven with gold, and adorned me with innumerable necklaces.

Psalm 4: Cum invocarem

When I call.

Fifth Antiphon

Mel et lac ex eius ore suscepi, et sanguis eius ornavit genas meas.

I have received milk and honey from his mouth, and his blood has adorned my cheeks.

Psalm 5: Verba mea

My words.

Sixth Antiphon

Ipsi soli servo fidem, ipsi me tota devotione committo.	I keep faith with him alone. To him, I commit myself with complete devotion.

Psalm 8: Domine dominus noster
    O Lord, our Lord.

Lessons 4-6 (Synopsis)

Agnes will not alter her position even after the prefect attempts to seduce her with flattery, threatens her, and appeals to her parents. Finally, he threatens her with the charge of blasphemy, giving her the choice of either sacrificing to the goddess Vesta or whoring with prostitutes in a brothel. Upon her refusal to sacrifice to Vesta, the prefect charges Agnes with blasphemy, and orders her to be stripped and led naked to a brothel. As soon as she is stripped, her hair becomes so thick that it hides her nakedness and she is surrounded by a wondrous light. When she prostrates herself in prayer to the Lord, the whitest possible outer garment appears before her eyes and the brothel becomes a place of prayer.

Fourth Responsory

℟) Induit me dominus vestimento salutis, et indumento laetitiae circumdedit me. *Et tanquam sponsam, decoravit me corona. ℣) Tradidit

℟) The Lord has clothed me with the garments of salvation, and has surrounded me with a robe of joy. *And He has adorned me with a crown

auribus meis inaestimabiles margaritas, et circumdedit me vernantibus, atque coruscantibus gemmis. // Et tanquam.

like a bride. *V)* He hung priceless pearls from my ears, and surrounded me with glittering and sparkling gems. // And He.

Fifth Responsory

𝕽*)* Mel et lac ex eius ore suscepi, *et sanguis eius ornavit genas meas. *V)* Ostendit mihi thesauros incomparabiles, quos mihi se donaturum repromisit. // Et sanquis.

𝕽*)* I have received milk and honey from his mouth, *and his blood has adorned my cheeks. *V)* He showed me incomparable treasures, which he promised to give to me. // And his blood.

Sixth Responsory

𝕽*)* Iam corpus eius corpori meo sociatum est, et sanguis eius ornavit genas meas: *cuius mater virgo est: cuius pater feminam nescit. *V)* Ipsi sum desponsata, cui angeli serviunt, cuius pulchritudinem sol et luna mirantur. // Cuius mater.

𝕽*)* Already, his body has been united with my body, and his blood has adorned my cheeks. *His mother is a virgin; his father has never known a woman. *V)* I am wedded to him whom the angels serve, whose beauty the sun and moon admire. // His mother.

Third Nocturn

Seventh Antiphon

Cuius pulchritudinem sol et
luna mirantur, ipsi soli servo
fidem.

Whose beauty the sun and
moon admire, I keep faith
with him alone.

Psalm 15: Domine quis

Lord who.

Eighth Antiphon

Christus circumdedit me
vernantibus, atque
coruscantibus gemmis
pretiosis.

Christ surrounded me with
glittering and sparkling,
precious gems.

Psalm 45: Eructavit

[My heart] overflows.

Ninth Antiphon

Ipsi sum desponsata, cui
angeli serviunt: cuius
pulchritudinem sol et luna
mirantur.

I am wedded to him whom
the angels serve, whose
beauty the sun and moon
admire.

Psalm 46: Deus noster refugium

God is our refuge.

The Legend of Saint Agnes of Rome as Source

Lessons 7-8 (synopsis)

The prefect's son comes to the brothel and, without reverence for the angelic light surrounding Agnes, rushes in with the intention of assaulting her. Before he can touch her, he falls on his face and dies. The crowd is convinced that Agnes has used sorcery to kill the young man. When the prefect approaches Agnes and asks her the reason for his son's death, Agnes explains that the young man was imprudent, not showing reverence before the angelic splendor. Agnes prays and the young man is raised and publicly confesses the Christian God. At this, the soothsayers and temple priests grow angry and demand that the prefect get rid of the sorceress. Appointing a deputy to deal with the uprising, the prefect leaves the scene. The deputy tries to burn Agnes, but the blaze does not touch her.

Seventh Responsory

℟) Ipsi sum desponsata, cui angeli serviunt, cuius pulchritudinem sol et luna mirantur. *Ipsi soli servo fidem. Ipsi me tota devotione committo. 𝒱) Dexteram meam, et collum meum cinxit lapidibus pretiosis: tradidit auribus meis inaestimabiles margaritas. // Ipsa soli.

℟) I am wedded to him whom the angels serve, whose beauty the sun and moon admire. *I keep faith with him alone. To him, I commit myself with complete devotion. 𝒱) My right hand and my neck he encircled with precious stones; he hung priceless pearls from my ears. // I keep.

Eighth Responsory

ℛ⟩ Omnipotens adorande, colende, tremende, benedico te; *Quia per filium tuum unigenitum, evasi minas hominum impiorum, et spurcitias diaboli, impolluto calle transivi. 𝒱⟩ Te confiteor labiis, te corde, te totis visceribus concupisco. ∥ Quia.

ℛ⟩ Almighty [Father], who inspires adoration, worship, and awe, I bless you; *because through your only begotten Son I have escaped the threats of impious persons and passed through the devil's impurities by an undefiled footpath. 𝒱⟩ I desire to confess you with my lips, with my heart, with my entire inmost being. ∥ Because.

Ninth Lesson (1ˢᵗ Part)

Tunc beata Agnes expandens manus suas in medio ignis his verbis orationem fudit ad dominum: Omnipotens, adorande, colende, tremende, Pater Domini nostri Iesus Christi, benedico te, quia per filium tuum unigenitum evasi minas hominum impiorum et spurcitias diaboli impolluto calle transivi. Ecce et nunc per Spiritum sanctum rore coelesti perfusa sum: focus juxta me moritur, flamma dividitur, et ardor incendii huius ad eos, a quibus

Then Blessed Agnes, stretching out her hands in the middle of the fire, poured out a prayer to the Lord in these words: "Almighty Father of our Lord Jesus Christ, who inspires adoration, worship, and awe, I bless you, because through your only begotten Son I have escaped the threats of impious persons and passed through the devil's impurities by an undefiled footpath. And now behold, I have been steeped in heavenly dew

ministratur refunditur.
Benedico te, Pater
praedicande, qui etiam inter
flammas intrepidam me ad te
pervenire permittis. Ecce
iam quod credidi, video;
quod speravi, iam teneo;
quod concupivi, complector.

through the Holy Spirit: the
altar-pyre near me dies; the
flame is divided; and the
heat of this fire is poured
back upon those by whom it
is supplied. I bless you,
Father, who must be praised,
for you permit me to come
to you without fear, even in
the midst of the flames.
Behold, what I believed, I
already see; what I have
hoped for, I already hold;
what I have desired, I
embrace.

Clare's Use of the Agnes Office in her Letters

Quotations

We have already noted that Clare rarely quotes her sources directly, but rather varies them to fit her purpose. It is not surprising, therefore, that most of her references to *The Legend of Saint Agnes of Rome* are paraphrases or allusions rather than direct quotations.

In *3LAg* 15, Clare writes: "And completely ignoring all those who in this deceitful and turbulent world ensnare their blind lovers, you might totally love him who gave himself totally out of love for you."[33] One could certainly read this statement with the legend in mind. Clare follows this with a quotation from the legend, 3rd lesson. Repeated in the 6th and 7th responsories, and in the 7th and 9th antiphons, the line plays like a refrain throughout the Office of Matins.

The Legend of Saint Agnes 3rd Lesson	*3LAg* 16
cuius pulchritudinem sol et luna mirantur [whose beauty the sun and moon admire].	**cuius pulchritudinem sol et luna mirantur** [whose beauty the sun and moon admire].

While this passage needs to be cited as Clare's only direct quote of the legend, it, as well the responsories and antiphons that quote it, cannot explain Clare's free construction around the *cuius* passages of the legend. The full passage of *3LAg* 16 reads: "whose beauty the sun and moon admire, and whose rewards, in both their preciousness and magnitude, are without end."[34] Obviously the rest of the passage will need another explanation.

Paraphrases

Clare's possible dependence upon the Agnes Office is shown most convincingly in her paraphrases and allusions to *The Legend of Saint Agnes of Rome.* Her dependence on this legend is especially obvious in her variations on passages from the legend that are not repeated in responsories or antiphons. In order to compose these variants, Clare most probably had knowledge of the legend itself.

Clare plays with the *cuius* construction found in *The Legend of Saint Agnes*, 2nd and 3rd lessons, in both her third and fourth letters. Although for the most part, she improvises rather freely using this construction, the use of her direct quote in the third letter, already noted as explaining only half of *3LAg* 16, and her variant, "whose fragrance will revive the dead" in the fourth letter make it clear that Clare is writing a variation on the legend. None of the antiphons and

The Legend of Saint Agnes of Rome as Source

responsories for the feast of Saint Agnes carry the repetitive *cuius* construction. Clare's source of this construction was the legend itself.

The Legend of Saint Agnes 3rd Lesson	4LAg 10-13
Cui angeli serviunt, **cuius pulchritudinem** sol et luna **mirantur. Cuius odore reviviscunt mortui,** cuius tacta foventur infirmi. Cuius opes numquam deficiunt, cuius divitiae non decrescunt [Angels serve him, whose beauty the sun and moon admire; by whose fragrance the dead revive; by whose touch the sick are relieved; whose wealth never fails; whose riches do not diminish].	**cuius pulchritudinem** omnia beata caelorum agmina incessabiliter ad**mirantur,** cuius affectus afficit, cuius contemplatio reficit, cuius implet benignitas, cuius replet suavitas, cuius memoria lucescit suaviter, **cuius odore mortui reviviscent,** cuiusque visio gloriosa beatificabit omnes cives supernae Ierusalem [whose beauty all the blessed hosts of the heavens unceasingly admire, whose affection moves, whose contemplation invigorates, whose generosity fills, whose sweetness replenishes, whose remembrance pleasantly brings light, whose fragrance will revive the dead, and whose glorious vision will bless all the citizens of the heavenly Jerusalem].

In *1LAg* 8, one finds a variant quotation from the 3rd lesson (repeated in the 3rd responsory), wherein Clare changes the text of the legend from the first to second person in order to address Agnes of Prague:

Clare's Letters to Agnes

The Legend of Saint Agnes 3rd Lesson	1LAg 8
Quem cum amavero, casta sum; cum tetigero, munda sum; cum accepero, virgo sum [Having loved him, I am chaste; having touched him, I am pure; having received him, I am a virgin].	Quem cum amaveritis, casta estis; cum tetigeritis, mundior efficiemini; cum acceperitis virgo estis [Having loved him, you are chaste; having touched him, you will be made more pure; having received him, you are a virgin].

In *1LAg* 9, Clare paraphrases a part of the 2nd lesson that is not repeated as either an antiphon or responsory.

The Legend of Saint Agnes 2nd Lesson	1LAg 9
cuius est generositas celsior, possibilitas fortior, adspectus pulchrior, amor suavior, et omni gratia elegantior [Whose nobility is higher, his power stronger, his appearance lovelier, his love sweeter, and his every grace more elegant].	Cuius possibilitas fortior, generositas celsior, cuius aspectus pulchrior, amor suavior et omnis gratia elegantior [His power is stronger, his nobility higher, his appearance lovelier, his love sweeter, and his every grace more elegant].

The first line of *1LAg* 10 is found only at the end of the 2nd lesson:

The Legend of Saint Agnes 2nd Lesson	1 LAg 10
iam amplexibus eius castis adstricta sum [already, I have been held fast in his chaste embraces].	Cuius estis iam amplexibus astricta [You are now held fast in the embraces of the one].

The other lines of *1LAg* 10 and the first two lines of *1LAg* 11 are also adapted from the 2nd lesson. Although the 2nd, 4th, and 7th responsories and the 2nd and 8th antiphons contain some of this same text, they do not use the verb *ornavit* which Clare borrows from the legend. To explain Clare's entire text, one must refer to the 2nd lesson of the legend.

The Legend of Saint Agnes 2nd Lesson	*1LAg* 10-11a
Ornavit inaestimabili dextrochirio dexteram **meam,** et collum meum cinxit **lapidibus pretiosis. Tradidit auribus meis inaestimabiles margaritas, et circumdedit** me **vernantibus atque coruscantibus gemmis** [He adorned my right hand with a priceless bracelet, and encircled my neck with precious stones. He hung priceless pearls from my ears, and surrounded me with glittering and sparkling gems].	qui pectus **vestrum ornavit lapidibus pretiosis et vestris auribus tradidit inaestimabiles margaritas.** Et totam **circumdedit vernantibus atque coruscantibus gemmis** [who has adorned your breast with precious stones and has hung priceless pearls from your ears. He has completely surrounded you with glittering and sparkling gems].

Clare expresses her eschatological joy at her privilege of being united to the Poor Christ using the words of the Agnes legend. In *3LAg* 5, Clare paraphrases Agnes of Rome stating that her joy is based on the fulfilled longing of her heart.

The Legend of Saint Agnes 9th Lesson	*3LAg* 6
Ecce iam quod credidi, video; quod speravi, **iam teneo; quod**	cum, **quod** sub caelo **cuncupivi iam tenens** [since I already possess

| concupivi, complector [Behold, what I believed, I already see; what I have hoped for, I already hold; what I have desired, I embrace]. | what under heaven I have yearned for]. |

In *3LAg* 7, Clare takes the scriptural image of a treasure hidden in a field (Mt 13:44; 2 Cor 4:7), and juxtaposes this scriptural allusion onto the incomparable treasures found in the Agnes legend, 2nd lesson and repeated in the 5th responsory. The adjective *incomparabiles* is not from Mt 13:44 or 2 Cor 4:7.

The Legend of Saint Agnes 2nd Lesson	3LAg 7
Ostendit mihi **thesauros incomparabiles,** quos mihi se donaturum si ei perserveravero repromisit [He showed me incomparable treasures, which he promised to give to me if I persevere with him].	absconsumque in agro mundi et cordium humanorum **thesaurum incomparabilem** [the incomparable treasure that lies hidden in the field of the world and the hearts of human beings].

Allusions

Instead of jumping directly into a paraphrase of *The Legend of Saint Agnes of Rome*, Clare prepares her readers with two allusions to the legend. In *1LAg* 5-7, which introduces text taken from the legend, Clare says:

> (5) I rejoice because you, more than others, could have enjoyed public ostentation, honors, and worldly status having had the opportunity to become, with eminent glory, legitimately married to the illustrious

emperor, as would befit your and his pre-eminence.
(6) Spurning all these things with your whole heart and
mind, you have chosen instead holiest poverty and
physical want, (7) accepting a nobler spouse, the Lord
Jesus Christ, who will keep your virginity always
immaculate and inviolate."[35]

Verses 5-6 could be imagined as an interesting synopsis of the
Agnes legend applied to Agnes of Prague. Clare seems to be
suggesting that Agnes of Prague is a new Saint Agnes.

The last phrase (7) contains two interesting and complex
ideas. The first is the acceptance of "a nobler spouse," the
second, the notion of immaculate and inviolate virginity.
Clare's idea of "accepting a nobler spouse" incorporates
vocabulary found in the 2nd lesson of the Agnes Office:

The Legend of Saint Agnes 2nd Lesson	*1LAg* 7
quia iam ab alio amatore praeventa sum, qui mihi satis meliora obtulit ornamenta, et annulo, fidei suae subarrhavit me, longe te **nobilior** et **genere** et dignitate [because I have already been taken by another lover, who presented me with even better ornaments than you have, and put me under a pledge with the ring of his fidelity, (who is) far nobler than you in birth and position].	sponsum **nobilioris generis** accipientes, Dominum Iesum Christum, qui vestram virginitatem semper immaculatam custodiet et illaesam [accepting a nobler spouse, the Lord Jesus Christ, who will keep your virginity always immaculate and inviolate].

The concept that the choice of Jesus Christ is the better
choice, taken from the Agnes legend and carrying overtones of
the Martha and Mary story (Lk 10:38-42), evolves into a
medieval theology of virginity. Although the idea of defining

a woman's choice of virginity as a spiritual marriage to Christ was not new to the twelfth and thirteenth centuries, the paradigm governing considerations on this theme, namely the nature of the marital bond between the Blessed Virgin and Joseph, was novel. Hugh of Saint Victor (d. 1141), suggested that the physical act of coition was foreign to the original nature of Adam and Eve's relationship in Eden before the Fall. According to Hugh, the ideal marriage is a spiritual bond and is experienced most fully when it is not consummated. The sacramentality of marriage is conceived as a spiritual union of love between two souls. "Chaste marriages," well known in the Franciscan tradition, were heir to this spirituality.

Hugh's system readily transferred to female monastic spirituality. Since sexuality is not necessary in marriage, a female religious could enjoy spiritual marital union with Jesus Christ. It logically followed that this marital union with Jesus Christ had more to recommend it than human marriage. Medieval women writers, who prayed matins for the feast of Saint Agnes annually, describe this union with Jesus Christ as more noble, more chaste, more rich, etc., often leaving the medieval man in rivalry for feminine affections with Jesus Christ, himself.[36]

Clare's second allusion to the Agnes legend in *1LAg* 7, is that Christ "will keep [*custodiet*] your virginity always immaculate and inviolate." In the 5th lesson, (part of the following text is repeated in lauds, 2nd antiphon),[37] Agnes of Rome says to the prefect who demands that she either sacrifice to the goddess Vesta or whore with the prostitutes in a brothel:

The Legend of Saint Agnes 5th **Lesson**	
Unde ego quia novi virtutem Domini mei Iesus Christi, secura contemno minas tuas, credens	Accordingly, because I know the excellence of my Lord Jesus Christ, I am tranquil and despise

quod neque sacrificem idolis tuis, neque polluar sordibus alienis. Mecum enim habeo **custodem** corporis mei angelum domini. Nam unigenitus Dei filius, quem ignoras, murus est mihi impenetrabilis, et **custos** mihi est numquam dormiens, et defensor mihi est numquam deficiens.	your threats, believing that I will neither sacrifice to your idols nor be defiled by others' filth. Indeed, I have with me my body's **guardian**, an angel of the Lord. For the only begotten Son of God, whom you do not know, is my impenetrable wall of defense, my **guardian** who never sleeps, and my defender who never fails.

This theme is reiterated in the 7th lesson. Here Agnes states:

The Legend of Saint Agnes 7th **Lesson**	
Quia universi dederunt honorem Deo, qui mihi misit angelum suum, qui et induit me hoc indumento misericordiae, et **custodivit** corpus meum, quod ab ipsis cunabulis Christo consecratum est et oblatum.	Because without exception they gave honor to God, who sent his angel to me, who clothed me in this garment of mercy, and **guarded** my body, which from the cradle itself has been consecrated and presented to Christ.

God's fidelity is demonstrated when Agnes's hair miraculously grows so long that it covers her body better than clothing.

The Franciscan sources contain clues other than this statement in Clare's first letter that suggest that Clare believed that Christ would literally protect her sisters from those who would disrespect their virginal way of life. In *The Acts of the Process of Canonization*, the ninth witness, Sister Francesca, tells how Clare asks Christ to defend her sisters from the invading Saracens who had already entered the San Damiano enclosure. In response to her urgent prayer, Christ responds "I will always defend you!,"[38] and with Clare's prayer the Saracens are scattered.

The harm and even the rape of nuns was not uncommon in the Middle Ages. Germanic invaders coming into Italy were accustomed to legal systems that were not much concerned with the protection of women.[39] Clare's use of the Agnes legend suggests that Clare believed that while God might allow martyrdom, God would protect the virginity of his faithful handmaids. The Saracen story seems to confirm her faith.

Using *1LAg* 11b as a hinge, Clare transitions from her paraphrase of the Agnes legend back into prose. *1LAg* 11a reads, "He has completely surrounded you with glittering and sparkling gems." This line, as has been cited, is a paraphrase of the legend. The line that follows it in the legend is, "He placed a seal/*signum* on my face." Using *signum* as a pivot, Clare brilliantly moves into Sirach 45:14, the primary source for *1LAg* 11b.

Legend of St. Agnes 2nd Lesson	Sirach 45:14	*1LAg* 11b
Posuit **signum** in faciem meam [He placed a seal on my face].	**Corona aurea** super mitram eius, lamina cum **signo sanctitatis** [Upon his turban a crown of gold, its plate wrought with the seal of holiness].	atque vos coronavit **aurea corona signo sanctitatis** expressa [and has placed on your head a golden crown engraved with the seal of holiness].

In *4LAg* 8, Clare plays wonderfully on Agnes's name, recalling Agnes of Rome without focusing on the liturgical texts. Note in the Latin, Clare's wonderful wordplay. Agnes of

Rome is referred to as *sancta Agnes,* while Christ is referred to as *Agno immaculato.* Their spousal bond makes them: *sancta Agnes, Agno immaculato.*

4LAg 8	
quia velut altera virgo sanctissima, **sancta Agnes, Agno immaculato,** qui tollit peccata mundi, es mirifice desponsata, sumptis omnibus vanitatibus huius mundi.	because like that other most holy virgin, **Saint Agnes,** you have been in an astonishing way espoused to the **immaculate Lamb**, who, having assumed responsibility for all the vanities of this world, takes away the sins of the world.

In the first lesson for the octave of the feast of Saint Agnes, Agnes's parents see their daughter after her death in a crowd of virgins and dressed in a garment of light. At her right hand is her spouse, a "lamb whiter than snow."

V. Summary and Conclusion

If one charts Clare's use of the Agnes Office, the following picture emerges.

Clare's Letters to Agnes

TYPE OF CITING	LETTERS OF CLARE	*THE LEGEND OF ST. AGNES OF ROME*
Quotations	*3LAg* 16	3rd lesson (repeated in the 6th and 7th responsories and in the 7th and 9th antiphons; need *cuius* construction found in the 2nd and 3rd lessons to explain the entire passage)
Paraphrases	*1LAg* 8	3rd lesson (repeated in the 3rd responsory)
	1LAg 9	2nd lesson
	First line of *1LAg* 10	2nd lesson
	1LAg 10-11a	2nd lesson (some text repeated from 2nd and 8th antiphons and the 2nd, 4th and 7th responsories, but one needs the 2nd lesson to explain the entire text)
	3 LAg 6	9th lesson and lauds Benedictus antiphon
	3 LAg 7	2nd lesson (repeated in the 5th reponsory)
	4 LAg 10-13	3rd lesson
Allusions	*1LAg* 7	2nd lesson. For the idea of Jesus Christ defending a woman's virginity, see the 5th-7th lessons.
	1LAg 11b	2nd lesson (repeated in the 3rd antiphon and the 2nd responsory)
	4 LAg 8—Word play on the name, "Agnes."	Allusion to the legend (see 1st lesson for the octave of Saint Agnes).

Given this picture, what might be concluded? Certainly one can be certain that Clare knew the Agnes legend well, through popular culture, and through the lessons of the annual Office of Matins for the feast of Saint Agnes. Clare draws upon her familiarity with the Agnes legend in writing her letters to Agnes of Prague, whose name recalled for her the famous virgin martyr of Rome.

Given Clare's creativity with embroidering texts into her letters, it is important in translating and in interpreting to understand Clare's use and source of the Agnes legend. One could hardly explain, for example, Clare's understanding of virginity with its relationship to martyrdom and to poverty without reading Clare's letters in light of the Agnes legend.

In postulating the Agnes Office as Clare's primary source of the Agnes legend, one notes that Clare's dependence upon the text of the Agnes legend is primarily reserved to the 2nd and 3rd lessons of the Agnes Office. The preponderance of the antiphons and responsories in the Office of Saint Agnes as well as the quotations from the legend found in the liturgy of the consecration of virgins are also from the 2nd and 3rd lessons. In restricting her paraphrasing to the 2nd and 3rd lessons, Clare follows liturgical precedent.

Although Clare paraphrases primarily from the 2nd and 3rd lessons, she does not restrict herself to the sections of these lessons that were repeated in the antiphons and responsories of the Agnes Office or in the liturgy of the consecration of virgins. This seems to imply that she had greater familiarity with the legend other than a simple reliance on the liturgy of the consecration of virgins or on the antiphons and responsories of the Agnes Office. In proposing a liturgical source for many of Clare's paraphrases and allusions to the legend, it seems more proper to cite the primary source as the legend while noting various repetitions found in the responsories and antiphons. To do this would be to prescind a bit from common practice.[40]

A number of witnesses in the *Acts of the Process of Canonization*[41] of Clare testify to Clare's love for prayer at night. Regarding the witness of these sisters, Regis Armstrong states: "The custom of celebrating Matins or the Office of Readings at midnight is not prescribed in the Form of Life of Saint Clare. Hence this information is invaluable in confirming a practice that still exists in many communities of the Sisters of Saint Clare."[42] Clare's creative use of the Agnes legend may give further evidence that Clare not only listened well to these texts, but also pondered and prayed them. Her freedom of spirit in quoting the prayer of the seasons, and her ability to freely improvise on these texts in liturgical style, may testify to Clare's profound love and knowledge of the Office of Matins.

In the end, the letters of Clare definitely demonstrate that Clare used *The Legend of Saint Agnes* and not simply the antiphons and responsories of the Agnes Office or the consecration of virgins liturgy in her letters to Agnes of Prague. Most likely she had knowledge of this legend from both popular and liturgical sources. She presumed that Agnes was also familiar with the legend of her own patron saint.

In studying the breviary manuscripts, it was hoped that one might prove Clare's further reliance upon other lessons from the Office of Matins, perhaps from the Marian feasts, to strengthen the hypothesis of Clare's reliance upon a breviary source of the Agnes legend. Despite a lengthy search, no such collaborating evidence was found.

Since both Clare and Agnes did share the experience of hearing *The Legend of Saint Agnes* annually, it seems that noting the lessons of the feast, with the pertinent repetitions in the antiphons and responsories, is a fair way to document Clare's source. In practice, however, while writing to Agnes, Clare's ear and heart most likely improvised on a popular memory that had been matured by contemplative, annual reflection on the Agnes story, but that still held on to the rhythms and poetry of the legend as she had heard it from popular sources as a child from her own mother, in parish churches, or in the squares of Assisi and Perugia.

Notes

[1]*Butler's Lives of the Saints*, January (Collegeville, MN: The Liturgical Press, 1995), 138.

[2]See M. Teresa Tavormina, "Of Maidenhood and Maternity: Liturgical Hagiography and the Medieval Ideal of Virginity," *American Benedictine Review* 31 (December 1980): 387.

[3]*Religious Movements in the Middle Ages*, trans. Steven Rowan (Notre Dame: University of Notre Dame Press, 1995), 192-93. Originally published as *Religiöse Bewegungen im Mittelalter* (Darmstadt: Wissenschaftliche Buchgesellschaft, 1935, 1961).

[4]In a recent correspondence, Sr. Edith Van den Goorbergh, OSC, kindly referred me to the use of *The Legend of Saint Agnes* in the writings of Saint Gertrude the Great. A liturgical analysis of Gertrude's *Spiritual Exercises* which amply illustrates Sr. Edith's point can be found in *The Exercises of Saint Gertrude*, with introduction, commentary and translation by a Benedictine nun of Regina Laudis (Westminster: MD: The Newman Press, 1956), 174-82. See also E. Ann Matter, "Il Cantico dei Cantici negli 'Exercitia Spiritualia' di Gertrude la Grande di Helfta," in *Chiara: Francescanesimo al Femminile*, ed. Davide Covi and Dino Dozzi (Roma: Edizioni Dehoniane, 1992), 46-54.

[5]See "Starting Points: Images of Women in the Letters of Clare," *GR* 7 (1993): 351-54.

[6](The Netherlands: Van Gorcum & Camp., 2000), 44.

[7]Michel Andrieu, *Le pontifical romain au moyen-âge,* tome II, *Le pontifical de la curie romaine au XIIIe siècle*, ST 87 (Città del Vaticano: Biblioteca Apostolica Vaticana, 1940), 414-18. In reading through various manuscript renditions of the rite of consecration of virgins, one finds more

and more lines from *The Legend of Saint Agnes* inserted into later versions of the consecration liturgy. However, none of these later rites does this so extensively as to be able to explain fully Clare's use of the legend. For these various texts see, Edmond Martène, *De Antiquius Ecclesiae Ritibus Libri*, tome II (Hildesheim: Georg Olms Verlagsbuchhandlung, 1967), cols., 517-59. For the history of the rite of the consecration of virgins see O. G. Harrison, "The Formulas *Ad virgines sacras*: A Study of the Sources," *Ephemerides liturgicae* 66 (1952): 252-73; and René Metz, *La consécration des vierges dans l'église romaine: Étude d'historie de la liturgie* (Paris: Presses Universitaires de France, 1954).

[8]Tavormina, note 1, pages 384-85, lists her sources as follows: *Liber Pontificalis Christopheri Bainbridge, Archiepiscopi Eboracensis*, ed. Willam G. Henderson, Surtees Society 61 (Durham 1875), 154-69; *Liber Pontificalis of Edmund Lacy, Bishop of Exeter*, ed. Ralph Barnes (Exeter 1847), 114-22; and *Missale ad Usum Ecclesiae Westmonasteriensis*, ed. J. Wickham Legg, Henry Bradshaw Society 1, 5, 12 (London 1891-1897), 2. cols., 1197-1212.

[9]Stephen J. P. Van Dijk and Joan Hazelden Walker, *The Ordinal of the Papal Court From Innocent III to Boniface VIII and Related Documents*, (Switzerland: The University Press Fribourg, 1975), XVII and XXIV-XXV.

[10]Manuscripts of the Regula breviary are listed in Stephen Van Dijk, *The Origins of the Modern Roman Liturgy: The Liturgy of the Papal Court and the Franciscan Order in the Thirteenth Century* (Westminster, MD: The Newman Press, 1960), 218-19.

[11]Van Dijk, *The Ordinal*, 363-65.

[12]Ibid., 364.

[13]Van Dijk, *The Origins*, 127.

[14]Sorores litteratae faciant divinum officium secundum consuetudinem fratrum minorum, ex quo habere poterunt breviaria, legendo sine cantu.

[15]Stephen J. P. Van Dijk, OFM, "*The Breviary of Saint Francis*," *FS* IX (1949): 17-19.

[16]*ChrJG* 57 says: "At the same general chapter (1230) breviaries and antiphonaries according to the usage of the Order were sent to the provinces [In eodem capitulo generali (Anno Domini 1230) breviaria et antiphonaria secundum Ordinem provinciae sunt transmissa]."

[17]*Butler's*, January (1995), 139.

[18]et ad aedificationem vestram, o Virgines, Christi, textum passionis eius credidi destinandum, obsecrans caritatem Spiritus sancti, ut labor noster in vestra imitatione fructum in conspectu Domini valeat invenire.

The Legend of Saint Agnes of Rome as Source

[19]Background information on *The Breviary of Saint Francis* can be found in Van Dijk, "*The Breviary of Saint Francis,*" 13-25; and Van Dijk and Walker, *The Origins,* 129-35.

[20]Van Dijk, *The Origins,* 131.

[21]Van Dijk, "*The Breviary of St. Francis,*" 17.

[22]Ibid.

[23]Van Dijk worked out his theories concerning *The Breviary of Saint Clare* in a series of articles. See "*The Breviary of St. Clare,*" *FS* VIII (1948): 25-46, and the continuation of this same article in *FS* IX (1949): 351-87. Van Dijk's final study of this breviary can be found in *The Origins,* 135-44.

[24]Van Dijk, *The Origins,* 135-36.

[25]Ibid., 140; 144.

[26]For a description of this manuscript see, Stephen J. P. Van Dijk, OFM, "Some Manuscripts of the Earliest Franciscan Liturgy," *FS* 14 (1954): 257-58.

[27]Van Dijk describes this manuscript in the continuation of his article, "Some Manuscripts of the Earliest Franciscan Liturgy," *FS* 16 (1956): 60-67.

[28]Van Dijk, *The Origins,* 214.

[29]For a description of these manuscripts see, Helena Soukupová, *Anežský klášter v Praze* (Praha: Odeon, 1989), 158-69. See also Helena Soukupová, "Illuminované rukopisy z kláštera bl. Anežky v Praze Na Františku," *Časopis Národního Muzea v Praze* 153 (1984): 69-95.

[30]See for example, Jan Kapistrán Vyskočil, *Legenda Blahoslavené Anežky* (Praha: Nakladatelství Universum, 1932), 177-78, and Regis Armstrong, OFM Cap., *Clare of Assisi: Early Documents* (St. Bonaventure, NY: Franciscan Institute Publications, 1993), 35 and 46, who cite only antiphons and responsories as the sources of specific verses of Clare's use of the Agnes legend.

[31]Translations of the lessons are by my colleague, Dr. Julia Fleming of Creighton University. Because of the length of the lessons, only those necessary for understanding the basic spirit of the Agnes Office and for studying Clare's use of the text in her letters will be reproduced in this essay. The full text of *The Legend of Saint Agnes of Rome* can be found on pages 253-65 in this volume.

[32]The lessons of this Office are divided according to Regula breviary manuscript, Assisi, Sacro Convento, 694.

[33]Et omnibus qui in fallaci mundo perturbabili suos caecos amatores illaqueant penitus praetermissis, illum totaliter diligas, qui se totum pro tua dilectione donavit.

[34]Cuius pulchritudinem sol et luna mirantur, cuius praemiorum et eorum pretiositatis et magnitudinis non est finis.

[35]Hinc est quod, cum perfrui potuissetis prae ceteris pompis et honoribus et saeculi dignitate, cum gloria excellenti valentes inclito Caesari legitime desponsari, sicut vestrae ac eius excellentiae decuisset, quae omnia respuentes, toto animo et cordis affectu magis sanctissimam paupertatem et corporis penuriam elegistis, sponsum nobilioris generis accipientes, Dominum Iesum Christum, qui vestram virginitatem semper immaculatam custodiet et illaesam.

[36]For further development of this theme in early medieval women's literature, see John Bugge, *'Virginitas:' An Essay in the History of a Medieval Ideal* (The Hague, Netherlands: Martinus Nijhoff, 1975), 80-90.

[37]Lauds, 2nd antiphon reads: "Mecum enim habeo custodem corporis mei, angelum Domini."

[38]"Io te defenderò sempre mai!," *Proc* 9:2.

[39]See Vern L. Bullough and James Brundage, *Sexual Practices and the Medieval Church* (New York: Prometheus Books, 1994), 142.

[40]Scholarly sources for studying the letters of Saint Clare quote responsories and antiphons and sometimes the legend or Office, but do not cite particular lessons of matins as Clare's source. In referring to the lessons, one must remember the fluidity of the divisions of the lessons for the feast of Saint Agnes of Rome in early 13th century breviaries. What is important is not the particular lesson divisions, but that the legend is cited as the source of Clare's paraphrases.

[41]1:7; 2:9; 10:3.

[42]*Clare of Assisi*, note c, 143.

The Primitive Franciscan Climate As Source
Clare's Letters and the Early Brothers

Saint Clare of Assisi wrote her letters to Saint Agnes of Prague amid the dawning of the Franciscan movement. While Clare's identification with and synthesis of Franciscan ideals were very much her own, many of the elements used in formulating her thoughts were common to the primitive Franciscan climate. With this as a given, it seems that pondering Clare's writings in light of other Franciscan sources might reveal more of the fullness and context of Clare's thought.

Supportive and appropriate mutuality between brothers and sisters was core to the vision of Clare. Clare held fast to two defining aspects of her Franciscan lifestyle: living without possessions and mutual relationships with the Franciscan brothers. Considering Clare's writings without examining mutual relationships would be foreign to Clare's spirit.[1]

Living without possessions and mutual relations are connected in that the friars served as questors for the sisters as well as chaplains and preachers providing the sisters with "spiritual food." This interconnectedness is illustrated by the *Legend of St. Clare* 37:7-10:

> Once when Lord Pope Gregory forbade any brother to go to the monasteries of the ladies without permission, the pious mother, sorrowing that her sisters would more rarely have the food of sacred teaching, sighed: "Let him now take away from us all the brothers since he has taken away those who provide us with the food that is vital." At once she sent back to the minister all the brothers, not wanting to have the questors who acquired corporal bread when they could not have the questors for spiritual bread. When Pope Gregory heard this, he

immediately mitigated that prohibition into the hands of the general minister.[2]

Because of Clare's integrity as a woman of intellectual and spiritual astuteness, there is no reason to fear that Clare's contribution to Franciscan theology and spirituality might be eclipsed by examining her writings in tandem with the writings of the early brothers. The sources give ample evidence that Clare was not easily intimidated.[3] When Clare's vocational identity and the integrity of her community were at stake, she stood her ground disagreeing both with Francis[4] and with papal authority.[5]

To proceed with this exercise, I began by investigating the apparati compiled by Giovanni M. Boccali in *Fontes Franciscani*.[6] Although not all available primitive Franciscan sources are included in the *Fonte Franciscani*,[7] Boccali's apparati seemed to be a good tool for facilitating a mutual reading. At times, I supplemented Boccali's apparatus with other appropriate texts.

The aim of this essay is to study mutual word sequences used by both Clare and the early brothers in order to examine Clare's letters within the theological and spiritual climate of the early Franciscan movement. Comparison of mutual word sequences within Franciscan sources will be presented both in English (within the text), and in Latin (in footnotes). For clarity, the word sequences under discussion are highlighted in both the English and Latin texts.[8] After a mutual reading for each of Clare's letters is explored, the dialogue will be summarized with suggested insights gleaned from this mutual reading. The conclusion will propose an evaluation of the value of the mutual reading technique for the study of Clare's letters.

Because of length, I had to make choices regarding Boccali's apparati. The focus on mutual relationships among friars and sisters presupposes that not all similar word patterns among the Clarian sources are included here. I omitted comparisons of formulaic expressions such as *in saecula saeculorum.* I also omitted minor apparati that offered no particular insight other than noting the recurring word sequence itself.

The First Letter

In *1LAg* 2,[9] Clare speaks of herself as the "useless handmaid of the enclosed **ladies of the Monastery** of San Damiano." *L3C* 73:1 repeats Clare's use of *dominarum. . .monasterii,* stating that the exterior honors of Francis's canonization, his translation to the grand Basilica of San Francesco, the rare and superb gift from the pope of a cross containing a relic of the true cross together with ornaments, vessels, and vestments, papal exemption from inferior jurisdiction, and the papal declaration signed and sealed by all the cardinals that San Francesco was to be the mother church of the entire Order, would count as nothing if after his death, Saint Francis had not continued to convert and heal both men and women. The author of *The Legend of the Three Companions* continues by saying that through the intercession of Francis many noble women, together with their daughters, "entered the **monasteries** of the Poor **Ladies**."[10] Entrance into the Friars Minor or into the monasteries of the Poor Ladies was seen by the early brothers as a grace given through the intercession of Francis.

AC 85:1[11] uses Clare's expression *dominarum/monasterii . . . Damiani.* Here Francis is on his deathbed composing for the consolation of "the Poor **Ladies of the Monastery of San Damiano**" the words and music for a canticle. Since Francis knew the tribulation that his sickness caused the sisters, and since his sickness prohibited Francis from visiting them, he composed the canticle and sent his brothers to give it to them.

AC 85 summarizes the gist of this canticle.[12] The sisters are to preserve themselves in mutual charity. Francis celebrates the sisters as the fruit of his preaching and example.

They are the joy and edification not only of the brothers, but also of the whole church. Francis begs the sisters to treat their bodies with discretion. He reminds the healthy sisters to bear patiently the fatigue of caring for the sick, and the sick sisters to bear their sickness with patience.

A letter from the ladies of the Monastery of San Damiano carried with it these memories of care between Francis and the founding community of sisters. *L3C* 24[13] suggests that Francis's care for the Poor Ladies existed even before Clare's acceptance of the Franciscan form of life. As Francis repaired the Church of San Damiano, he prophesied in French: "Come and help me in the work of the Church of **San Damiano**, which, in the future, will be a monastery of **ladies** through whose fame and life our heavenly Father will be glorified throughout the church."

In *1LAg* 2,[14] Clare uses the expression, "**enclosed** ladies of the **Monastery** of San Damiano." *2C* 106:5[15] also uses *inclusarum monasterii* in reference to the Damianite community. The reference records a meeting at a poor enclosed monastery between a vain man of the world who is visiting a relative, and Saint Francis who was visiting the sisters. Francis preached to the man, who was so moved that he joined the friars as Brother Pacifico. The passage gives evidence that the enclosed monastery had provisions for visiting relatives and certainly for visiting friars. One would expect that a place dedicated to prayer and poverty might also at times be the occasion of great, and even life-changing grace for those who visited.

In *1LAg* 6,[16] Clare acknowledges that Agnes has chosen the "**holiest poverty**." *Sanctissimam paupertatem* is found in various places in Clare's writings (*1LAg* 13; *2LAg* 7; *RCl* 6:6, 8). It is also cited by the brothers in *LR* 5:5,[17] *1C* 39:5; *L3C* 39:8. Describing the communal life of the early friars, *1C* 39:5[18] outlines the essence of their poverty: "As followers of the **holiest poverty**, since they had nothing, they loved nothing, so they feared losing nothing." *1C* 39:6-11, goes on to describe the lifestyle of the "holiest poverty." Celano's description portrays the brothers being content with poor clothing, being protected from worrying about anything because they had nothing, spending cold nights in caves, doing day labor, staying often at the houses of lepers, and not wishing to accept positions that might give rise to scandal.

L3C 38:3-39:8 recounts the story of the brothers who in journeying through Florence were deprived of a place to stay and of blankets on a cold night by a husband of a woman who had been initially willing to allow the brothers the use of a portico. The next morning in church, a man named Guido began to give alms. Brother Bernard refused these alms explaining that the poverty of the brothers was not destitution, but voluntary poverty. The author, after suggesting that Brother Bernard was believed to be a saint, explains that Bernard "persevered to the end in the **holiest poverty**."[19] Again the mention of this "holiest poverty" is surrounded by descriptions of concrete difficulties resulting from the hardships of living life without possessions or status. When Clare speaks about "holiest poverty," she is not speaking of vague spiritual poverty, but of a poverty that concretely embraces the reality of the poor themselves. In embracing a lifestyle without property, guaranteed income, or status, both Clare and her brothers realize that theirs is a voluntary poverty, a state that, while difficult, will always differ from true destitution.

After recognizing Agnes's choice of the "holiest poverty," Clare continues in *1LAg* 7,[20] "accepting a nobler **spouse**, the Lord Jesus **Christ**, who will keep your virginity always immaculate and inviolate." Clare repeats the word pattern *sponsum. . .Christum* again in *1LAg* 12:[21] "Therefore, dearest sister—or should I say, most venerable lady, because you are the **spouse** and mother and sister of my Lord Jesus **Christ**."

Saint Francis, himself, uses the word pattern *sponsum. . .Christum* in *1LtF* 1:7 (cf., *2LtF* 50). In *1LtF* 1:7,[22] Francis explains that those who live a life of penance "are children of the heavenly Father," and "are **spouses**, brothers, and mothers of our Lord Jesus **Christ**." *1LtF* 1:1-4 outlines this life of penance in five steps. To live such a life, penitents must: (1) "love the Lord with their whole heart, with their whole soul and mind, with their whole strength;" (2) "love their neighbors as themselves;" (3) "hate their bodies with their vices and sins;" (4) "receive the Body and Blood of our Lord Jesus Christ;" and (5) "produce worthy fruits of penance." By doing these things with perseverance, Francis explains, those who do penance will find beatific happiness because "the Spirit of the Lord will rest upon them." In *1LtF* 1:8[23] (cf., *2LtF* 51), Francis explains that "We are **spouses** when the faithful soul is joined by the Holy Spirit to our Lord Jesus **Christ**." One who chooses a life of penance as outlined above, will be gifted with the Holy Spirit. The Holy Spirit will effect spousal relationship between the soul and Jesus Christ.

It is interesting that Clare refers to Agnes as *sponsum . . .Christi*, which, as seen from the above, has overtones from Francis concerning the embrace of a lay penitential life. In her letters to Agnes, Clare never uses *sponsa Spiritus Sancti*, which is used of Mary in the antiphon of *The Office of the Passion* that Clare loved and prayed. Rather, Clare repeatedly refers to Agnes as the spouse of Christ (cf., *1LAg* 12, 24; *2LAg* 1; *4LAg* 1, 7, 8, 15).

In *1LAg* 12,[24] Clare rhetorically addresses Agnes: "Therefore, dearest **sister**—or should I say, most venerable **lady**." The pattern *soror. . .domina* is found again in *2LAg* 24. In *2LAg* 24,[25] Clare recognizes Agnes as sister and lady because of her spousal relationship with Jesus Christ: "Farewell, dearest **sister** and **lady** for the sake of the Lord, your spouse." Clare affirms Agnes's royalty as enhanced by her spousal relationship with Jesus Christ.

In *1LAg* 13,[26] Clare exhorts: "be strenghtened in the holy service begun in you out of a burning desire for the **Poor Crucified**." The word sequence *pauperis Crucifixi* is found also in *1C* 151:2 and *LMj* 2:7:2. Celano asks those who have read and heard his biography of Francis to remember him, a sinner. He begs them to do this "for the love of the **Poor Crucified**, and by his sacred stigmata which the blessed Father Francis bore in his body" (*1C* 151:2).[27]

In *LMj* 2:7:2[28] Bonaventure says that Francis overcame his embarrassment in begging stones from the people of Assisi for repairing the Church of San Damiano "out of love of the **Poor Crucified**." In both *1LAg* 13 and *LMj* 2:7:2, "love of the **Poor Crucified**" seems to be the source of the Franciscan vocation. One chooses a life of penance and poverty because of this "burning desire." This was true for Francis, and Clare assumes that this "burning desire for the **Poor Crucified**," was also the founding motivation for Agnes.

1LAg 14[29] states: "**For** all of us he endured the **passion** of the cross." Clare begins her thought by encouraging Agnes in the holy service begun in her out of a burning desire for the one who endured **for** all of us the **passion**. The word sequence *pro. . .passionem* is also found in *Adm* 6:1.[30] Here, Francis encourages his brothers to look to the Good Shepherd "who bore **for** his sheep the **passion** of the cross." The sheep follow the Good Shepherd in tribulation and persecution, in insult and hunger, in infirmity and temptation, and in everything else. As a result, they receive everlasting life. He reserves his point until the end: "Therefore, it is a great shame for us, the servants of God, that the saints have accomplished great things, and we want only to receive glory and honor by recounting them (*Adm* 6:3)."[31] The one with "burning desire for the Poor Crucified" wishes to follow him in tribulation, persecution, and insult.

The word sequence *paupertas/Dominus. . .Christus* found in Clare's poetic *1LAg* 17 is a very popular Franciscan sequence. The passages are perhaps best contemplated synoptically.

Clare's Letters to Agnes

---

paupertas/Dominus. . .Christus

1LAg 17[32]
O pious **poverty**,
that the **Lord Jesus Christ**, who ruled and is ruling heaven and earth,
and who spoke and all things were made,
deigned to embrace before anything else!

ER 9:1[33]
Let all the brothers strive to follow the humility and **poverty** of our **Lord Jesus Christ** and let them remember that we should have nothing else in the whole world except, as the Apostle says, having food and clothing, we are content with these.

RCl 6:7-8[34]
I, Brother Francis, the little one, wish to follow the life and **poverty** of our most high **Lord Jesus Christ** and of his most holy mother and to persevere in this until the end. And I beg and counsel you, my ladies, that you might always live in this most holy life and in poverty.

AC 114:11[35] (cf., *1MP* 42:10, *2MP* 37:7)
(After punishing a brother for uncharitably judging a poor man, Francis teaches):
This man's poverty and weakness are a mirror for us in which we should see and consider lovingly the **poverty** and weakness of our **Lord Jesus Christ** which he endured in his body for the salvation of the human race.

Francis's last will for the sisters of San Damiano, which Clare copies verbatim into the heart of her Rule, is essential to consider here. The embrace of poverty, following the example of the poor crucified Lord Jesus Christ, is the life of the Poor Sisters. This poverty is concrete and practical (*ER* 9:1), and its nobility shines through not only in a chosen lifestyle of living without possessions and privileges, but also in the all too human, and at times inconvenient and ungainly limitations of the poor themselves (*AC* 114:11).

The Primitive Franciscan Climate As Source

Clare's quotation of Lk 9:58 is a scriptural text frequently used in the early Franciscan movement.

Luke 9:58
1LAg 18[36] **For foxes have dens, he says, and the birds of the sky have nests, but the Son of Man, who is Christ, has nowhere to lay his head;** instead, bowing his head, he handed over his spirit.
2C 56:1-2[37] He [Francis] taught his own to build poor little dwellings out of wood, and not stone, and how to build these according to a crude plan. Often, when he spoke to the brothers about poverty, he would insist on that saying of the Gospel: **Foxes have dens and the birds of the sky have nests; but the Son of Man has nowhere to lay his head.**
2C 122:3[38] When he [Francis] was alone, he poured out long and very devout prayers to the Lord. Finally he looked around for a **place to lay his head** so he could sleep.
LMj 7:2:3-4[39] Often when he spoke to the brothers about poverty, he would insist on the saying of the Gospel: **"Foxes have dens, and the birds of the sky have nests; but the Son of Man has nowhere to lay his head."** Because of this, he taught the brothers to build, like the poor, poor little houses, which they should inhabit not as their own but, like pilgrims and strangers, as belonging to others.
AC 57:13[40] (cf., *2MP* 9:7) (After Francis moves out of a cell because another brother refers to it as "his cell"): We who were with him often heard him repeat the saying of the holy Gospel: **"Foxes have dens and the birds of the sky have nests, but the Son of Man has nowhere to lay his head."**

> **ScEx 19[41]**
> He was placed in a manger, the Evangelist said, because there was no room for him in the inn. Thus, always inseparable from him, you accompanied him so that throughout his life, when he was seen upon earth and conversed with human beings, **while foxes have dens and the birds of the sky nests, he** nevertheless **had nowhere to lay his head.**

It is obvious from this collage of Franciscan texts, that scriptural allusions to Lk 9:58 refer to the practical question of housing. Jaroslav Polc suggests that Agnes's cloister was planned and erected between 1232-1240, with the actual building of the monastery beginning before the arrival of the sisters from Trent.[42] If this is true, and the date of Clare's letter is 1234, Clare's Franciscan citing of Lk 9:58, perhaps in reference to the call to live in poor housing, is particularly pertinent. Clare does not give Agnes specific instructions regarding the physical poverty of her monastery. Rather, she simply cites Lk 9:58, inviting Agnes to love the Poor Crucified who had no place to lay his head.

1LAg 19 contains the word phrase, *pauper in mundo,* another sequence common to early Franciscan writings.

> **pauper in mundo**
>
> **1LAg 19[43]**
> If, then, so great as such a Lord who, coming into the virgin's womb, chose to appear contemptible, needy, and **poor in** this **world.**
>
> **RCl 8:1-3[44]**
> Let the sisters not appropriate anything, neither a house nor a place nor anything at all; instead, as pilgrims and strangers in this world who serve the Lord in poverty and humility, let them confidently send for alms. Nor should they be ashamed, since the Lord made himself **poor in** this **world** for us.

1C 76:9[45] (cf., *LJS* 45:7)

Anyone who curses the poor insults Christ whose noble banner the poor carry, since Christ made himself **poor** for us **in** this **world**.

LR 6:2-3[46]

As pilgrims and strangers in this world, serving the Lord in poverty and humility, let them go seeking alms with confidence, and they should not be ashamed because, for our sakes, our Lord made himself **poor in** this **world**.

2C 74:1-3[47] (cf., *AC* 51:5; *2MP* 18:5)

At first he [Francis] often used to go for alms by himself, both to train himself and to spare embarrassment for his brothers. But seeing that many of them were not giving due regard to their calling, he once said: "My dearest brothers, the Son of God was more noble than we are, and yet for our sake he made himself **poor in** this **world**. For love of him we have chosen the way of poverty. So we should not be ashamed to go for alms."

(*2C* 74:5[48] continues in a way reminiscent of Agnes's reality):
"I say to you that many noble and wise persons will join our order and will consider it an honor to beg for alms."

The above passages allow one to ponder *1LAg* 19 in terms of overcoming the embarrassment of asking for alms. To "become **poor in** this **world**" suggests that one needs to depend upon the goodness of others. One should not be ashamed of this, since the Lord, who is nobler than we, became **poor** for our sake **in** this **world**. Following this, Clare's use of *egenus et pauper* in *1LAg* 19, is found also in *OfP* 8:6:[49] "But I am **afflicted and poor**. God, help me!"

One finds the expression *laetitia spiritali* in *1LAg* 21, with parallels as follows:

laetitia spiritali
1LAg 21[50]   exult exceedingly and rejoice, filled with great joy and **spiritual happiness**.
2C 125:1[51]   Saint Francis insisted that **spiritual happiness** was an infallible remedy against a thousand snares and tricks of the enemy.
2C 128:5-6[52]   He so loved the man filled with **spiritual happiness** that at one chapter he had these words written down as a general admonition: "Let them be careful not to appear outwardly as sad and gloomy hypocrites but show themselves joyful, cheerful, and consistently gracious in the Lord."
1MP 23:3[53] (cf., *AC* 120:13)   From the beginning of his conversion to the day of his death, blessed Francis had always been hard on his body. But his primary and main concern was always to possess and preserve **spiritual happiness** interiorly and exteriorly.
2MP 95:1,[54] 3,[55] 7[56]   Blessed Francis had always the highest and particular desire to continually have, outside times of prayer and Divine Office, interiorly and exteriorly **spiritual happiness**. . . . He used to say, "If the servant of God strives to obtain and preserve both interiorly and exteriorly **spiritual happiness** that springs from purity of heart and is acquired through devout prayer, the devils have no power to hurt him." . . . "Therefore, my brothers, since this **spiritual happiness** springs from cleanness of heart and the purity of continuous prayer, it must be your first concern to acquire and preserve these two virtues, so as to possess this **spiritual happiness** interiorly and exteriorly that I so greatly desire and love to see both in you and myself, and which edify our neighbor and reproach our enemy. For it is the lot of the devil and his minions to be sorrowful, but ours always to be happy and rejoice in the Lord."

> *2MP* 96:8-9[57]
> It should not be imagined that our Father, who loved mature and reputable behavior wished this happiness to be shown in levity or vain words, for these things are not evidence of **spiritual happiness** but of vanity and folly.

In the Franciscan tradition, spiritual happiness is a discipline springing from the virtues of purity of heart and constant prayer, and it is possessed both interiorly and exteriorly. Its power drives away the enemy and edifies the neighbor. Spiritual happiness is not feigned levity, but a genuine cheerful expression of inward purity, simplicity, and Trinitarian relationship.

Clare uses the expression **"contempt of the world"** (*contemptus saeculi*) in *RCl* 6:2:[58] "When the Blessed Father saw we had no fear of poverty, hard work, trial, shame or **contempt of the world**, but instead, regarded such things as great delights, moved by compassion he wrote a form of life for us." In *1LAg* 22,[59] Clare suggests to Agnes that she can have spiritual joy because she understands contempt for the world: "Because—since **contempt of the world** has pleased you more than its honors; poverty more than temporal riches; and storing up treasures in heaven rather than on earth." *2C* 15:1[60] speaks of Brother Bernard before his entrance into the order as contemplating the contempt of the world: "A certain Bernard from the town of Assisi, who later became a son of perfection, planned **to reject the world** perfectly after the example of the man of God." It is interesting that all three cases speak of this contempt of the world at the beginning of entrance into the Franciscan lifestyle. Since, at least for the earliest Franciscans, there was little status in joining a new community without resources or juridical standing, joining this community automatically resulted in the contempt of the world. What is interesting, however, is that the early

Franciscans did not focus on the contempt the world had for them, but rather on the contempt they had for the world. Clare's reference in *1LAg* 22 to *thesauros in caelo*, "**treasures in heaven**," (cf., Mt 6:20), is found also in *L3C* 29:2.[61] Francis, Bernard, and Peter open the Gospels to Mt 19:21: "If you wish to be perfect, go, sell everything that you possess, and give to the poor, and you will have a **treasure in heaven.**" *Adm* 28:1[62] turns "treasure" into a verb: "Blessed is the servant who **treasures in heaven** the good things that God has revealed to him and does not want to reveal them to people under the guise of a reward, because the Most High himself will reveal his deeds to whomever he pleases. Blessed is the servant who safeguards the secrets of the Lord in his heart." With the practical dimensions of a life without possessions in place, Francis can proceed to the poverty of heart that entrusts to God's generosity, one's radical act of surrender.

Clare's continued allusion to Mt 6:20, "**where neither rust consumes them, nor moth destroys them, and thieves do not dig them up and steal them,**" (*ubi. . .furantur*), in *1LAg* 23,[63] is echoed in *ScEx* 31:[64] "Do not store up for yourselves treasures on earth, **where rust and moth consume, and where thieves break in and steal.**" *ScEx* 31 is part of a simple listing of scripture passages regarding poverty. It seems that Mt 6:20 was one of the primary scriptural texts of the early Franciscan movement. Its call to poverty is the simple one: "You can't take it with you!"

The allusion to Mt 5:12,[65] "**your most abundant reward is in heaven,**" (*merces. . .caelis*) in *1LAg* 23,[66] is also found in *ER* 16:16:[67] "Rejoice and be glad on that day because **your reward is great in heaven.**" In *ER* 16:16, the passage appears in a list of scripture passages dealing primarily with persecution encountered when preaching the Gospel. The allusion to Mt 5:12 was a favorite of the early Franciscans. Persecution for following the Poor Crucified had to be accepted as a given, for one's reward would not be found on earth. An advantage of choosing voluntary poverty was to learn the discipline of valuing a treasure that was not of this world.

The sequence *soror/sponsa/mater*, which Clare uses in *1LAg* 24 and reorders in *1LAg* 12, is common especially in Franciscan epistolary literature. Although not including *soror*, I agree with Boccali that the *OfP Antiphon* 2 is worth noting in this context.

---

soror/sponsa/mater

1LAg 24[68]
And you have quite fittingly deserved to be called **sister, spouse, and mother** of the Son of the most high Father and the glorious Virgin.

1LAg 12[69]
Therefore, dearest sister—or should I say, most venerable lady, because you are **spouse and mother and sister** of my Lord Jesus Christ.

1LtF 1:7-10[70] (cf., *2LtF* 50-53)
They are children of the heavenly Father whose works they do, and they are **spouses**, brothers, and **mothers** of our Lord Jesus Christ. We are **spouses** when the faithful soul is joined by the Holy Spirit to our Lord Jesus Christ. We are brothers to him when we do the will of the Father who is in heaven. We are **mothers** when we carry him in our heart and body through a divine love and a pure and sincere conscience and give birth to him through a holy activity that must shine as an example before others.

OfP Antiphon 2[71]
Daughter and handmaid of the most high and supreme King and of the Father in heaven, **mother** of our most holy Lord Jesus Christ, **spouse** of the Holy Spirit.

One can begin to observe here the dynamism of Franciscan Trinitarianism. From the *OfP Antiphon* 2, the Virgin Mary is understood to be the mother of Jesus Christ and the spouse of the Holy Spirit. In Francis's letter, those who do penance are spouses, brothers, and mothers of Jesus Christ. The spousal relationship results when the faithful soul is joined by the Holy Spirit to Jesus Christ. One becomes a brother by doing the will of the Father. One is a mother, when one gives birth to Jesus Christ "through a holy activity that must shine as an example before others (*1LtF* 1:10)." In *1LAg* 24, Clare speaks of Agnes as the "**sister, spouse, and mother** of the Son of the most high Father and of the glorious Virgin."

Clare's use of *cum nudo* was a familiar slogan within the Franciscan movement. Taken from Gregory the Great's *Homilia in Evangelia* II, 32, 2,[72] the early Franciscans understood nudity as an advantage in fighting the eschatological battle. In Clare, as well as in the works of Celano and Bonaventure, nakedness is seen as an advantage in the struggle against the naked enemy. Nakedness is not necessarily virtuous by itself, but it is a wise way of being in the world. Even the enemy knows that it is better to enter into the struggle naked. To be naked, to enter spiritual combat without possessions, is simply good spiritual sense.

---

cum nudo

1LAg 27[73]
You also know that a person wearing clothing cannot fight **with** another who is **naked**, because the one who has something that might be grasped is more quickly thrown to the ground.

1C 15:6[74]
(In the context of Francis stripping before the bishop):
Look! Now he wrestles naked **with the naked**. After disposing of everything that is of this world, he is mindful only of divine justice.

2C 214:6[75] (cf., *LMj* 14:3:2; *LMn* 7:3:3)
As he was wasted by that grave illness which ended all his sufferings, he had himself placed naked on the naked ground, so that in that final hour, when the enemy could still rage, he might wrestle naked **with the naked**.

The Primitive Franciscan Climate As Source

Clare's allusion in *1LAg* 29 to Mt 7:13-14[76] in regard to entering the kingdom of heaven via the narrow road (*arctam. . . introire; arctam. . .viam*), and constricted gate (*angustam portam*), is commonplace in Franciscan literature.

Matthew 7:13-14
1LAg 29 (arctam viam et angustam portam)[77]   so that you may enter the kingdom of heaven by the **narrow road** and **constricted gate.**
L3C 45:7 (arctam viam)[78]   As they advanced on the way of the cross and the paths of justice, they cleared all hindrances from the **narrow road** of penance and of the observance of the Gospel, that they might make a smooth and safe path for the future.
ER 11:13 (arctam. . .introire)[79]   (In the context of a passage admonishing the brothers not to slander or engage in disputes):   Let them struggle to enter through the **constricted gate,** for the Lord says: **The gate is constricted and the road** that leads to life is **narrow**; those who find it are few.
ScEx 13 (arctam. . .portam)[80]   (In the context of Francis's search for Lady Poverty): Blessed Francis understood this and said to them: **"The road is narrow,** brothers, and **the gate** that leads to life is **constricted.** There are few who find it."

Allusions to Mt 7:13-14 in Franciscan literature refer to the choice of embracing a life of penance. This penance involves particularly the disciplines of poverty and the practice of persevering in spiritual happiness. Within the context of *1LAg* 29, Clare's reference to the "narrow road and constricted gate" most likely refers to the choice of poverty.

Clare's allusion to Mt 19:29[81] in *1LAg* 30,[82] *centuplum/recipere*, "**To receive a hundredfold** instead of one, to have a happy, eternal life" is also found in the *ER* 1:5:[83] "Everyone who has left father or mother, brothers or sisters, wife or children, houses or lands because of me, will **receive a hundredfold** and will possess eternal life."

Summary

Reading Clare's first letter together with the writings of the early Franciscan brothers has surfaced insights worthy of particular note. The fraternal overtones to Clare's reference to the "enclosed ladies of the Monastery of San Damiano" could be greatly amplified. Clare sees her life of poverty in mutual relationship with the life of the Poor Brothers.

The embrace of the holiest poverty by both the brothers and the sisters involves a physical want that truly affects one's body. The renunciation of material property and wealth, seen as ludicrous by those focused on worldly gain, will often result in tribulation, persecution, and insult. Contemplating the Poor Christ in the midst of insult and persecution enables one to be open to receiving the grace of compassion for and solidarity with the "Poor Crucified." Clare's embrace of poverty, insistent in its refusal to accept individually or communally any form of immoveable property, is able to stand the test of trial and, through contemplation on the "Poor Crucified," matures into profound contemplative union with Jesus Christ. Because Clare has experienced this union, she is able to stand fast in her insistence upon living without possessions and privileges as a way of holiness.

One embraces poverty because of the resurrected promise of eschatological beatitude. If one had to choose one line from scripture that would summarize Clare's letters, the choice for this passage might be Mt 5:3: "Blessed are the poor in spirit, for theirs is the kingdom of heaven." Those who are "poor in spirit," meaning for Clare that they embrace solidarity with the crucified Christ through living in poor housing, giving up riches, and choosing a lifestyle that will earn them contempt in this world, receive eschatological happiness. This happiness is practiced as a spiritual discipline and is fostered both interiorly and exteriorly. Note that the mention of "spiritual happiness" (*1LAg* 21), implies Trinitarian relationships (*1LAg* 24).

The Second Letter

Clare begins her letter citing again the relationships of *filiae/ancillae/sponsae* within the dynamism of Trinitarian relationship. The pattern is also found in *RCl* 6:3, and in *OfP Antiphon* 2, and will be further explored in considerations of the third letter.

filiae/ancillae/sponsae
2LAg 1[84] To the **daughter** of the King of kings, **handmaid** of the Lord of lords, most worthy **spouse** of Jesus Christ.
OfP Antiphon: 2[85] **Daughter** and **handmaid** of the most high and supreme King and Father in heaven, **mother** of our most holy Lord Jesus Christ, **spouse** of the Holy Spirit.
RCl 6:3[86] Because by divine inspiration you have made yourselves **daughters** and **handmaids** of the most high King, the Father of heaven and have **espoused** yourselves to the Holy Spirit.

In using *pauperum dominarum*, (cf., *dominarum pauperum* in *3LAg* 2), in referring to herself and her sisters, Clare repeats a word phrase that was used extensively in primitive Franciscan literature and that seems to be the expression of choice in referring to the early Damianite community.

pauperum dominarum
2LAg 2[87] Clare, useless and unworthy handmaid of the **Poor Ladies**.
3LAg 2[88] Clare, most humble and unworthy handmaid of Christ and servant of the **Poor Ladies**.
1C 116:4[89] he arrived at the place where he first planted the religion and the Order of the consecrated virgins and **Poor Ladies**.
LJS 13:3[90] (cf., *1C* 18:4; *L3C* 24:7) This place [San Damiano] is worthy of renown, for it was here that the Order that is endowed with the fullness of so many virtues, namely the religion of the **Poor Ladies** and holy virgins, was happily founded by the same holy man about six years after his conversion.
LJS 23:9[91] The Second Order, the Order of the **Poor Ladies** and virgins of the Lord, also mentioned above, likewise took its fruitful origin from him.
LJS 72:4[92] (During Francis's funeral procession): They showed him to his daughters, that is, the **Poor Ladies** and holy virgins, whom he had planted there.
LMj 4:6:4[93] she who was the daughter in Christ of our holy father Francis, the little poor man, and the mother of the **Poor Ladies**.

The allusion in *2LAg* 15 to Ps 119:32,[94] "I run the way of your commands" is found also in *1C* 55:1. It is interesting that in the story of Francis making his way to the East in *1Cel* 55-57, "walking in the way of God's commands," implies tribulation, courage, generosity of heart, virtue, alacrity of mind, and the pursuit of perfection. Clare's meaning is similar. For Clare, walking "the way of the Lord's commands" presupposes careful discernment even of authoritative pronouncements (*2LAg* 14), fidelity and courage in the midst of tribulation (*2LAg* 14), a kind of lightness of spirit that allows one to move with clarity (*2LAg* 12-13), and perseverance in one's resolve (*2LAg* 11, 14).

mandatorum/viam perambules
2LAg 15[95] Now concerning this, so that you may **walk** more tranquilly along **the way of the** Lord's **commands**.
1C 55:1[96] (Before telling of Francis's desire for martyrdom and first attempted missionary journey to Syria): Burning with divine love, the most blessed father Francis was always eager to try his hand at brave deeds, and **walking in the way of** God's **commands** with a heart wide-open, he longed to reach the summit of perfection.
2C 214:2[97] (In introducing the death scene of Francis): **Running** eagerly **the way of God's commands** he scaled the steps of all the virtues until he reached the very summit.

In *2LAg* 15, Clare repeats the formula *fratris. . .ministri* that Francis also uses in *LtOrd* 2, 38. Although one is to obey the *fratris. . .ministri*, the Franciscan focus for Francis and certainly for Clare is on sisterhood, brotherhood, and servanthood. Although Francis specifically mentions the minister of the Order in his *Letter to the Entire Order*, this mentioning is both times in the context of a list that includes all in the brotherhood.

---

fratris. . .ministri

2LAg 15[98]
follow the advice of our venerable father, our **Brother** Elias, **minister** general.

LtOrd 2[99]
To all my reverend and dearly beloved brothers; to **Brother** A., the **minister** general of the Order of Friars Minor, its lord, and the other general ministers who will come after him, and to the ministers, custodians, humble priests of this same brotherhood in Christ, and to all simple and obedient brothers, from the first to the last.

LtOrd 38[100]
to **Brother** H., the **minister** of our Order as my venerable lord, to the priests of our Order and all my other blessed brothers.

Agnes is to "**walk** more tranquilly along **the way of the Lord's commands**," by following "the advice of our venerable father, our **Brother** Elias, **minister** general (*2LAg* 15)." Agnes is to prefer this advice "to the advice of others and consider it more precious to you than any gift (*2LAg* 16)."[101] The relationship to Elias is not one of unthinking obedience as can be deduced from *2LAg* 17:[102] "Indeed, if someone tells you something else, or suggests anything to you that may hinder your perfection and that seems contrary to your divine vocation, even though you must respect him, still, do not follow his advice." Advice is only to be followed if it is judged to be in conformity with one's divine vocation. Clare accepts Elias's advice as authoritative primarily because she trusts that he will support the form of life given to her by Saint Francis. Advice opposing Francis's vision would need to be respectfully rejected as contrary to Clare's divine vocation.

Clare's interesting understanding of her relationship with the minister general of the Friars Minor is faithful to the early spiritual reciprocity between Francis and the Poor Ladies. One sees this in Francis's last will that he wrote for the Poor Ladies, which Clare inserts into her Rule (*RCl* 6:7-9).[103] Francis does not admonish the Poor Ladies under the strictures of obedience, but rather begs them and advises them:

> I, Brother Francis, the little one, wish to follow the life and poverty of our most high Lord Jesus Christ and of his most holy mother and to persevere in this until the end. And I beg and counsel you, my ladies, that you might always live in this most holy life and in poverty. Guard yourselves assiduously so that you may never stray from this in any respect whatsoever neither because of the teaching nor because of the advice of anyone.

Summary

Reading Clare's second letter in dialogue with other early Franciscan literature illuminates Clare's relationship with the minister general of the Franciscan Order. Clare exhorts Agnes to walk along the way of the Lord's commands by valuing and following the advice of the minister general, Elias, who can be trusted, in Clare's mind, to preserve Agnes in the holiest poverty. For Clare, "walking along the way of the Lord's commands" requires an alacrity of mind focused on one's vocational identity. Outside influences need to be weighed and discerned in light of one's foundational grace. In regard to preserving the vocational integrity of the Poor Ladies, it seems that Clare is confident that Elias's counsel can be completely trusted.

The Third Letter

The word phrase *summo/Regi* (*3LAg* 1), also *summi Regis*, (*4LAg* 17), is repeated throughout the sources.

summo/Regi (also summi Regis)
3LAg 1[104] To Agnes, most venerable lady and sister in Christ, deserving of love before all other mortals, blood-sister of the illustrious king of Bohemia, but now sister and spouse of the **most high King** of the heavens.
4LAg 17[105] adorned in the same manner with flowers and garments made of all the virtues as is proper, dearest daughter and spouse of the **most high King**.
RCl 6:3[106] Because by divine inspiration you have made yourselves daughters and handmaids of the **most high King**, the Father of heaven, and have espoused yourselves to the Holy Spirit, choosing to live according to the perfection of the holy Gospel, I resolve and promise for myself and for my brothers to always have that same loving care and solicitude for you as I have for them.
1C 120:1[107] While he still lived among sinners, Francis traveled the whole world preaching; but now reigning with the angels on high, he flies quicker than a thought as the herald of the **most high King**, bringing wonderful gifts to all peoples.

LMj 1:3:1[108]
The following night, when he had fallen asleep, the divine kindness showed him a large and splendid palace with military arms emblazoned with the insignia of Christ's cross. Thus it vividly indicated that the mercy he had exhibited toward the poor knight for love of the **most high King** would be repaid with an incomparable reward.

LMj 12:12:4[109]
the marks of the **most high King** imprinted on his body.

LMj 15:3:3[110]
His sons were weeping at the loss of so lovable a father, but they were also filled with no little joy while they kissed the marks of the **most high King** in his body.

By using the expression "**most high King**," is Clare referring to God the Father or to Jesus Christ? Clare's Trinitarian language is difficult. One is sister, spouse, and daughter of the "**most high King**." In *RCl* 6:3, Clare's sense is easier to decipher. Quoting from Francis's form of life for Clare and her sisters, the expression "you have made yourselves daughters and handmaids of the **most high King**, the Father of heaven, and have espoused yourselves to the Holy Spirit,"[111] seems to be lifted from the *OfP Antiphon* 2. In speaking of Mary in this antiphon, Francis prays: "Daughter and handmaid of the **most high** and supreme **King** and Father in heaven, mother of our most holy Lord Jesus Christ, spouse of the Holy Spirit." In referring to Clare and her sisters as other Marys in the passage found in *RCl* 6:3, Francis understands them as daughters and handmaids of the Father, and as spouses of the Holy Spirit. It is interesting that in this passage, Francis does not project Clare as another mother of the Lord Jesus Christ.

While Francis seems to sidestep portraying Clare as the mother of Christ, Clare refers to Agnes specifically as the mother of Jesus Christ. In *3LAg* 24-25[112] Clare writes: "So, just as the glorious Virgin of virgins carried him physically, so, you too, following in her footsteps especially those of humility and poverty, can without any doubt, always carry him spiritually in your chaste and virginal body." Here Agnes has become, as Clare carefully distinguishes, not a physical but a spiritual mother of Christ. This possibility of Clare and her sisters literally following the mother of Christ is reinforced by Sister Francesca in *Proc* 9:4. Here Francesca says under oath that she witnessed a child, whom she felt sure was Jesus Christ, sitting on the lap of Clare before her breast. She adds that she saw "above Lady Clare's head two wings, brilliant as the sun, which at times were raised on high and at other times covered Lady Clare's head."[113]

Following the concept of Agnes as mother of Jesus Christ, one would expect Clare to follow Francis's lead from the form of life and refer to Agnes also as the spouse of the Holy Spirit. Instead, Clare speaks of Agnes as the spouse of Jesus Christ. She does this in a very literal way. Agnes has chosen to be spouse of the most high King, rather than spouse of the German emperor. Referring to Jesus Christ as the "most high King" is also the obvious meaning of the passages charted above from Bonaventure. While her reference to *summo sponsae* in *4LAg* 17 could be imagined to refer to Jesus Christ or to the Father, *4LAg* 7-32 is specifically Christological. It seems correct, therefore, to interpret *summo/Regi* in *3LAg* 1, as a Christological reference.

Although the fluidity of Clare's Trinitarian language may prove to be a bit bewildering at first glance, one needs to understand Clare's perception in the context of the medieval world where family relationships, especially noble and royal family relationships, were extremely fluid. Certain scenarios, almost incomprehensible to moderns, as for instance, imaging oneself as daughter-in-law and spouse of the same man as was almost the case for Agnes with Frederick II, were real possibilities for upper class medieval women. Within a household one lived with in-laws and family of all ages. One's blood mother was often not the woman who raised one. One's "sisters and brothers" may be in-laws rather than blood relatives. Marriage proposals were made for political purposes, often abandoning considerations of both preference and age. Women were engaged to men who could have been their fathers or sons.

Whatever one might feel about the plight of women in the above situations, it is interesting to note that Clare's experience as a medieval woman seems to have taken her into the very depths of Trinitarian mysticism. The scene of the dying Clare in *Proc* 3:20 helps one catch a glimpse of this profundity. Near death, Clare says: '"Go (my soul) calmly in peace, for you will have a good escort, because he who created you has sent you the Holy Spirit and has always guarded you as a mother does her child who loves her.'[114] She added: 'O Lord, may you who have created me, be blessed.'"[115] The witness follows Clare's words with this comment: "She said many things about the Trinity, so softly that the sisters were not able to understand her well."[116]

In the end, what might one say regarding Clare's expression of Trinitarian relationships? Three things seem clear. First, Clare avoided modalist tendencies. She does not embrace a "job description" view of the Trinity—i.e., God is only creator, the Son is only redeemer, the Spirit is only sanctifier, etc. In this respect, she is solidly orthodox. Second, the fluidity of medieval relationships seems to be expressed in Clare's Trinitarian experience. Although relational possibilities always have limits, i.e., I'm doubtful that being "mother of the Spirit," for instance, was an imagined possibility for Clare, Clare, it seems, did imagine more relational possibilities than modern women might. An outline of the Trinitarian relationships that Clare expresses in her letters and in the sixth chapter of her Rule demonstrates the breadth of these relational images.

Father: Daughter (*2LAg* 1; *RCl* 6:3)
            Handmaid (*2LAg* 1; *RCl* 6:3)
Son: Sister (*1LAg* 12, 24; *3LAg* 1)
            Spouse (*1LAg* 7, 12, 24; *2LAg* 1, 20, 24;
                  3LAg 1; *4LAg* 1, 4, 7, 8, 15, 17)
            Daughter (*4LAg* 17)
            Mother (*1LAg* 12, 24)
            Handmaid (*3LAg* 2)
            Queen (*4LAg* 1, 15, 27)
Spirit: Spouse (*RCl* 6:3)

Third, Clare's relational imaginings helped her to enter into an experience of a profound and dynamic Trinitarian union. The profundity of this union empowers the depth and sensitivity of her relationships with her sisters.

It is helpful to read *3LAg* 12,[117] "place your soul in the **splendor of glory**," *splendore gloriae*, in light of *4LAg* 14:[118] "because the vision of him [Christ] is the **splendor of** everlasting **glory**, the radiance of everlasting light and a mirror without tarnish." Clare's next phrase, *3LAg* 13,[119] contains scriptural illusions that are helpful in discerning Clare's sense: "place your heart in the figure of the divine substance (Heb 1:3); and, through contemplation, transform your entire being into the image of the Divine One himself (2 Cor 3:18)." The two scripture passages seem to be the source of Clare's vision. Heb 1:3[120] reads: "He is the **splendor of** God's **glory** and the figure of God's substance, and he upholds all things by his powerful word." 2 Cor 3:18[121] reads: "For we all, seeing the glory of the Lord with unveiled faces, are being transformed into the same image from glory into glory as it were, by the Spirit of the Lord." The **splendor of** God's **glory** is a Christological reference. One contemplates the **splendor of** God's **glory**, Jesus Christ, and through contemplation of Jesus Christ, one is transformed into the image of Jesus Christ.

The word sequence, *caeli. . .poterant*, found in *3LAg* 18, "May you cling to his most sweet Mother, who gave birth to the kind of Son whom the **heavens** could not **contain**,"[122] perhaps hints at the theology that undergirded Clare's fasting practices. A medieval religious woman might fast so that she could be emptied of all that was not of God. If she fed upon the Eucharist, she might imagine herself carrying God as Mary did. Clare warns Agnes that nothing created can make itself empty enough for God, who chose to dwell physically within Mary, by sheer, unrepeatable grace: "and yet, she carried him in the tiny enclosure of her sacred womb, and held him on her young girl's lap (*3LAg* 19)."[123] In *3LAg* 20,[124] Clare reminds Agnes that force cannot bring about the grace of God's indwelling: "Who would not abhor the treachery of the enemy of humanity who, by means of the pride that results from fleeting and false glories, compels that which is greater than heaven to return to nothingness?" Clare suggests that the way to invite God's indwelling presence is not through extreme and self-destructive fasting, but through poverty and humility: "so, you too, following in her [Mary's] footsteps especially those of humility and poverty, can without any doubt, always carry him spiritually in your chaste and virginal body (*3LAg* 25)."[125]

Clare repeats her use of the *caeli. . .poterant* in *3LAg* 21-22.[126] "See, it is already clear that the soul of a faithful person, the most worthy of God's creations through the grace of God, is greater than heaven, since the **heavens** and the rest of creation together **cannot** contain their Creator and only the soul of a faithful person is his dwelling and throne and this is possible only through the charity that the wicked lack." The spirit of this passage is very similar to *1LtF* 1:5-7; 10,[127] (cf., *2LtF* 48-50; 53), wherein Francis writes: "O how happy and blessed are these men and women while they do such things and persevere in doing them, because the Spirit of the Lord will rest upon them and make its home and dwelling place among them, and they are children of the heavenly Father whose works they do, and they are spouses, brothers, and mothers of our Lord Jesus Christ. . . . We are mothers when we carry him in our heart and body through a divine love and a pure and sincere conscience and give birth to him through a holy activity which must shine as an example before others." Clare invites Agnes to refocus her energies on sacramental contemplation and on faithful discipleship. Fasting practices are only a means to an end. The experience of being filled by God is a sheer grace and cannot be manipulated or forced. In the midst of this, Clare introduces the word sequence *fidelis anima* (*3LAg* 22).[128] The expression is found also in *1LtF* 1:8[129] (cf., *2LtF* 51): "We are spouses when the **faithful soul** is joined by the Holy Spirit to our Lord Jesus Christ." The key for Clare is fidelity to one's vocational calling, represented in one's initial *propositum*. This *propositum* for Clare is fidelity to live without possessions and the privileges that arise from possessions. Since particular fasting regulations are not essential to the Damianite lifestyle, the particularities of fasting rules might be changed without compromising fidelity.

The word group *mansionem. . .faciemus* of *3LAg* 23:[130] "For the Truth says: The one who loves me, will be loved by my Father, and I shall love him and we shall come to him and **make our dwelling place** with him," quotes the Johannine reference (Jn 14:23), also found in *1LtF*. According to *1LtF* 1:6[131] (cf., *2LtF* 48), the Spirit of the Lord "**will make its dwelling place**" among those who choose a life of penance.

In *ER* 22:27-31,[132] Francis places the reference to Jn 14:23 within the context of a discussion on constant prayer: "**Let us** always **make** a home and a **dwelling place** there for him who is the Lord God Almighty, Father, Son, and Holy Spirit, who says: Be vigilant, praying constantly that you may be considered worthy to escape all the evils that are to come and to stand before the Son of Man. When you stand to pray, say: Our Father who is in heaven. And let us adore him with a pure heart, because it is necessary to pray always and not lose heart; for the Father seeks such worshipers. God is Spirit, and those who adore him must adore him in spirit and in truth." It seems that Clare is evoking both the sense of living a life of penance and the sense of constant prayer. In *3LAg* 23, one receives the indwelling and thus carries Christ through following in the Virgin's footsteps of humility and poverty. This "carrying" for Clare is the gift of constant prayer, the gift of contemplative presence.

"**Following** in her **footsteps**" is a common expression in Franciscan literature. While most of the sources speak of following in the footsteps of Christ, Clare, following her image of carrying Christ "spiritually in your chaste and virginal body," transposes the expression into a Marian key. While Clare does not restrict herself to Marian images of discipleship, the Marian image is the one she is exploring here. One should not simplistically mistake these lines, however, for a gender specific spirituality. As Francis pictures himself both as a mother and as a disciple "on the way," so does Clare. Franciscan men and women contemplate the Christological mystery through the use of both masculine and feminine images.

---

sequens. . .vestigia

3LAg 25[133]
so, you too, **following in her footsteps**, especially those of humility and poverty, can without any doubt, always carry him spiritually in your chaste and virginal body.

ER 1:1[134]
The rule and life of these brothers is this, namely: to live in obedience, in chastity, and without anything of their own, and to **follow** the teaching and **footsteps** of our Lord Jesus Christ.

ER 22:1-2[135] (same as *FR* 1:1)
All my brothers: let us pay attention to what the Lord says: "Love your enemies and do good to those who hate you," for our Lord Jesus Christ, whose **footsteps** we must **follow**, called his betrayer a friend and willingly offered himself to those who crucified him.

2LtF 13[136]

(In speaking about the conformity of Jesus' will with the Father's):
leaving us an example that we might **follow** his **footsteps.**

LtL 3[137]

In whatever way it seems better to you to please the Lord God and to **follow** his **footstep** [sic] and poverty, do this with the blessing of the Lord God and my obedience.

LtOrd 51[138]

Inwardly cleansed, interiorly enlightened, and inflamed by the fire of the Holy Spirit, may we be able to **follow** in the **footsteps** of your beloved Son, our Lord Jesus Christ.

1C 84:1[139]

Francis's highest intention, his foremost desire, his uppermost purpose was to observe the Holy Gospel in all things and through all things and, with perfect vigilance, with all zeal, with all the longing of his mind and all the fervor of his heart, "to **follow** the teaching and the **footsteps** of our Lord Jesus Christ."

2C 148:9[140] (similar to *AC* 49:9 and *2MP* 43:8)

Their [the brothers'] vocation teaches them to stay down to earth, and to **follow** the **footsteps** of the humble Christ, so that in the end they may be exalted above the rest in the sight of the saints.

Using the word sequence *Natalis. . .bis,* from Clare's instructions in *3LAg* 33:[141] "except on Sundays and on the Lord's **Nativity**, when we ought to eat **twice** a day," is echoed in *RCl* 3:9:[142] "They may eat **twice** on **Christmas**, however, no matter on what day it happens to fall." In regard to fasting, it is perhaps also helpful to ponder the word group *sacrificium/sale conditum.* Clare urges Agnes toward discretion saying: "I am asking and begging in the Lord that you be restrained wisely, dearest one, and discreetly from the indiscreet and impossibly severe fasting that I know you have imposed upon yourself, so that living, you might profess the Lord, and might return to the Lord your reasonable worship and your **sacrifice** always **seasoned with salt** (*3LAg* 40-41).[143] In *2C* 22:6,[144] Francis, after eating with a brother who could not tolerate the hunger of the early community, illustrated the necessity of discretion: "He ordered them always to give to the Lord a **sacrifice seasoned with salt**, and carefully admonished each one to consider his own strength in the service of God." All penance must be undertaken with both generosity and discretion.

Summary

Clare's third letter illustrates the fluidity of Clare's sense of Trinitarian relationship. Clare's sense of being spouse, sister, mother, and daughter within Trinitarian dynamism demonstrates a theological richness unavailable to contemporaries whose relational images are often limited to the "nuclear family." For Clare, contemplating Trinitarian splendor from the vantage of a plethora of relationships transforms one into Trinitarian glory.

As a model for this contemplation, Clare recommends Mary. Mary's poverty, humility, and openness to God transformed and filled her. This transformation cannot be forced or manipulated; it can only be invited. One invites grace by being faithful to one's initial *propositum*, to one's vocational calling. According to one's vocational grace, one becomes "full of grace," and rejoices and contemplates the wonder of the Trinity making their home within one.

The key to the dialectic between active asceticism and receptive *fiat* is discretion. Although one invites by abstinence, fasting, and other expressions of poverty, spiritual disciplines are mitigated when they undermine one's ability to live. The practicality of listening to the limits of one's body is a key component of inviting transforming Trinitarian relationship.

The Fourth Letter

In *4LAg* 2, the word group *Clara/monasterio. . .Assisio*; variant *Clara/Sancti. . .Assisio* is also found in *AC* 13:1[145] (cf., *1MP* 18:1 and *2MP* 108:1). In *AC* 13:1, "**Lady Clare,** . . . abbess of the Poor Ladies of the **Monastery** of **San** Damiano in **Assisi**," is herself ill and fearful that she will not see Francis again. Early writers, including Clare herself, identified Clare as belonging to the Assisi monastery. While the friars are missioned all over the known world, there is a strong sense of stability to Clare's form of life. In his letter of 1216 concerning the "Lesser Brothers and Lesser Sisters," Jacques de Vitry identifies stability and mobility as differentiating the sisters and the brothers. De Vitry writes: "The women dwell together near cities in various hospices."[146]

Cuius pulchritudinem, "**whose beauty** all the blessed hosts of the heavens unceasingly admire," (*4LAg* 10[147]) is taken from *The Legend of St. Agnes of Rome*.[148] While we have discussed Clare's use of this phrase in our previous essay, one parallel text from *First Celano* is worth considering in this context. On Mount LaVerna, Francis experiences a vision in which he sees a seraph: "Moreover, he greatly rejoiced and he was much delighted by the the kind and gracious look that he saw the Seraph gave him, **whose beauty** was beyond comprehension." The seraph, although inestimably beautiful, was also experienced in profound suffering: "but the fact that the Seraph was fixed to a cross and the bitter suffering of that passion thoroughly frightened him (*1C* 94:4[149])." For both Francis and Clare, beauty is found in profound compassion that, if suffered in union with Christ, is the fruit of profound suffering. In gazing upon the mirror of Christ, Clare invites Agnes to gaze upon Christ's poverty, humility, and charity (*4LAg* 15-26).

This charity is experienced precisely in the depths of Christ's suffering. It is in the depths of Christ's poverty, humility, and charity preserved amid ultimate desolation that Christ's beauty is to be found.

The word pair *interius et exterius* is common to Franciscan sources. While Clare uses the expression once in her writings, the writings of the brothers attest to its widespread use in the early Franciscan movement. The following is a sampling from the sources:

interius et exterius
4LAg 15-16[150]   Look into this mirror every day, O queen, spouse of Jesus Christ, and continually examine your face in it, so that in this way you may adorn yourself completely, **inwardly and outwardly**, clothed and covered in multicolored apparel.
Adm 23:3[151]   Faithful and prudent is the servant who does not delay in punishing himself for all his offenses, **inwardly** through contrition and **outwardly** through confession and penance for what he did.
1C 72:1[152]   He used to struggle hand to hand with the devil, who, in those places, would not only assault him **internally** with temptations but also frighten him **externally** with ruin and undermining.
1C 95:2[153]   Those marks on the **inside** of his hands were round, but rather oblong on the **outside**.
1C 96:5[154]   For he had met some people who agreed with him **outwardly** but **inwardly** disagreed, applauding him to his face but laughing behind his back.

2C 211:18[155]

And that is why the stigmata shone **outwardly** in his flesh, because **inwardly** that deeply set root was sprouting forth from his spirit.

3C 124:5[156]

One of them, however, the granddaughter, was deprived of the light of her **exterior** eyes, though her **inner** sight, which sees God, was sharp and clear.

LJS 33:9-10[157]

Seeking to attain the highest level of every kind of perfection, he used to avoid human favor by every means, so that, with his conscience as witness, he might possess the vessel of sanctification **internally**, and **externally** become, to himself, a broken vessel.

LMj 3:10:1[158]

The servant of Almighty God giving himself totally to prayer, obtained through his devout prayers both what he should say **outwardly** and what the pope should hear **inwardly**.

LMj 5:2:1[159]

Once when he was asked how he could protect himself against the bite of the winter's frost with such thin clothing, he answered with a burning spirit: "If we were touched **within** by the flame of desire for our heavenly home, we would easily endure that **exterior** cold."

LMn 1:4:2-3[160]

His soul melted at the sight, and the memory of Christ was so impressed on the innermost recesses of his heart, that with the eyes of his mind continually, as it were, he discerned **inwardly** the wounds of his crucified Lord and could scarcely restrain his **outward** tears and sighs.

2MP 9:2-3[161]

Blessed Francis said, "This cell is too fine. . . . If you wish me to stay here, have a cell made with branches and ferns as its only covering **interiorly and exteriorly**."

The Primitive Franciscan Climate As Source

2MP 95:3-4[162]

He used to say, "If the servant of God strives to obtain and preserve both **outwardly and inwardly** the joyful spirit that springs from purity of heart and is acquired through devout prayer, the devils have no power to hurt that person, and say, 'We can find no way to get at or hurt the person, because this servant of God preserves joy both in trouble and in prosperity.'"

Franciscan literature suggests that it is problematic to have one's heart and one's deeds/words out of sync (*1C* 96:5). Growing into *interius et exterius* integration requires spiritual discipline (*Adm* 23:3); it implies growth in virtue (*4LAg* 15-16). One's external manner of living reflects what is in one's heart (*2MP* 9:3; *LMj* 5:2:1). Even the devils understand this basic anthropological premise, since they, who are by nature subject to sloth, find it necessary to attack the maturing Christian both through interior temptations and through outward disturbances (*1C* 72:1).

When the interior and exterior are out of sync, human persons suffer frustration. The blind girl with extraordinary interior sight (*3C* 124:5) is deprived of exterior sight. Her family begs Francis for mercy. Francis heals the girl's deformity, suggesting that interior sight without exterior sight is not ideal. In light of this, one ponders the dying, blind Francis whose hands are wounded interiorly and exteriorly (*1C* 95:2). Even in submitting to human vulnerability, the embodied soul accosted by suffering and evil and the enspirited body subjected to illness and decay must cry out in both love and anguish (*LMn* 1:4:3).

As anyone who has listened to the blind or has experienced blindness knows, interior sight is not bereft of physicality. Those who are blind find other avenues of sense perception sharpened. Those who physically see can be blind to the understanding and compassion of the "seer." What is required is a dance among and between the inner and the outer. In this dance, the interior and exterior senses while distinct, suffer neither division nor fusion.

The discipline and gift of joy is found within the integration of the *interius et exterius*. Joy is a disciplined choice in that one "obtains" it and "preserves" it. It springs from a heart that is not duplicitous. It is found in dancing with the rhythm of life, so that there is "no way to get at or hurt the person, because this servant of God preserves joy both in trouble and in prosperity" (*2MP* 95:3-4).

The *interius et exterius* is choreographed not only anthropologically but also within Trinitarian relationship. The *interius et exterius* fruits of Francis's prayer are manifested in his relationships; i.e. Francis understands what he "should say **outwardly**," and through prayer understands "what the pope should think **inwardly**" (*LMj* 3:10:1). This does not mean that relationships will always be successful, since human relationships are always subject to limitation, insensitivity, and indifference. What it does mean is that praying persons who discipline themselves interiorly and exteriorly and who are open to the work of the Spirit of God will discover the dynamism of God's grace in their world. Within this dynamism, one can sometimes identify a Pentecostal moment when God's grace finds paschal fecundity through human openness. As *LMj* 3:10:1 suggests, communities are born in these moments.

In *4LAg* 19,[163] Clare refers to "the poverty of him **placed in a manger** (*positi/in praesepio*)." The same word pattern is found in *OfP* 15:7: "For the most holy beloved child has been given to us, and he has been born for us on the way and **placed in a manger** because there was no place for him in the inn."[164] The passage from the *Office of the Passion* continues by breaking into praise as Clare also does.

One looks into the mirror by examining the poverty of Christ as a baby (*4LAg* 19), by pondering the poverty of his public life (*4LAg* 22), and by contemplating his death on the cross (*4LAg* 23-26). Clare repeats the word group *in praesaepio. . .involuti* in *RCl* 2:24:[165] "And for love of the most holy and beloved child who was **wrapped** in such poor little swaddling clothes and laid **in a manger** and of his most holy Mother, I admonish, beg, and exhort my sisters always to wear poor garments." For Clare, an exterior fruit of the contemplation of the Poor Christ wrapped in swaddling clothes and laid in a manger is shown in wearing poor garments. Again one sees the relationship between the interior and exterior.

This integrity of the inner and outer can also be seen in Francis's use of a word phrase that Clare also uses in *4LAg* 20, *O miranda humilitas.* In *LtOrd* 27,[166] Francis speaks of Christ's eucharistic presence. At the thought of this presence, Francis exclaims: "O **wondrous** loftiness and stupendous dignity! **O sublime humility! O humble sublimity!**" Francis, like Clare, expresses the mystical concretely in the exterior. Francis goes on to say: "Humble yourselves that you may be exalted by him. Hold back nothing of yourselves for yourselves, that he who gives himself totally to you may receive you totally" (*LtOrd* 28-29).[167] "**O sublime humility! O humble sublimity!**" with its practical application of humbling oneself allows the Franciscan to participate in the very depths of the hypostatic unity of Christ. One becomes divinized by embracing the Christic depths of one's creaturehood. While utterly profound, this participation is practical and simple.

In *4LAg* 21, Clare speaks of Jesus Christ as "The **King** of the angels, the Lord of heaven and **earth**."[168] The sequence *Rex. . .terrae* is also found in the *ER* 23:1[169] where Francis addresses God: "All-powerful, most holy, most high and supreme God, holy and just Father, Lord **King** of heaven and **earth**."[170] Francis's *Praises of God* 2[171] reads: "You are strong. You are great. You are the most high. You are the almighty King. You, holy Father, are **King** of heaven and **earth**." Finally in *The Office of the Passion*, one reads: "My holy Father, **King** of heaven and **earth**, do not leave me for trouble is near and there is no one to help (1:5),"[172] and "I will praise you, Lord, most holy Father, **King** of heaven and **earth**, because you have consoled me (14:1)."[173] It is interesting to note that in these writings of Francis, the "King" referred to is God the Father. Clare, on the other hand, speaks of Jesus Christ both as the "Lord of heaven and earth," and as the "King of the angels."

In *4LAg* 21, this "King of the angels" is "**laid to rest in** a manger (*in. . .reclinatur)*."[174] As noted above, the word group is found in RCl 2:24[175] and the poverty of this infant is connected with the practice of wearing poor garments. Recalling the Christmas at Greccio, *1C* 84:8[176] uses this same word group: "For I wish to enact the memory of that baby who was born in Bethlehem: to see as much as is possible with my own bodily eyes the discomfort of his infant needs, how he **lay in** a manger, and how, with an ox and an ass standing by, he rested on hay." In *AC* 14:4-5[177] (cf., *1MP* 19:5, *MP* 114:3-4), Francis dreams of speaking to the emperor and asking that the birds and domesticated animals might be fed by the people on the feast of Christmas. In regard to domesticated animals, he says: "Also out of reverence for the Son of God, whom his Virgin Mother on that night **laid in** a manger between an ox and an ass, everyone should have to give brother ox and brother ass a generous portion of fodder on that night. Likewise, on the Nativity of the Lord, all the poor should be fed their fill by the rich."

Calling to mind the infant lying in a manger requires concrete responses from both Clare and Francis. For Clare, the thought of the infant inspires the practical wearing of poor garments. For Francis, Christmas inspires the concrete staging of the manger scene and the practical distribution of food and other gifts to the poor as well as to wild and domesticated animals.

The passage from Lamentations 1:12, which Clare cites in *4LAg* 25[178]: "**O all you who pass by this way, look and see if there is any suffering like my suffering,**" is also used by

Francis in *OfP* 6:1. Clare is creative in her use of this passage and does not seem to be relying on the *OfP*. The word sequence *eiulanti/voce* found in *4LAg 26* is repeated in *L3C* 14:4-7[179] (cf., *AC* 78:1; *2MP* 92:1): "Once he [Francis] was roaming about alone near the church of Saint Mary of the Portiuncula, weeping and **lamenting** with a loud **voice**. A certain spiritual man, overhearing him, thought he was suffering from some sickness or pain, asked pityingly the reason for his distress. Francis replied: 'I weep for the passion of my Lord; and I should not be ashamed to go weeping through the whole world for his sake.' Then the other man fell to crying and lamenting with him." It is in the contemplation of the passion, that Clare also invokes "crying out and **lamenting**."[180]

The word group *benigne/suscipias* used by Clare in *4LAg* 37 is found liberally throughout the Franciscan sources.

benigne/suscipias
4LAg 37[181] I beg you to **receive** these words with **kindness** and devotion, seeing in them at least the motherly affection, by which every day I am stirred by the fire of love for you and your daughters.
ER 2:1, 3[182] If anyone, desiring by divine inspiration to accept this life, comes to our brothers, let him be **received** by them with **kindness**. . . . On his part, let the minister **receive** him with **kindness,** encourage him and diligently explain the tenor of our life to him.
ER 7:14[183] Whoever comes to them, friend or foe, thief or robber, let him be **received** with **kindness.**

1LtF 2:19[184]
In the love that is God, we beg all those whom these words reach to **receive** those fragrant words of our Lord Jesus Christ written above with divine love and **kindness**.

2LtF 88[185]
And may the Father and the Son and the Holy Spirit bless all those men and women who **receive** them [these words] with **kindness**, understand them, and send copies of them to others, if they have persevered to the end in them.

LtR 6[186]
Therefore I strongly advise you, my lords, to put aside all care and anxiety and **receive** the most holy Body and Blood of our Lord Jesus Christ **kindly** in holy remembrance of him.

1C 32:8-9[187]
Saint Francis also approached the reverend lord bishop of Sabina, named John of Saint Paul, who, among the other princes and great men at the Roman Curia, seemed to despise earthly things and love heavenly things. He **received** Francis **kindly** and charitably, and praised highly his desire and proposal.

L3C 35:1-2,5[188] (cf., *AP* 17:2)
After a few days had elapsed, however, three other men from Assisi, Sabbatino, Morico, and John of Capella, came to them, begging blessed Francis to receive them as brothers. He **received** them humbly and **kindly**. . . . The bishop of the city of Assisi, to whom the man of God would frequently go for counsel, **receiving** him **kindly**, told him. . . .

AP 29:1[189]
When people who were rich in worldly goods came to the brothers, the brothers **received** them eagerly and **kindly** and sought to invite them away from sin and to prompt them to do penance.

Although one might reduce Clare's use of *benigne/suscipias* to epistolary formulation, the tradition of receiving another kindly is highly valued in the Franciscan sources. New members are to be received with kindness (*ER* 2:1, 3). Whoever comes, friend, foe, thief, or sinner should be received with kindness (*ER* 7:14). The Word of God and the Eucharist should be received with kindness (*1LtF* 2:19; *LtR* 6). A receptive curia receives Francis with kindness (*1C* 32:8-9). The spiritual principle of accepting the good of another with openness rather than with testing or suspicious judgment is central to the spirit of Francis and Clare. To remain faithful in one's embrace of poverty, one must receive others and their words and actions with gracious kindness, just as God receives with kindness the poverty of all humanity.

Summary

Clare's fourth letter reveals the spiritual maturity of the dying Clare. Reading Clare in dialogue with her Franciscan brothers helps one appreciate more fully the Franciscan hypostasis of radical divinization with concrete devotion and practical behavior. One finds the heights of beauty in the depths of suffering. One welcomes divinity by embracing with Christ the fragility of one's humanity. The interior profundity of a heart totally devoted to the contemplative praise of God is manifested exteriorly in the practicality of concrete devotion, penitential practices, choice of clothing, housing, and even the feeding of birds on Christmas day! Because God is found in the midst of the world, even in the depths of desolation, physical hardship, and human fragility, one is free to accept with kindness whatever and whoever life brings.

Conclusion

The dialogue between Clare and her beloved brothers could certainly be contemplated with greater fullness. The above is merely a sample exercise in studying the mutuality between brothers and sisters in the primitive Franciscan climate. Even though not all possible word sequences have been studied here, three points seem obvious.

First, a mutual reading of Clare's letters with the sources of the brothers brings about a clearer and a fuller contextual reconstruction of the primitive Franciscan climate. Mutual study identifies recurring idioms, word sequences, and hermenuetics. Studying these idioms, word sequences, and hermenuetical applications in differing primitive Franciscan contexts, helps the scholar imagine in a more satisfying way the foci and parlance common to primitive Franciscanism.

Second, the language of primitive Franciscanism with its corresponding practices of penitential behavior and contemplative prayer enables the reader to reconstruct Clare's theology and spirituality. This theology, although "lay" in origin, is remarkable in depth, practicality, subtlety, and nuance. Clare's letters read in dialogue with the writings of the brothers demonstrate a subtlety in Christological understandings, a profound Trinitarian dynamism, a transforming sacramental vision, the integration of contemplative prayer with simple devotion, and a relational understanding of faith and works. The theologian stands in awe of this profound intellectual and practical integration revealed more fully in a mutual reading.

Third, for modern Franciscans interested in recovering the contribution of Clare in order to more faithfully live the fullness of their Franciscan life, a mutual reading helps one peel back mitigations, stagnant expressions of piety, and ahistorical interpretations in order to better understand the initial energy and genius of the primitive Francisan movement. Although Franciscanism will never again be lived literally in its medieval form, understanding the initial intuition, preaching, prayer, energy, and life of the early Francisans can help contemporaries renew and create faithful Franciscan lifestyles.

Notes

[1]Further insight into poverty and mutual relationships between the early brothers and sisters can be found in Margaret Carney, *The First Franciscan Woman: Clare of Assisi and her Form of Life* (Quincy, IL: Franciscan Press, 1993), particularly pages 132-35; see also Lázaro Iriarte, OFM Cap., "Clara de Asís in la tipologia hagiográfica," *Laurentianum* 29 (1988): 416-61; translated by Ignatius McCormick, OFM Cap., as "Clare of Assisi: Her Place in Female Hagiography," *GR* 3 (August 1989): 173-206, particularly pages 190-94.

[2]Cum semel dominus Papa Gregorius prohibuisset, ne aliquis frater ad monasteria dominarum sine sua licentia pergeret, dolens pia mater cibum sacrae doctrinae rarius habituras Sorores, cum gemitu dixit: Omnes nobis auferat de cetero Fratres, postquam vitalis nutrimenti nobis abstulit praebitores. Et statim omnes Fratres ad Ministrum remisit, nolens habere eleemosynarios qui panem corporalem acquirerent, postquam panis, spiritualis eleemosynarios non haberent. Quod cum audiret Papa Gregorius statim prohibitum illud in generalis Ministri manibus relaxavit.

[3]*Proc* 3:18-19; 9:2-3.

[4]*Proc* 6:15.

[5]*Proc* 1:13; 2:22; 3:14; *LegCl* 14, 37. See also Sigismund Verheij, "Persönliches Berufungsbewusstsein und kirchliche Autorität am Beispiel der Klara von Assisi," *FranzStud* 69 (1987): 79-87; translated by Ignatius McCormick, OFM Cap., as "Personal Awareness of Vocation and Ecclesiastical Authority as Exemplified in St. Clare of Assisi," *GR* 3 (1989): 35-42.

[6](S. Maria degli Angeli—Assisi: Edizioni Porziuncola, 1995).

[7]The second volume of *Fontes Franciscani* has not yet been published.

[8]The first and second volumes of *Francis of Assisi: Early Documents* (Hyde Park, NY: New City Press, 1999, 2000), has been our guide for translations of the writings and legends of Francis. For the writings of Clare other than her letters, Regis J. Armstrong, OFM Cap, *Clare of Assisi: Early Documents* (St. Bonaventure, NY: Franciscan Institute Publications, 1993), was consulted. At times the author found it necessary to rework the above translations in order to show more clearly in English the Latin parallelism between various sources.

[9]Clara indigna famula Iesu Christi et ancilla inutilis **dominarum inclusarum monasterii** Sancti Damiani, sua ubique subdita et ancilla, recommendationem sui omnimodam cum reverentia speciali aeternae felicitatis gloriam adipisci.

[10]Verum quia parum esset sanctum Dei rebus insensibilibus honorari nisi per eum, corpore mortuum et spiritu viventem in gloria, Dominus quamplurimos converteret et sanaret, non solum promiscui sexus personae indifferentes post eius obitum meritis ipsius ad Dominum sunt conversae, sed etiam multi magni et nobiles cum filiis suis habitum sui ordinis susceperunt, reclusis propriis uxoribus et filiabus suis in **monasteriis** pauperum **dominarum**.

[11]Similiter illis diebus et in eodem loco, postquam beatus Franciscus composuit Laudes Domini de creaturis, fecit etiam quedam sancta verba cum cantu pro maiori consolatione **dominarum** pauperum **monasterii** Sancti **Damiani**, maxime quia de eius infirmitate ipsas sciebat nimis tribulari.

[12]The canticle referred to in *AC* 85:1 is *CtExh*.

[13]Venite et adiuvate me in opere ecclesia **Sancti Damiani** quae futura est **monasterium dominarum**, quarum fama et vita in universali ecclesia glorificabitur Pater noster caelestis.

[14]See note 9.

[15]Occurrunt sibi invicem divina providentia beatus Franciscus et ipse ad quoddam **monasterium** pauperum **inclusarum**.

[16]quae omnia respuentes, toto animo et cordis affectu magis **sanctissimam paupertatem** et corporis penuriam elegistis.

[17]This addition to Boccali's apparati was brought to my attention by Edith van den Goorbergh, OSC, and Theodore Zweerman, OFM.

[18]**Paupertatis sanctissimae** sectatores quia nihil habebant, nihil amabant: nihil proinde perdere verebantur.

[19]perseverans usque in finem in **sanctissima paupertate**.

[20]**sponsum** nobilioris generis accipientes, Dominum Iesum **Christum**, qui vestram virginitatem semper immaculatam custodiet et illaesam.

[21]Ergo, **soror** carissima immo **domina** veneranda nimium, quia **sponsa** et mater estis et soror Domini mei Iesu **Christi**.

[22]et sunt filii patris caelestis, cuius opera faciunt, et sunt **sponsi**, fratres et matres Domini nostri Iesu **Christi**.

[23]**Sponsi** sumus, quando Spiritu Sancto coniungitur fidelis anima Domino nostro Iesu **Christo**.

[24]See note 21.

[25]Vale, carissima **soror** et **domina**, propter Dominum tuum sponsum.

[26]in sancto servitio confortamini, **pauperis Crucifixi** ardenti desiderio inchoato.

[27]Obsecro propter amorem **pauperis Crucifixi** et per sacra stigmata eius, quae beatus pater Franciscus portavit in corpore suo, universos ista legentes, videntes et audientes, ut coram Deo mei meminerint peccatoris.

[28]Depositaque omni verecundia propter amorem **pauperis Crucifixi**.

[29]Qui **pro** nobis omnibus crucis sustinuit **passionem**.

[30]Attendamus, omnes fratres, bonum pastorem, qui **pro** ovibus suis salvandis crucis sustinuit **passionem**.

[31]Unde magna verecundia est nobis servis Dei, quod sancti fecerunt opera et nos recitando ea volumus recipere gloriam et honorem.

[32]O pia **paupertas** quam **Dominus Iesus Christus**, qui caelum terramque regebat et regit, qui dixit etiam et sunt facta, dignatus est prae ceteris amplexari!

[33]Omnes fratres studeant sequi humilitatem et **paupertatem Domini** nostri **Iesu Christi** et recordentur, quod nihil aliud oportet nos habere de toto mundo, nisi, sicut dicit apostolus, habentes alimenta et quibus tegamur, his contenti sumus.

[34]Ego frater Franciscus parvulus volo sequi vitam et **paupertatem** altissimi **Domini** nostri **Iesu Christi** et eius sanctissimae matris, et perseverare in ea usque in finem. Et rogo vos, dominas meas, et consilium do vobis, ut in ista sanctissima vita et paupertate semper vivatis.

[35]nam paupertas et infirmitas istius est quoddam speculum nobis, per quod speculari et considerare cum pietate debemus **paupertatem** et infirmitatem **Domini** nostri **Iesu Christi**, quas in suo corpore pertulit pro salvatione humani generis.

[36]**Vulpes enim foveas, inquit, habent et volucres caeli nidos, Filius autem hominis, id est Christus, non habet ubi caput reclinet**, sed, inclinato capite, tradidit spiritum.

[37]Docebat suos habitacula paupercula facere, ligneas, non lapideas, easque vili schemate casellas erigere. Saepe vero de paupertate sermonem faciens ingerebat fratribus evangelicum illud: "**Vulpes foveas habent et volucres caeli nidos, Filius autem Dei non habuit ubi caput reclinaret**."

[38]Cum ergo solus persisteret orationes longas ac devotissimas Domino fundens, circumspicit tandem, **ubi caput** ad dormiendum **reclinet**.

[39]Saepe vero de paupertate sermonem faciens, ingerebat fratribus evangelicum illud: "**Vulpes foveas habent et volucres caeli nidos, Filius autem hominis non habet ubi caput suum reclinet.**" Propter quod docebat fratres, ut pauperum more pauperculas casas erigerent, quas non inhabitarent ut proprias, sed sicut peregrini et advenae alienas.

[40]Nos vero qui cum ipso fuimus multotiens audivimus ipsum dicentem illud verbum sancti Evangelii: **Vulpes foveas habent et volucres celi nidos, Filius autem hominis non habet ubi caput suum reclinet.**

[41]Positus est, inquit Evangelista, in presepio, quia non erat ei locus in diversorio. Et sic semper inseparabiliter comitata es ipsum, ut in omni vita sua, quando in terris visus est et cum hominibus conversatus est, cum **vulpes foveas haberent et volucres Celi nidos, ipse nihilominus non habuit ubi caput suum reclinaret.**

[42]*Agnes von Böhmen 1211-1282: Königstochter-Äbtissin-Heilige* (München: R. Oldenbourg Verlag, 1989), 115-16.

[43]Si, ergo, tantus et talis Dominus in uterum veniens virginalem, despectus, **egenus, et pauper in mundo** voluit apparere.

[44]Sorores nihil sibi approprient, nec domum nec locum, nec aliquam rem; et tanquam peregrinae et advenae in hoc saeculo, in paupertate et humilitate Domino famulantes, mittant pro eleemosyna confidenter; nec oportet eas verecundari, quia Dominus pro nobis se fecit **pauperem in** hoc **mundo**.

[45]Aiebat namque: "Qui pauperi maledicit, Christo iniuriam facit, cuius portat nobile signum, qui 'se pro nobis fecit **pauperem in** hoc **mundo.**'"

[46]Et tanquam peregrini et advenae in hoc saeculo in paupertate et humilitate Domino famulantes vadant pro eleemosyna confidenter, nec oportet eos verecundari, quia Dominus pro nobis se fecit **pauperem in** hoc **mundo**. Edith van den Goorbergh, OSC, and Theo Zweerman, OFM suggested this addition to Boccali.

[47]Nonnumquam vero seipsum exercitans et fratrum verecundiae parcens, ipse solus in principio pro eleemosyna discurrebat. Videns autem plures vocationem suam non debite attendentes, semel aliquando dixit: "Carissimi fratres, Dei Filius nobilior nobis erat, qui 'pro nobis se fecit **pauperem in** hoc **mundo.**' Suo amore viam paupertatis elegimus; non debemus confundi pro eleemosynis ire."

[48]"Dico vobis, multos nobiles et sapientes nostrae congregationi iungendos, qui pro honore ducent eleemosynas mendicare."

[49]Ego vero **egenus et pauper** sum. Deus, adiuva me.

[50]exsultate plurimum et gaudete, repletae ingenti gaudio et **laetitia spiritali**.

[51]Tutissimum remedium contra mille inimici insidias vel astutias **laetitiam spiritualem** sanctus iste firmabat.

[52]Tantum autem diligebat virum **spirituali laetitia** plenum, quod pro generali commonitione in quodam capitulo scribi fecit haec verba: "Caveant fratres, ne se ostendant extrinsecus nubilosos et hypocritas tristes, sed ostendant se gaudentes in Domino, hilares et iucundos, et convenienter gratiosos."
[53]licet a principio sue conversionis usque ad diem sue mortis valde afflixerit corpus suum, videlicet quod semper fuit sollicitus interius et exterius habere et conservare **letitiam spiritualem.**
[54]In hoc autem summum et praecipuum studium semper habuit beatus Franciscus ut extra orationem et divinum officium haberet continue interius et exterius **laetitiam spiritualem.**
[55]Dicebat enim quod "si servus Dei studuerit habere et conservare interius et exterius **laetitiam spiritualem,** quae provenit ex munditia cordis et acquiritur per devotionem orationis, daemones nihil possunt ei nocere."
[56]Quia ergo, fratres mei, ex munditia cordis et puritate continuae orationis provenit haec **laetitia spiritualis,** circa illa duo acquirenda et conservanda principaliter est studendum, ut **ipsam laetitiam,** quam in me et in vobis summo affectu cupio et diligo cernere et sentire, possitis habere interius et exterius ad aedificationem proximi et vituperium inimici. Ad ipsum enim et ad membra eius pertinet contristari, ad nos autem laetari semper in Domino et gaudere."
[57]Non quidem intelligendum est vel credendum quod pater noster, omnis maturitatis et honestatis amator, voluerit hanc laetitiam ostendi per risum vel etiam per nimium verbum vanum, cum per hoc non **laetitia spiritualis** sed vanitas et fatuitas potius ostendatur.
[58]Attendens autem beatus pater quod nullam paupertatem, laborem, tribulationem, vilitatem et **contemptum saeculi** timeremus, immo pro magnis deliciis haberemus, pietate motus scripsit nobis formam vivendi.
[59]Quia—cum vobis magis placuisset **contemptus saeculi** quam honores; paupertas quam divitiae temporales; et magis **thesauros in caelo** recondere quam in terra.
[60]Bernardus quidam de civitate Assisii, qui postea filius fuit perfectionis, cum viri Dei exemplo disponeret **saeculum** perfecte **contemnere.**
[61]Et in prima eius apertione occurrit illud consilium Domini: "Si vis perfectus esse, vade et vende omnia quae habes et da pauperibus et habebis **thesaurum in caelo.**"
[62]Beatus servus, qui **thesaurizat in caelo** bona, quae Dominus sibi ostendit et sub specie mercedis non cupit manifestare hominibus, quia ipse altissimus manifestabit opera eius quibuscumque placuerit. Beatus servus qui secreta Domini observat in corde suo.

[63]ubi nec rubigo consumit, nec tinea demolitur, et fures non effodiunt, nec furantur—merces vestra copiosissima est in caelis.
[64]Nolite thesaurizare vobis thesauros in terra, **ubi erugo et tinea** demolitur et **ubi fures effodiunt et furantur**.
[65]quoniam merces vestra copiosa est in caelis.
[66]merces vestra copiosissima est in caelis.
[67]Gaudete in illa die et exsultate, quoniam **merces vestra multa est in caelis.**
[68]et fere digne meruistis **soror, sponsa et mater** altissimi Patris Filii et gloriosae Virginis nuncupari.
[69]Ergo, soror carissima—immo domina veneranda nimium, quia **sponsa et mater estis et soror** Domini mei Iesu Christi.
[70]et sunt filii patris caelestis, cuius opera faciunt, et sunt **sponsi, fratres et matres** Domini nostri Iesu Christi. **Sponsi** sumus, quando Spiritu Sancto coniungitur fidelis anima Domino nostro Iesu Christo. **Fratres** ei sumus, quando facimus voluntatem patris qui in caelis est. **Matres**, quando portamus eum in corde et corpore nostro per divinum amorem et puram et sinceram conscientiam; parturimus eum per sanctam operationem, quae lucere debet aliis in exemplum.
[71]**filia** et **ancilla** altissimi summi Regis Patris caelestis, **mater** sanctissimi Domini nostri Iesu Christi, **sponsa** Spiritus Sancti.
[72]*PL* 76, 1233b.
[73]et vestitum **cum nudo** certare non posse, quia citius ad terram deicitur, qui habet unde teneatur.
[74]Ecce iam nudus **cum nudo** luctatur, et depositis omnibus quae sunt mundi, solius divinae iustitiae memoratur.
[75]Confectus namque infirmitate illa tam gravi, quae omni languori conclusit, super nudam humum se nudum fecit deponi, ut hora illa extrema, in qua poterat adhuc hostis irasci, nudus luctaretur **cum nudo**.
[76]**Intrate** per **angustam portam**, quia lata porta et spatiosa via, quae ducit ad perditionem, et multi sunt, qui intrant per eam; quam **angusta porta** et **arta via**, quae ducit ad vitam, et pauci sunt, qui inveniunt eam!"
[77]ut per **arctam viam** et **angustam portam** possitis regna caelestia **introire**.
[78]Per viam crucis et semitas iustitiae incedentes, de **arcta via** poenitentiae et observationis evangelicae offendicula removebant, ut posteris iter planum fieret et securum.
[79]Et contendant **intrare** per **angustam portam**, quia dicit Dominus: **Angusta porta** et **arcta via** est, quae ducit ad vitam; et pauci sunt, qui inveniunt eam.
[80]Quod intelligens, beatus Franciscus dixit eis: "**Arta est via**, fratres, et **angusta porta** que ducit ad vitam, et pauci sunt qui inveniunt eam."

[81]Et omnis, qui reliquit domos vel fratres aut sorores aut patrem aut matrem aut filios aut agros propter nomen meum, **centuplum accipiet** et vitam aeternam possidebit.

[82]**centuplum** pro uno **recipere**, ac beatam vitam perpetuam possidere.

[83]Et: Omnis, qui reliquerit patrem aut matrem, fratres aut sorores, uxorem aut filios, domos aut agros propter me, **centuplum accipiet** et vitam aeternam possidebit.

[84]**Filiae** Regis regum, **ancillae** Domini dominantium, **sponsae** dignissimae Iesu Christi.

[85]See above 71.

[86]Quia divina inspiratione fecistis vos **filias** et **ancillas** altissimi summi Regis, Patris caelestis, et Spiritui Sancto vos **desponsastis**.

[87]Clara, **pauperum dominarum** ancilla inutilis et indigna.

[88]Clara, humillima et indigna Christi ancilla et **dominarum pauperum** serva.

[89]perventum esset ad locum in quo religionem et ordinem sacrarum virginum et **Dominarum pauperum** ipse primo plantavit.

[90]Hic est ille locus celebri memoria dignus, in quo illa tantarum virtutum plenitudine praedita, **pauperum** videlicet **Dominarum** virginumque sanctarum religio, ab eodem sancto viro quasi post sextum suae conversionis annum felix exordium sumpsit.

[91]Secundus etiam, qui supra memoratus est, **pauperum Dominarum** et virginum felix ab eo sumpsit exordium.

[92]eumque filiabus ipsius, quas ibidem plantaverat, **pauperibus** videlicet **Dominabus** et sacris virginibus, ostenderunt.

[93]quae filia fuit in Christo sancti patris Francisci pauperculi et mater **Pauperum Dominarum.**

[94]**Viam mandatorum tuorum curram.**

[95]In hoc autem, ut **mandatorum** Domini securius **viam perambules.**

[96]Amore divino fervens, beatissimus pater Franciscus studebat semper ad fortia mittere manum, et dilatato corde **viam mandatorum** Dei **ambulans**, perfectionis summam attingere cupiebat.

[97]Qui **mandatorum** Dei **viam** mentis alacritate **percurrens**, per omnium virtutum gradus ad summa pervenit.

[98]venerabilis patris nostri **fratris** nostri Heliae, generalis **ministri**, consilium imitare.

[99]Reverendis et multum diligendis fratribus universis, **fratri A.**, generali **ministro** religionis minorum fratrum.

[100]**fratri H. ministro** religionis nostrae.

[101]quod praepone consiliis ceterorum et reputa tibi carius omni dono.

[102]Si quis vero aliud tibi dixerit, aliud tibi suggesserit, quod perfectionem tuam impediat, quod vocationi divinae contrarium videatur, etsi debeas venerari, noli tamen eius consilium imitari.

[103]Ego frater Franciscus parvulus volo sequi vitam et paupertatem altissimi Domini nostri Iesu Christi et eius sanctissimae matris, et perseverare in ea usque in finem. Et rogo vos, dominas meas, et consilium do vobis, ut in ista sanctissima vita et paupertate semper vivatis. Et custodite vos multum ne doctrina vel consilio alicuius ab ipsa in perpetuum ullatenus recedatis.

[104]Agneti, illustris regis Bohemiae germanae, sed iam **summo** caelorum **Regi** sorori et sponsae.

[105]omnium virtutum floribus et vestimentis pariter adornata, sicut decet, filia et sponsa carissima **summi Regis**.

[106]Quia divina inspiratione fecistis vos filias et ancillas altissimi **summi Regis**, Patris caelestis, et Spiritui Sancto vos desponsastis eligendo vivere secundum perfectionem sancti Evangelii, volo et promitto per me et fratres meos semper habere de vobis tanquam de ipsis curam diligentem et sollicitudinem specialem.

[107]Vivens adhuc inter peccatores universum peragrat et praedicat orbem: regnans iam cum angelis in excelsis facilius cogitatu volat tamquam nuntius **summi Regis** et populis omnibus praestat beneficia gloriosa.

[108]Nocte vero sequenti, cum se sopori dedisset, palatium speciosum et magnum cum militaribus armis crucis Christi signaculo insignitis clementia sibi divina monstravit, ut misericordiam pro **summi Regis** amore pauperi exhibitam militi praeostenderet incomparabili compensandam esse mercede.

[109]**summi** quoque **Regis** signacula per modum sigilli corpori eius impressa.

[110]Lacrimabantur filii pro subtractione tam amabilis Patris, sed et non modica perfundebantur laetitia, dum deosculabantur in eo signacula **summi Regis**.

[111]See above, note 85.

[112]Sicut ergo Virgo virginum gloriosa materialiter, sic et tu, sequens eius vestigia, humilitatis praesertim et paupertatis, casto et virgineo corpore spiritualiter semper sine dubietate omni portare potes.

[113]Ancho disse che allora epsa vidde sopra el capo de epsa madonna Chiara doi ale splendide come el sole, le quale alcuna volta se levavano in alto, et alcuna volta coprivano el capo de la predicta madonna.

[114]"Va secura in pace, però che haverai bona scorta, però che quello che te creò, innanti te sanctificò, et poi che te creò mise in te lo Spirito Sancto, et sempre te ha guardata como la matre lo suo figliolo lo quale ama."

[115]"Tu, Signore, sii benedecto, lo quale me hai creata."

[116]Et molte cose disse parlando de la Trinità così sutilmente, che le Sore non la potevano bene intendere.

[117]pone animam tuam in **splendore gloriae**.

[118]quae cum sit **splendor** aeternae **gloriae**, candor lucis aeternae et speculum sine macula.

[119]pone cor tuum in figura divinae substantiae et transforma te ipsam totam per contemplationem in imagine divinitatis ipsius.

[120]qui, cum sit **splendor gloriae** et figura substantiae eius et portet omnia verbo virtutis suae.

[121]Nos vero omnes revelata facie gloriam Domini speculantes, in eandem imaginem transformamur a claritate in claritatem tamquam a Domini Spiritu.

[122]Ipsius dulcissimae matri adhaereas, quae talem genuit Filium, quem **caeli** capere non **poterant**.

[123]et tamen ipsa parvulo claustro sacri uteri contulit et gremio puellari gestavit.

[124]Quis non abhorreat humani hostis insidias, qui per fastum momentaneorum et fallacium gloriarum ad nihilum redigere cogit quod maius est caelo?

[125]sic et tu, sequens eius vestigia, humilitatis praesertim et paupertatis, casto et virgineo corpore spiritualiter semper sine dubietate omni portare potes.

[126]Ecce iam liquet per Dei gratiam dignissimam creaturarum fidelis hominis animam maiorem esse quam caelum, cum **caeli** cum creaturis ceteris **capere** nequeant Creatorem, et sola **fidelis anima** ipsius mansio sit et sedes, et hoc solum per caritatem qua carent impii."

[127]O quam beati et benedicti sunt illi et illae, dum talia faciunt et in talibus perseverant, quia requiescet super eos spiritus Domini et faciet apud eos habitaculum et mansionem, et sunt filii patris caelestis, cuius opera faciunt, et sunt sponsi, fratres et matres Domini nostri Iesu Christi. . . . Matres, quando portamus eum in corde et corpore nostro per divinum amorem et puram et sinceram conscientiam.

[128]See above 124.

[129]Sponsi sumus, quando Spiritu Sancto coniungitur **fidelis anima** Domino nostro Iesu Christo.

[130]Veritate dicente: Qui diligit me diligetur a Patre meo, et ego diligam eum, et ad eum veniemus et **mansionem** apud eum **faciemus**.

[131]quia requiescet super eos spiritus Domini et **faciet** apud eos habitaculum et **mansionem**.

[132]et semper **faciamus** ibi habitaculum et **mansionem** ipsi, qui est Dominus Deus omnipotens, Pater et Filius et Spiritus Sanctus, qui dicit: Vigilate itaque omni tempore orantes, ut digni habeamini fugere omnia

mala, quae ventura sunt et stare ante Filium hominis. Et cum stabitis ad orandum dicite: Pater noster qui es in caelis. Et adoremus eum puro corde, quoniam oportet semper orare et non deficere; nam Pater tales quaerit adoratores. Spiritus est Deus et eos qui adorant eum, in spiritu et veritate oportet eum adorare.

[133]sic et tu, **sequens** eius **vestigia**, humilitatis praesertim et paupertatis, casto et virgineo corpore spiritualiter semper sine dubietate omni portare potes.

[134]Regula et vita istorum fratrum haec est, scilicet vivere in obedientia, in castitate et sine proprio, et Domini nostri Iesu Christi doctrinam et **vestigia sequi**.

[135]Attendamus omnes fratres quod dicit Dominus: Diligite inimicos vestros et benefacite his qui oderunt vos, quia Dominus noster Iesus Christus, cuius **sequi vestigia** debemus, traditorem suum vocavit amicum et crucifixoribus suis sponte se obtulit.

[136]relinquens nobis exemplum, ut **sequamur vestigia** eius.

[137]In quocumque modo melius videtur tibi placere Domino Deo et **sequi vestigiam** et paupertatem suam, faciatis cum beneditione Domini Dei et mea obedientia.

[138]ut interius mundati, interius illuminati et igne sancti spiritus accensi **sequi** possimus **vestigia** dilecti Filii tui, Domini nostri Iesu Christi.

[139]Summa eius intentio, praecipuum desiderium, supremumque propositum eius erat sanctum Evangelium in omnibus et per omnia observare ac perfecte omni vigilantia, omni studio, toto desiderio mentis, toto cordis fervore, "Domini nostri Iesu Christi doctrinam **sequi** et **vestigia**" imitari.

[140]Docet vocatio in plano subsistere, et humilitatis Christi **sequi vestigia**, quo tandem in respectione sanctorum plus aliis exaltentur.

[141]exceptis diebus dominicis et **Natalis** Domini, in quibus **bis** in die comedere deberemus.

[142]In **Nativitate** vero Domini quocumque die venerit, **bis** refici possint.

[143]a quadam indiscreta et impossibili abstinentiae austeritate quam te aggressam esse cognovi, sapienter, carissima, et discrete te retrahi rogo et in Domino peto, ut vivens confiteris Domino, rationabile tuum Domino reddas obsequium et tuum **sacrificium** semper **sale conditum**.

[144]**Sale conditum sacrificium** Deo semper reddere iubet, et ut vires proprias in Dei obsequio unusquisque consideret, monet attente.

[145]domina **Clara**, Ordinis sororum prima plantula, abbatissa sororum pauperum **monasterii Sancti** Damiani de **Assisio**."

[146]Mulieres vero iuxta civitates in diversis hospitiis simul commorantur. The Latin text of Jacques de Vitry's letter can be found in P. Girolamo Golubovich, OFM, *Biblioteca Bio-Bibliografica della Terra*

The Primitive Franciscan Climate As Source

Santa e dell'Oriente Francescano, tomo I, 1215-1300 (Quaracchi: Collegio di S. Bonaventura, 1906), 5-6.

[147]**cuius pulchritudinem** omnia beata caelorum agmina incessabiliter admirantur.

[148]*AASS*, January 21.

[149]Gaudebat quoque plurimum et vehementius laetabatur in benigno et gratioso respectu, quo a Seraphim conspici se videbat, **cuius pulchritudo** inaestimabilis erat nimis, sed omnino ipsum crucis affixio et passionis illius acerbitas deterrebat.

[150]Hoc speculum cottidie intuere, o regina, sponsa Iesu Christi, et in eo faciem tuam iugiter speculare, ut sic totam **interius et exterius** te adornes amictam circumdatamque varietatibus.

[151]Fidelis et prudens servus est, qui in omnibus suis offensis non tardat **interius** punire per contritionem **et exterius** per confessionem et operis satisfactionem.

[152]Manu ad manum cum diabolo confligebat, cum in eiusmodi locis non solum tentationibus ipsum pulsaret **interius**, verum etiam **exterius** ruinis et subversionibus deterreret.

[153]Erant enim signa illa rotunda **interius** in manibus, **exterius** autem oblonga.

[154]Invenerat enim aliquos sibi **exterius** concordantes **et interius** dissidentes, applaudentes coram, irridentes retro.

[155]Et ideo stigmata **exterius** fulgebant in carne, quia **intus** radix altissima excrescebat in mente.

[156]Verumtamen una istarum, neptis scilicet, privata erat **exteriorum** lumine oculorum, cum tamen **interiores** eius, quibus Deus videtur, mira conspicuitate clarescerent.

[157]In omni genere perfectionis usque ad summum apicem pertingere cupiens, favorem summopere devitabat humanum, et ut conscientia teste vas sanctificationis **interius** possideret, factus est sibimetipsi **exterius** tamquam vas perditum.

[158]Omnipotentis autem Dei famulus, totum se conferens ad orandum, precibus devotis obtinuit et quid **exterius** ipse proferret, **et** quid **interius** Papa sentiret.

[159]Interrogatus aliquando, quomodo vestitu tam tenui se posset ab hiemalis algoris asperitate tueri, in spiritus fervore respondit: "Si supernae patriae flamma per desiderium contingeremur **interius**, frigus istud **exterius** facile portaremus."

[160]Nam et ad praemissae visionis contuitum liquefacta est anima eius, et memoria passionis Christi visceribus cordis ipsius adeo impressa medullitus, ut et crucifixi Domini plagas oculis mentis **interius** quasi iugiter cerneret **et** vix **exterius** a lacrimosis gemitibus continere valeret.

[161]"Nimis est pulchra cella ista!" . . . "Si ergo vis quod maneam ibi, facias sibi fieri unum vestimentum **interius et exterius** de filicibus et ramis arborum."

[162]Dicebat enim quod "si servus Dei studuerit habere et conservare **interius et exterius** laetitiam spiritualem, quae provenit ex munditia cordis et acquiritur per devotionem orationis, daemones nihil possunt ei nocere dicentes: Ex quo in tribulatione et prosperitate habet laetitiam servus Dei, non possumus invenire aditum intrandi ad ipsum nec sibi nocere."

[163]Attende, inquam, principium huius speculi paupertatem **positi** siquidem **in praesepio** et in panniculis involuti.

[164]Quia sanctissimus puer dilectus datus est nobis et natus fuit pro nobis in via et **positus in praesepio** quia non habebat locum in diversorio.

[165]Et amore sanctissimi et dilectissimi pueri pauperculis panniculis **involuti, in praesepio reclinati**, et sanctissimae matris eius moneo, deprecor et exhortor sorores meas, ut vestimentis semper vilibus induantur.

[166]O ad**miranda** altitudo et stupenda dignatio! **O humilitas sublimis! O sublimitas humilis.**

[167]humiliamini et vos, ut exaltemini ab eo. Nihil ergo de vobis retineatis vobis, ut totos vos recipiat, qui se vobis exhibet totum.

[168]**Rex** angelorum, Dominus caeli et **terrae.**

[169]Omnipotens, sanctissime, altissime et summe Deus, Pater sancte et iuste, Domine **rex** caeli et **terrae.**

[170]Omnipotens, sanctissime, altissime et summe Deus, Pater sancte et iuste, Domine **rex** caeli et **terrae.**

[171]Tu es fortis, tu es magnus, tu es altissimus, tu es rex omnipotens, tu pater sancte, **rex** caeli et **terrae.**

[172]Mi pater sancte, **rex** caeli et **terrae**, ne discesseris a me quoniam tribulatio proxima est et non est qui adiuvet.

[173]Confitebor tibi, Domine, sanctissime Pater, **Rex** caeli et **terrae** quoniam consolatus es me.

[174]**in** praesepio **reclinatur.**

[175]See note 162.

[176]"Volo enim illius pueri memoriam agere, qui in Bethlehem natus est, et infantilium necessitatum eius incommoda, quomodo **in** praesepio **reclinatus** et quomodo, adstante bove atque asino, supra foenum positus exstitit, utcumque corporeis oculis pervidere."

[177]"ut habeant ad comedendum, maxime sorores laudae et aliae aves, in die tantae solemnitatis. Et quod ad reverentiam Filii Dei, quem **in** presepio inter bovem et asinum **reclinavit** beata Virgo mater eius tali nocte omnis homo in ipsa nocte satis debeat dare de annona fratribus bobus et asinis; similiter quod in Nativitate Domini omnes pauperes a divitibus debeant saturari."

[178]O vos omnes qui transitis per viam, attendite et videte si est dolor sicut dolor meus. [179]Quadam autem vice, solus ibat prope ecclesiam Sanctae Mariae de Portiuncula, plangendo et **eiulando** alta **voce**. Quem audiens, quidam vir spiritualis putavit ipsum pati infirmitatem aliquam vel dolorem, et pietate motus circa eum, interrogavit illum cur fleret. At ille dixit: "Plango passionem Domini mei, pro quo non deberem verecundari alta voce ire plorando per totum mundum." Ille vero coepit cum ipso similiter plangere alta voce.

[180]respondeamus, inquit, ei clamanti et **eiulanti** una **voce**, uno spiritu.

[181]Oro **benigne** ac devote **suscipias** attendens in eis saltem affectum maternum, quo circa te ac filias tuas caritatis ardore afficior omni die, quibus me ac filias meas in Christo plurimum recommenda.

[182]Si quis divina inspiratione volens accipere hanc vitam venerit ad nostros fratres, **benigne recipiatur** ab eis. . . . Minister vero **benigne** ipsum **recipiat** et confortet et vitae nostrae tenorem sibi diligenter exponat.

[183]Et quicumque ad eos venerit amicus vel adversarius, fur vel latro **benigne recipiatur**.

[184]Omnes illos quibus litterae istae pervenerint, rogamus in caritate quae Deus est, ut ista supradicta odorifera verba Domini nostri Iesu Christi cum divino amore **benigne recipiant**.

[185]Et omnes illi et illae, qui ea **benigne recipient**, intelligent et mittent aliis in exemplum, et si in ea perseveraverint usque in finem, benedicat eis Pater et Filius et Spiritus Sanctus. Amen.

[186]Unde firmiter consulo vobis, dominis meis, ut omni cura et sollicitudine posthabitis et sanctissimum corpus et sanctissimum sanguinem Domini nostri Iesu Christi in eius sancta commemoratione **benigne recipiatis**.

[187]Accessit praeterea sanctus Franciscus ad reverendum dominum episcopum Sabinensem, nomine Iohannem de Sancto Paulo, qui inter alios Romanae curiae principes et maiores videbatur "terrena despicere et amare caelestia." Qui eum "**benigne** atque charitative" **suscipiens**, ipsius voluntatem et propositum plurimum commendavit.

[188]Paucis autem diebus elapsis, venerunt ad eos tres alii viri de Assisio, videlicet Sabbatinus, Moricus et Iohannes de Capella, supplicantes beato Francisco ut eos in fratres reciperet. Et ipse **recepit** eos humiliter et **benigne**. . . . Episcopus vero civitatis Assisii, ad quem pro consilio frequenter ibat vir Dei, **benigne** ipsum **recipiens** dixit ei.

[189]Quando autem declinabant ad eos divites huius mundi, **recipiebant** eos alacriter et **benigne**, et eos invitabant ut revocarent eos a malo et ad faciendam paenitentiam provocarent.

The Privilege of Poverty As Source: Clare's Letters Amid Papal and Royal Correspondence

The insistence of both Clare of Assisi and Agnes of Prague to live faithfully the poverty of Saint Francis generated admiration as well as civil and ecclesiastical juridical difficulties. These difficulties prompted an abundance of correspondence between the papacy, Agnes, and the royal Přemyslid family. One can understand Clare's letters to Agnes more clearly if one reads them within the context of this papal and royal correspondence.

Clare and Agnes envisioned for their monasteries a Franciscan economy of living without possessions. A spirituality that advocated the following of the Poor Christ served as the inspiration for this lifestyle. Practices embodying the sisters' commitment to following the Poor Christ included the relinquishment of both personal and communal property, the giving of one's goods to the poor as a prerequisite for entrance, the choice not to engage in quarrels and litigation, the commitment to do manual labor, and the care of the sick and poor.

Essential to the workings of the sisters' economy were the Franciscan brothers who lived in the friaries attached to the sister's monasteries. These brothers were assigned to care for the spiritual and temporal needs of the sisters. In exchange, the sisters prayed for the spiritual and temporal needs of the Friars Minor. The austere fasting practices of the sisters made it possible for the brothers to shoulder the burden of begging for their needs, and made credible the spiritual efficacy of the sisters' lives.

When Pope Gregory IX sought to regularize under his own Rule the many independent women's monasteries in central and northern Italy, Clare feared that the corporate poverty of her monastery might be undermined. Unable to convince Clare to abandon her founding ideal, Pope Gregory IX, in his

September 17, 1228 letter, *Sicut manifestum est*,[1] granted the San Damiano monastery the Privilege of Poverty. The first part of *Sicut manifestum est* was most likely, according to custom, paraphrased from a petition written by the sisters of San Damiano themselves.

> As is clear, by your desire to be dedicated to the Lord alone you have given up your appetite for temporal matters. For this reason, having sold everything and distributed it to the poor, you propose to have no possessions whatsoever, in every instance clinging to the footsteps of him, who was made poor for our sakes and is the Way, the Truth, and the Life. The lack of goods from this *propositum* does not frighten you, for the left hand of your heavenly spouse is under your head to uphold the weaknesses of your body that you have submitted to the law of the soul through your well-ordered love. Accordingly, he who feeds the birds of the sky and clothes the lilies of the field will not fail you in matters of food and of clothing until, passing among you, he serves himself to you in eternity when indeed his right arm will more blissfully embrace you in the greatness of his vision.[2]

If we speculate that the core of this text originates with the sisters of San Damiano, Clare's theology of the Privilege of Poverty comes to light. This theology is an eminently practical one and can be outlined simply as the *sacrum commercium*— the giving of one's temporalities to the poor in imitation of the Poor Christ in exchange for needed food and clothing, marriage with Jesus Christ, and eschatological vision.

As such, the Privilege of Poverty served as more than just an economy; it was a reworking of the practice and theology of medieval monastic life. This Franciscan style of following the Poor Christ demanded that the San Damiano monastery adopt an administrative structure, disciplinary and prayer practices, as well as an economy and politics substantially different from that of the Benedictine reforms favored by the papacy. Clare's agenda, however, was eschatological rather than economic or liberationist—one follows the Poor Christ in order to obtain the fullness of eschatological vision.

Pope Gregory IX had plenty of experience in dealing with small women's monasteries with pauperistic aspirations. Knowing that the radical nature of Clare's ideal could compromise his administrative objective of unifying the women's monastic movement in central and northern Italy and beyond, Gregory IX approved Clare's Privilege of Poverty with an important qualification. He changed the wording of the *propositum* of Clare and her sisters from "you propose to have no possessions whatsoever, [nullas omnino possessiones habere proponitis]," to "you cannot be compelled by anyone to receive possessions, [recipere possessiones a nullo compelli possitis]."

This reworking of Clare's request is an important one. It is the sisters of San Damiano, not the laws of Rome that will insure fidelity to the Privilege of Poverty. The Privilege is an exception to the law given only to a particular monastery. With changing administrations and tightening papal policies, such exemptions could easily be undermined. Sister Filippa alludes to this precariousness in Clare's *Process of Canonization*:

> She [Clare] could never be persuaded by the pope or the bishop of Ostia to receive any possessions. The Privilege of Poverty granted to her was honored with great reverence and kept well and with great diligence since she feared she might lose it.[3]

Clare's First Letter to Agnes

Agnes's Entrance

In the salutation of her first letter to Agnes, Clare states that she is writing in the hope that Agnes attain "the glory of everlasting happiness" (*1LAg* 2)[4]—an eschatological objective. Clare structures the beginning her first letter following the twofold theological outline of the 1228, Privilege of Poverty. The choice of poverty, meaning the following in the footsteps of the Poor Christ, is initiated by the giving of one's possessions to the poor. Agnes has rejected a marriage to Frederick II with all its pomp and glory. Instead of Frederick, she has chosen to accept "a nobler spouse, the Lord Jesus Christ" (*1LAg* 7).[5] To embrace this singular dedication, Agnes spurned "public ostentation, honors, and worldly status" (*1LAg* 5)[6] and chose instead "holiest poverty and physical want" (*1LAg* 6).[7]

In exchange for her rejection of temporalities, Agnes receives marital union with Jesus Christ, adequate food and clothing for this life, and eschatological glory. This is "indeed a great and praiseworthy exchange, to give up the temporal for the everlasting, to merit the heavenly rather than the earthly, to receive a hundredfold instead of one, to have a happy, eternal life" (*1LAg* 30).[8] Agnes's "most abundant reward is in heaven" (*1LAg* 23),[9] and she has "quite fittingly deserved to be called sister, spouse, and mother of the Son of the most high Father and the glorious Virgin" (*1LAg* 24).[10]

The giving up of all of one's worldly possessions to the poor was no simple task for the royal daughter of Bohemia. Following the example of her cousin, Elizabeth of Hungary, Agnes established the Hospital of Saint Francis in Prague (*LegAg* 3:2).[11] She also erected a monastery (*LegAg* 3:3),[12] and shortly before November 11, 1233,[13] welcomed five sisters from Trent who were associated with the Monastery of San Damiano (*LegAg* 3:3).[14] On November 11, 1233, the feast of

Saint Martin of Tours, seven noble Bohemian women entered the monastery (*LegAg* 3:3).[15]

In the March 21, 1234 declaration, *Actiones humanae*,[16] Agnes's brother, King Wenceslas I placed both Agnes's monastery and Hospital of Saint Francis under royal patronage.[17] With great solemnity on the following Pentecost, June 11, 1234,[18] Agnes herself entered the monastery (LegAg 3:4).[19] Writing to Agnes for the occasion of her entrance, Pope Gregory IX, in his August 30, 1234 letter, *Sincerum animi tui*,[20] compared Agnes of Prague to Agnes of Rome, as Clare does in her first letter, and accepted from Wenceslas I, Agnes's monastery and the Hospital of Saint Francis.[21]

Pope Gregory IX was certainly aware of the pauperistic aspirations of Agnes. *Sincerum animi tui* embraces the vocabulary of the *sacrum commercium*, although Gregory IX focuses more on Agnes's juridical status than upon the Franciscan eschatology found in the Privilege of Poverty.

> Considering the favors of the world and the riches of earthly affairs to be of no account, you compelled the flesh to serve the spirit so that, having left behind everything transitory, you might choose in cleanliness of heart and body to serve your heavenly Spouse in the religious community of poor enclosed nuns, dedicating yourself to him with a solemn vow and desiring to become, instead of a queen, the handmaid of him who, humbling the loftiness of his divinity and taking up the form of a slave, raises up the humble into salvation.[22]

The Support of the Přemyslid Family

On October 2, 1234,[23] Agnes's brother Přemysl, the margrave of Moravia, gave the estate of Rakšice "with all its accessories, meadows, pastures, woods, fields, waters, valleys, and all its appurtenances which at a previous time we had given to our illustrious sister, the virgin Agnes,"[24] to the

Hospital of Saint Francis. Přemysl is clear that the estate is donated to the hospital, at Agnes's request, not to the monastery.[25] King Wenceslas I confirmed this gift.[26]

Agnes's mother, Queen Constance, also endowed the Hospital of Saint Francis with a number of estates. In her February 12, 1235 letter, *Noverit tam praesens*,[27] Constance bequeathed a number of estates to the hospital of the Cloister of Saint Francis in Prague and set herself up as steward of this endowment.[28]

In her first letter, Clare confirms Agnes's pauperistic aspirations and places them within the theological economy of the *sacrum commercium*. The Přemyslid family, as can be seen in their generosity toward the Hospital of Saint Francis and their legal care in endowing the hospital rather than the monastery, demonstrated understanding and support for the economic and eschatological implications of Agnes's choice. The papacy, on the other hand, while mouthing the vocabulary of the *sacrum commercium*, focused on the juridical rather than the eschatological implications of Agnes's vocational decision. This seemingly benign difference in theological vision will make coming to agreement in practical matters concerning the life and economy of the Prague monastery difficult.

Clare's Second Letter to Agnes

Gregory IX and the Question of Endowment

On May 18, 1235, Gregory IX wrote two letters, *Filius summi Regis*[29] and *Filius Summi Regis*[30] both addressed to the rector and brothers of the Hospital of Saint Francis in Prague. In the first of these letters, Gregory IX confirmed the donations of Přemysl, margrave of Moravia, and in the second, the donations of Queen Constance. He also confirmed that both donations listed the Hospital of Saint Francis as the beneficiary. According to Gregory IX, these donations were given at the request of Agnes, with the agreement of King Wenceslas I.

While the royal Přemyslid family obviously understood Agnes's desire to establish her monastery without possessions, Gregory IX was nervous about the legal situation Agnes was creating. The properties given to the Hospital of Saint Francis by Queen Constance and by Agnes's brother, Přemysl were substantial enough to warrant his attention.

In yet another letter dated May 18, 1235, *Cum relicta seculi*,[31] addressed to Agnes and her sisters, Gregory IX contradicts the wishes of Agnes and her family by unilaterally conceding the Hospital of Saint Francis with its appurtenances to the monastery. In doing this, he made it clear that he would not entertain legal arguments to the contrary. Moreover, the pope specified that the goods that had specifically been donated to the hospital by members of the royal family were also to endow and thus provide a regular and permanent income to the monastery.[32]

Gregory's letter contradicts Agnes's founding vision for a number of reasons. First, he extended the ownership of the landed endowment from the hospital to the monastery, an action that Agnes and her family had carefully avoided. Second, he legally bound the hospital to the monastery making Agnes and her sisters the co-beneficiaries of the large financial endowment originally intended solely for the charitable works of the hospital. Third, his actions virtually guaranteed not only the survival, but also the prosperity of both the monastery and the hospital. Not wanting to be responsible for destitute sisters, and certainly not wanting a daughter of Otakar Přemysl living in wanton poverty under the auspices of the Roman church, Gregory insisted that Agnes's monastery retain the goods that her family explicitly gave to the Hospital of Saint Francis along with the revenues that these goods would produce in perpetuity.

Shortly after, on July 25, 1235, in his bull, *Prudentibus Virginibus*,[33] Gregory IX firmly established the Prague monastery as a Hugolinian monastery. One can appreciate the devastation that Agnes must have felt upon receiving this document. Her dream of following the Poor Christ by living without personal or communal possessions was being thoroughly undermined.

Moreover, let whatever possessions and goods that same monastery and hospital might now possess as their own goods legally and canonically, or which you will in the future receive with God's help from a concession from popes, the largess of kings or princes, an offering of the faithful, or in other just ways, remain firm and untouched for you and your successors. We have decided that these items under discussion ought to be clearly and specifically described as being that place, in which the aforesaid monastery is located, with that hospital and all its appurtenances; the estate of Hloubětín, with all the small estates pertaining thereto, namely Humenec and Hnidošice, the estate of Borotice and Dražetice, the estate of Rybník, with all its appurtenances, the estate of Rakšice, with all its appurtenances, and your other possessions, with fields, vineyards, lands, woods, properties held in usufruct, and pastures, with all other freedoms and their immunities regarding forest and field, waters and mills, and streets and paths.[34]

Not content to give Agnes's original donation back to the monastery, to place the donations of Queen Constance and Margrave Přemysl under the monastery, and to insure that the endowments of both dowry and donations would return to the monastery, Gregory continued by exempting the monastery from all tithes: "Let no one presume to demand or exact from you a tithe from the fields that you cultivate for your own use, from which no one has yet taken a collection, or from the food for your animals."[35] Beyond this, the diocesan bishop was obligated to give to the monastery from the resources of the

The Privilege of Poverty as Source

people: "Let no one dare to exact anything from you under the pretext of custom or in any other way for the consecration of your altars or church, for making the holy oil or any type of church sacrament, but let the diocesan bishop freely pay for all these things for you by our authority."[36]

Gregory's intention for the Monastery of Saint Francis was to establish it as a prosperous, endowed, and well-regulated Benedictine or Cistercian style monastery. He juridically situated the monastery with every ability to accumulate wealth, and with no civil or ecclesiastical obligations to share this wealth in the form of taxes or tithes. Agnes had founded her monastery hoping to serve the poor in Prague by following the vision of Saint Francis. Gregory IX's ruling jeopardized the charismatic foundation of her monastery.

The Role of Elias

Clare wrote her second letter to Agnes sometime during the 1234-1239 generalate of Brother Elias. Given Clare's directives, it would seem that her letter may have been written in response to Agnes's distress over the July 25, 1235 issue of *Prudentibus Virginibus*. The focus of the second letter is again found in the salutation to, "always live in the utmost poverty" (*2LAg* 2).[37]

In her second letter, Clare's *sacrum commercium* theology of the Privilege of Poverty is again evident. In response to the fact that Agnes despised "the heights of an earthly kingdom and the less than worthy offers of an imperial marriage" (*2LAg* 6),[38] and has "clung to the footsteps" (*2LAg* 7)[39] of the Poor Christ, Christ will unite Agnes "to himself in marriage in heaven's bridal chamber" (*2LAg* 5).[40] Although Agnes has a papal directive, she is not to capitulate because only "one thing is necessary" (*2LAg* 10)—her initial commitment to following the Poor Christ.

But because one things is necessary, I invoke this one thing and advise you, by the love of him to whom you have offered yourself as a holy and pleasing sacrifice, . . . trusting in no one and agreeing with no one insofar as he might want to dissuade you from pursuing your founding purpose or might place a stumbling block in your way, preventing you, in that perfection with which the Spirit of the Lord has called you, from fulfilling your vows to the Most High" (*2LAg* 10, 14).[41]

For support during this difficult time, Agnes is to rely on Elias, the minister general and to value his counsel over the counsel of others as "more precious to you than any gift" (*2LAg* 16).[42] Clare's advice to Agnes regarding the directive of Pope Gregory IX could hardly be clearer.

Indeed, if someone tells you something else or suggests anything to you that may hinder your perfection and that seems contrary to your divine vocation, even though you must respect him, still, do not follow his advice; instead, poor virgin, embrace the Poor Christ (*2LAg* 17-18).[43]

Poverty as Vocational Identity

Clare insists that even the pope himself cannot tamper with Agnes's vocational call. Relinquishing her call to embrace life without possessions, would be to put her very eschatological relationship with Christ in jeopardy. Although Gregory IX deserves Agnes's respect, any directive that would jeopardize her embrace of the Poor Christ should not be obeyed.

In the interim, Agnes is to contemplate the Poor Christ who "made himself contemptible" for her sake (2LAg 19).[44] By following Christ in the poverty of ridicule and contempt incurred through faithfulness to her vocational identity, Agnes will receive "the glory of the heavenly kingdom rather than what is earthly and transitory, eternal goods instead of those that perish, and why you will live forever and ever" (*2LAg* 23).[45] In addition, her name "will be recorded in the *Book of Life* and will bring [her] glory among men and women" (*2LAg* 22).[46] Only by embracing the poverty of the contemptible Christ will Agnes receive the glory of the heavenly kingdom.

In her advice, Clare spoke with the authority of one who had suffered. In Clare's *Process of Canonization*, Sister Pacifica states:

> She [Pacifica] also said that she [Clare] particularly loved poverty, but she could never be persuaded to desire anything for herself, or to receive any possession for herself or the monastery. Asked how she knew this, she replied that she had seen and heard that the Lord Pope Gregory of happy memory wanted to give her many things and buy possessions for the monastery, but she would never consent (*Proc* 1:13).[47]

Following Sister Pacifica, Sister Benvenuta of Perugia also recalled Clare and Gregory IX's disagreement.

> She [Benvenuta] also said that she [Clare] had an especially great love of poverty. Neither Pope Gregory nor the bishop of Ostia [Cardinal Rainaldo] could ever make her consent to receive any possessions (*Proc* 2:22).[48]

It seems, therefore, that Clare's second letter is a response to Agnes's concerns regarding Gregory IX's, May 18, 1235 letter, *Cum relicta seculi*, and his subsequent July 25, 1235 letter, *Prudentibus Virginibus*. Agnes's very vocational identity was at risk. To help her navigate this precarious situation, Clare encouraged Agnes to remain faithful to her founding ideal, and to follow the counsel of Brother Elias, minister general of the Franciscans.

Clare's Third Letter to Agnes

Agnes's Privilege of Poverty

Knowing the entrenched position of Gregory IX, Agnes solicited the support of her brother, King Wenceslas I. In his letter *Primum quidem excellentissime*[49] of February 5, 1237, Wenceslas sides with his sister and demonstrates a clear understanding of the issue at hand. He begins by thanking Gregory IX for the affection and favors that he has shown Agnes in regard to the Order of Poor Ladies. He assures Gregory IX of his devotion and reminds the pope that this devotion lies in his kingdom, family, in-laws, and friends.

Wenceslas then proceeds to the point of his letter. He tells Gregory that his devotion will be more prompt if the Holy See grants Agnes's request. In other words, from the point of view of the Bohemian royal family, Gregory IX's response to Agnes's request for a Franciscan form of life could have political ramifications.[50]

Although the letter does not exist, it is obvious from both Wenceslas's letter and from the replies of Gregory IX that Agnes also wrote to the pope with specific requests. Her letter(s) included: 1) the petition to disengage her monastery from the hospital; 2) a request for permission to hear mass in the monastery choir; 3) a request for mitigations for clothing and fasting for the sisters at Prague; and perhaps, 4) an affirmation of Agnes's trust in the guidance of Brother Elias.

The letters of Agnes and King Wenceslas placed Gregory IX in a political quandary. On the one hand, Gregory wanted to place Agnes's monastery securely under the umbrella of his Order of Poor Enclosed Nuns who followed the Rule of Saint Benedict with his own Hugolinian constitutions. On the other hand, he could not politically tolerate a breach with the king of Bohemia.

In the end, Agnes's strategy prevailed and on April 14, 1237, Gregory reissued *Prudentibus Virginibus*.[51] There are important differences between the July 25, 1235 and the April 14, 1237 versions of this papal bull. In 1235, Gregory accepted under the patronage of Rome "the Monastery of Saint Francis in Prague with your hospital."[52] In 1237, the text mentions only the monastery. The 1235 document establishes Agnes's monastery according "to God and the Rule of Blessed Benedict."[53] In 1237, Gregory IX establishes the monastery according "to God, the Rule of Blessed Benedict, and the Institute of Enclosed Nuns of San Damiano in Assisi."[54] The papal tax for the monastery is reduced from one bezant in 1235, to one gold obol in 1237.

On the same day, April 14, 1237, Gregory IX wrote to the master and brothers of the Hospital of Saint Francis. In this letter, *Omnipotens Deus*,[55] he affirmed that Agnes had indeed given away her possessions to the poor: "Also for reasons of piety and compassion, she built and donated a hospital for the needs of the poor and sick, in which you have been bound to divine service."[56] Most likely because the hospital needed a substantial endowment in order to pursue its charitable objectives, Gregory IX, certainly with the blessing and most probably the recommendation of Agnes, gave to the brothers of the hospital the Rule of Saint Augustine, not the Rule of Saint Francis.

Negotiating a Franciscan Rule

Having regained the intended independence of the monastery from the hospital, Agnes still remained uneasy. Although we do not have the letter, Pope Gregory IX acknowledges that Agnes wrote to him sending her correspondence through the prior of the Hospital of Saint Francis in Prague.[57] Agnes's letter was most likely written in the year's interval between April 14, 1237 and April 15, 1238. From the papal response it is clear that Agnes requested that the pope confirm with apostolic authority a new Rule for her monastery created out of the original form of life given to the sisters of San Damiano by Saint Francis, and the Rule of the Order of Saint Damian.

We possess seven papal documents, both juridical and pastoral in nature, that were prompted by Agnes's request for this new Rule. In the first, *Pia credulitate tenentes*,[58] issued on April 15, 1238, Pope Gregory IX grants the Privilege of Poverty to Agnes's monastery. The juridical language of the Privilege is identical to that used by Gregory IX in the 1228 bull, *Sicut manifestum est*.[59]

> Hence it is the case that, bound by your prayers and tears, we grant with the authority of the present document that you can not be forced to receive unwillingly any possessions in the future. We do so having received your free resignation of the Hospital of Saint Francis of the Diocese of Prague that was conceded with all its legal rights and appurtenances to you, and through you to your monastery, by the apostolic see. For you, having scorned the visible and hastened to the delights of the invisible, are eager to avoid the obstacle of the thorns of temporal goods that is accustomed to arise for those seeking the unoffended face of God.[60]

In the April 22, 1238 bull, *Vota devotorum Ecclesiae*,[61] addressed to the Dominican Order, Gregory IX gives the Dominicans the duty of visitation for the Hospital of Saint Francis in consultation with Brother John, the provincial minister of the Order of Friars Minor. Needing to provide the hospital with local stewardship, Gregory IX, in his April 27, 1238 bull, *Carissima in Christo*,[62] gave the hospital to the Order of hospitaler brothers founded by Agnes.[63] The listing of properties making up the hospital's endowment is impressive and had already been outlined in the April 14, 1237 bull, *Omnipotens Deus*.[64]

The Privilege of Poverty as Source

We have decided that these items under discussion ought to be clearly and specifically described as being that place, in which the aforesaid hospital is located, with all its appurtenances, the estate of Hloubětín, with all the small estates pertaining thereto, namely Humenec and Hnidošice, the estate of Borotice, with all the small estates pertaining thereto, namely Županovice and Dražetice, the estate of Rybník, with all its appurtenances, the estate of Rakšice, with all its appurtenances, and your other possessions, with fields, vineyards, lands, woods, properties held in usufruct, and pastures, with all other freedoms and their immunities regarding forest and field, waters and mills, and streets and paths.[65]

The Question of Fasting

While conceding to Agnes's choice to live without property, Gregory IX still wanted to ensure the security of Agnes's monastery within his Hugolinian structure. It is therefore not surprising that less than one month after *Pia credulitate tenentes*, the pope attempted a significant mitigation of the fasting regulations for the Monastery of Saint Francis. The laws of fasting within a monastery associated with the Franciscan women's charism was not a periphery matter. Agnes's sisters were provided for by brothers who begged for their sustenance. Excessive legislation regarding what the sisters could or could not eat, or a laxity that allowed them the possibility of eating more, would make caring for them difficult—a difficulty that could undermine the Franciscan economy of the Prague monastery.

Pope Gregory IX had envisioned at the outset that monasteries of women following his Rule would be governed by strict prescriptions for fasting. Mitigations were made not by changing the text of the Rule, but by papal dispensations. The Hugolinian text concerning fasting reads as follows:[66]

> Let them hold this observance for fasting: They are to fast every day at all times, abstaining on the Wednesdays and Fridays outside of Lent from *pulmentum*[67] and wine, unless it happens that the principal feast of some saint needs to be observed at that time. On these days, that is Wednesdays and Fridays, if raw fruits or vegetables are available, they may be given to the sisters for their refreshment. During the week, on four days during Lent, and on three days during the Lent of Saint Martin, they are to fast on bread and water; if they wish, they may also do so on the vigils of all solemnities. The very young and the old, however, and those who are bodily sick and infirm are in no way permitted to observe this law of fasting and abstinence; rather, a dispensation for food and fasting is to be made mercifully for them in accordance with their weakness.[68]

Gerard Pieter Freeman's[69] hierarchy of abstinence foods is helpful for interpreting these fasting regulations. Freeman posits that when one particular rung of the hierarchy is cited by medievals, foods below this rung were allowed, while those above were excluded. In laws of abstinence, animal products were forbidden. Fish was allowed because medievals believed that fish were sexless. It was also noted that Christ ate fish after the resurrection.

Freeman's Fasting Hierarchy

Non-Fasting Foods
- Meat
- Fat
- Milk, milk products, and eggs

The Privilege of Poverty as Source

Fasting Foods (*cibus quadragesimalis*)
- Fish
- Wine and other *pulmenta* (cooked foods namely legumes, cake, gruel)
- Raw vegetables, fruit and nuts, oil
- Water, bread, and salt
- Eat nothing

If one examines the legislation of the Hugolinian constitutions according to this hierarchy, Hugolino regulated that at all times the fast consisted of water, bread, salt, raw vegetables, fruit, nuts, oil, wine, *pulmenta* (cooked foods namely legumes, cake, and gruel), and fish. This meant that the sisters were never allowed to consume meat, fat, milk, milk products, and eggs. During Wednesdays and Fridays outside of Lent, they were to omit fish, cooked foods (legumes, cake, and gruel), and wine from the above diet, unless these days fell on a principle feast. Gregory IX specifically points out that the level of raw vegetables was allowed on Wednesdays and Fridays. Each week during the great Lent, the sisters were to fast four days on bread and water, and each week during the Lent of Saint Martin they were to fast three days on bread and water. Discreet dispensations were to be made for the very young, old, and the debilitated.

At the request of the sisters of Agnes's monastery, Gregory IX, in the April 9, 1237 bull, *Cum sicut propositum*,[70] had given the abbess of the Monastery of Saint Francis in Prague permission to mitigate the fasting requirements "due to excessive cold and intemperate weather [propter nimium frigus, et aeris intemperiem]." According to this document, the abbess could "relax the regulation for continuous fasting [relaxando continuo jejunio]."

Fasting and the Privilege of Poverty

Not even one month after Agnes received her Privilege of Poverty, Gregory IX, in the May 5, 1238 letter, *Pia meditatione pensantes,*[71] regulated a further mitigation of the fasting laws for the monastery at Prague. He did this again because of "the coldness of the country [ex frigida dispositione patriae]." This dispensation had not been solicited by the sisters.

Thus we grant to you by the authority of the present document that on Sundays and Thursdays you may eat twice and be refreshed with dairy products, even though according to that Rule you ought to fast on Lenten food all the time. During Easter week and on the solemnities of the Blessed Virgin Mary, and also on those of the apostles, or on the feast of the Nativity of the Lord, and besides these, in times of clear necessity such as illness, none of you is held to the fast.

Moreover, if perchance some one of you should become ill, the abbess has the power of making dispensations for fasting and food, as does the senior sister as well. In addition, we wish that on those days during Lent and Advent on which, according to your Rule, you are obliged to fast on bread and water, you have refreshment of all sorts, just as on other fast days.[72]

The dispensation is a substantial one. Freeman calculates that the sisters of Prague could by means of this mitigation add milk products and eggs to their diet on ninety-one days during the year. Gregory IX abolished the law, "fast always" for Thursdays and Sundays and adds dairy products to the list of foods permitted on these days. Both the senior sister (Agnes) and the abbess were authorized to give even further dispensations in regard to fasting. On the four weekly fasting days of Lent and on the three weekly fasting days of Advent,

The Privilege of Poverty as Source

the sisters were to follow the Wednesday and Friday rules for fasting in which they could eat bread, water, salt, raw vegetables, fruit, nuts, and oil. During Easter week, the solemnities of the Virgin Mary and the apostles, and on Christmas, the sisters were not obliged to fast.

Arriving with the May 5, 1238 fasting mitigation, *Pia meditatione pensantes*, was the May 11, 1238 bull, *Angelis gaudium,*[73] with its accompanying missive, *Cum omnis vera religio.*[74] In *Angelis gaudium*, Gregory refused Agnes's request for a Franciscan Rule and spurns her attempt to integrate into the Rule of the Order of Saint Damian the form of life given to Clare by Francis. The form was in Gregory's mind only a "draught of milk, [potem lactis]," and "was suitable for those who were like newborns [quibus tamquam modo genitis]."

Gregory proceeds to give Agnes three reasons why the approval of her Rule is not possible. First, Clare and her sisters have professed the Hugolinian Rule with a mitigation (the Privilege of Poverty). This Rule along with this mitigation was, according to Gregory, accepted by Francis. Second, Clare and her sisters put aside the form of life given them by Francis and "have observed that same Rule in a praiseworthy fashion from the time of their profession to the present day."[75] Third, since it was uniformly observed, Gregory feared that certain sisters of the Order might "falter due to disturbed considerations regarding its [the Rule's] observance."[76] With his reasons in place, Gregory assured Agnes that she was not obligated by her Franciscan profession because this profession was not approved by the apostolic see and, according to Gregory, was not the form of life followed by the sisters of San Damiano in Assisi.

Angelis guadium concludes by dispensing Agnes from any obligation that she might feel toward Francis's form of life, and commands Agnes under obedience to accept the Hugolinian Rule together with the papal dispensations granted to her monastery. Gregory IX further assures Agnes that he is most willing to grant her any other dispensations that might be necessary to accommodate the spiritual and physical needs of the Prague monastery.

Most probably devastated that her efforts to secure a Franciscan Rule for the monasteries united by Clare's spirit had failed, Agnes wrote to Clare after May 11, 1238. From Clare's response, it is evident that Agnes shared with Clare her triumph in receiving the Privilege of Poverty [April 15, 1238, *Pia credulitate tenentes*], and that she also voiced apprehension regarding Gregory IX's further mitigations of the Hugolinian fasting practices. Agnes feared that Gregory IX had placed fasting regulations upon the Monastery of Saint Francis in Prague that would be inconsistent with the practices at San Damiano. Obviously, despite Gregory IX's belittlement of Francis's form of life, Agnes was still very concerned about being faithful to the early directions that Saint Francis had given to the sisters of San Damiano.

The Choice of Joy

In her third letter, Clare commends Agnes for her perseverance and dubs her as "God's own helper" (*3LAg* 8).[77] The point of the letter is to send Agnes the hope that she might have "the joys of salvation in him who is the Author of Salvation and for everything better that can be desired" (*3LAg* 2).[78] Clare exhorts Agnes to "always rejoice in the Lord" (*3LAg* 10)[79] and to let go of bitterness and confusion (*3LAg* 11).[80]

Agnes is to let go of her worries by placing her "mind in the mirror of eternity" (*3LAg* 12),[81] her "soul in the splendor of glory" (*3LAg* 12),[82] her "heart in the figure of the divine substance" (*3LAg* 13),[83] and by transforming through contemplation her "entire being into the image of the Divine One himself (*3LAg* 13).[84] Agnes is to "totally love him who gave himself totally out of love for you" (*3LAg* 15).[85] The eschatology here is simultaneously present, future, eucharistic, and nuptial. As her model in how to integrate all of this, Agnes is to "cling to his most sweet Mother" (*3LAg* 18).[86]

In Clare's mind, Agnes, who has now succeeded in her struggle for the Privilege of Poverty, already possesses heaven. Anything that would erode the eschatological joy that the embrace of poverty brings is the work of an evil spirit: "Who would not abhor the treachery of the enemy of humanity who, by means of the pride that results from fleeting and false glories, compels that which is greater than heaven to return to nothingness" (*3LAg* 20)?[87]

Fasting at San Damiano

In regard to the directive for fasting that Francis had given the San Damiano sisters, Clare gives Agnes the following information:

> Indeed, your prudence knows that, with the exception of the weak and the sick, for whom he advised and authorized us to use every possible discretion with respect to any foods whatsoever, none of us who are healthy and strong ought to eat anything other than Lenten fare, on both ordinary days and feastdays, fasting every day except on Sundays and on the Lord's Nativity, when we ought to eat twice a day. And, on Thursdays in Ordinary Time, fasting should reflect the personal decision of each sister, so that whoever might not wish to fast would not be obligated to do so. All the same, those of us who are healthy fast every day except Sundays and Christmas. Certainly, during the entire Easter week, as Blessed Francis states in what he has written, and on the feasts of holy Mary and the holy apostles, we are also not obliged to fast, unless these feasts should fall on a Friday; and, as has already been

said, we who are healthy and strong always eat Lenten fare (3LAg 31-37).[88]

The differences between Clare's directives and those of *Pia meditatione pensantes* are substantial. Clare mandated fasting on all days except Sundays, with optional fasting on Thursdays; Gregory, on the other hand, exempted both Sundays and Thursdays for all the sisters. Gregory permitted dairy products on Sundays and Thursdays, while Clare's directives allowed no dairy products—only Lenten fare. Clare's instructions exempted Christmas from fasting. Fasting was optional during Easter week and on the feasts of Mary and the apostles. Gregory exempted the sisters from fasting both on Christmas and on the days of Clare's "optional" fasting. Clare's directions dispense the ill from fasting but do not clarify who will do this dispensing. In *Pia meditatione pensantes* it is clear that the ill are dispensed from fasting by the abbess or the senior sister. Finally on the days of fasting during Lent and Advent, Clare permits only bread and water. Gregory IX allows wine and *pulmenta*, which also, according to Freeman's hierarchy, automatically also includes vegetables, fruit, nuts, and oil.

That the fasting regulations followed by the sisters of Prague was not the apostolic see's primary concern in issuing *Pia meditatione pensantes* seems clear from the fact the papal directives establish norms for fasting practices on the strictest days during Lent and Advent that are not any stricter than the fasting on all the other days of the year. If fasting practices were Gregory IX's primary concern, this canonical sloppiness would not have passed unnoticed.

The Privilege of Poverty as Source

Clare's Third Letter and Fasting Regulations

Surely Agnes recognized this oversight, and with Clare's response in hand, wrote to the pope probably during the fall of 1238. In her letter, she included the information that Clare had given her, reminded the pope of his expressed willingness to grant the Prague monastery appropriate dispensations, and perhaps reiterated the unity argument that Gregory IX himself had used in *Angelus gaudium*. Concerned less with particular fasting practices than with the more global juridical issue of the Rule, Gregory IX willingly capitulated. In his letter of December 18, 1238, *Ex parte Carissimae*,[89] Gregory quotes and concedes to Agnes's *propositum* concerning fasting.

> A *propositum* has come before us from our very dear daughter in Christ, Agnes, . . .that you have been obligated to follow a particular observance for fasting which is as follows: Sisters who are healthy and strong are to fast on Lenten food every day, whether an ordinary or a feastday, with the exception of Sundays and Christmas, although they are in no way held to fast during Easter week, and on the solemnities of the Blessed Virgin and the apostles, unless they occur on a Friday. Also those who do not wish to do so do not fast on Thursday, except during Lent and Advent. Those who are infirm of body or ill, will by no means be allowed to observe this law of fasting and abstinence, but according to their illness or weakness, they are to be given dispensations for eating and fasting by the abbess or the senior sister.[90]

The fasting practices outlined in Clare's third letter, in *Pia meditatione pensantes* of May 5, 1238, and in *Ex parte Carissimae* of December 18, 1238, might be charted as follows. One can clearly see the influence of Clare's letter in the December 18, 1238, papal response to Agnes.

Clare's Letters to Agnes

FASTING: Clare's Third Letter and the Papal Letters of 1238		
Clare's *Third Letter* July-October, 1238	*Pia meditatione pensantes* May 5, 1238	*Ex parte Carissimae* December 18, 1238
Indeed, your prudence knows that, with the exception of the weak and the sick, for whom he [Francis] advised and authorized us to use every possible discretion with respect to any foods whatsoever	in times of clear necessity such as illness, none of you is held to the fast. Moreover, if perchance some one of you should become ill, the abbess has the power of making dispensations for fasting and food, as does the senior sister as well.	Those who are infirm of body or ill, will by no means be allowed to observe this law of fasting and abstinence, but according to their illness or weakness, they are to be given dispensations for eating and fasting by the abbess or the senior sister. **(Note that "abbess" and "senior sister" are taken from *Pia meditatione pensantes*).**
none of us who are healthy and strong ought to eat anything other than Lenten fare, on both ordinary days and feastdays, fasting every day except on Sundays and on the Lord's Nativity, when we ought to eat twice a day.	Thus we grant to you by the authority of the present document that on Sundays and Thursdays you may eat twice and be refreshed with dairy products, even though according to that Rule you ought to fast on Lenten food all the time. **(Clare's instructions directly contradict this mitigation).**	Sisters who are healthy and strong are to fast on Lenten food every day, whether an ordinary or a feastday, with the exception of Sundays and Christmas **(Note that the papal text deletes Clare's note about eating twice a day on Sundays and Christmas).**

The Privilege of Poverty as Source

	In addition, we wish that on those days during Lent and Advent on which, according to your Rule, you are obliged to fast on bread and water, you have refreshment of all sorts, just as on other fast days. **(Clare does not permit this).**	
And, on Thursdays in Ordinary Time, fasting should reflect the personal decision of each sister, so that, whoever might not wish to fast would not be obliged to do so.	**(Directions regarding Thursdays are above. The construction of** *Ex parte Carissimae* **follows Clare's third letter, not** *Pia meditatione pensantes*).	Also those who do not wish to do so do not fast on Thursday, except in Lent and Advent. **(Clare's pastoral note is shortened).**
All the same, those of us who are healthy fast every day except Sundays and Christmas.		**(Clare's personal reference is edited out of this letter).**
Certainly, during the entire Easter week, as Blessed Francis states in what he has written, and on the feasts of holy Mary and of the holy apostles, we are also not obliged to fast, unless these feasts should fall on a Friday; and, as has already been said, we who are healthy and strong always eat Lenten fare.	During Easter week and on the solemnities of the Blessed Virgin Mary, and also on those of the apostles, or on the feast of the Nativity of the Lord, . . . none of you is held to the fast. **(The prescription for Christmas is placed differently. Ordinary Friday fasts have precedence over feastdays).**	although they are in no way held to fast during Easter week and on the solemnities of the Blessed Virgin and the apostles, unless they occur on a Friday. **(Note that Gregory IX has edited out both of Clare's references to Saint Francis).**

Although Agnes's attempt to obtain a specifically Franciscan Rule including Francis's own form of life given to Clare and the first sisters failed, Agnes did make progress toward assuring the ability of her monastery to follow the Poor Christ by living without possessions during 1237-1238. Agnes secured, during this year, the Privilege of Poverty for her monastery and, with the encouragement and information given to her in Clare's third letter, was able to have the pope confirm fasting practices that, according to Clare, Francis himself had given to the sisters of San Damiano.

Clare's Fourth Letter To Agnes

The Issue of the Brothers

After the victory of her Privilege of Poverty (April 15, 1238, *Pia credulitate tenentes*), and the reinstatement of fasting practices consistent with Francis's instructions (December 18, 1238, *Ex parte Carissimae*), Agnes seems to have remained relatively quiet during the rest of Gregory IX's term of office. There was one aspect, however, intimately connected to her Privilege of Poverty that Agnes continued to pursue.

The September 28, 1230 bull, *Quo elongati*,[91] had prohibited the Franciscan brothers from entering the cloister, living quarters, and the inner shops of monasteries of nuns. In order to obtain access to these monasteries, the brothers needed expressed papal permission. The response of Clare to *Quo elongati* is described in *The Legend of Saint Clare* 37:

> The pious mother, sorrowing that her sisters would more rarely have the food of sacred teaching, sighed: 'Let him now take away from us all the brothers since he has taken away those who provide us with the food that is vital.' At once she sent back to the minister all the brothers, not wanting to have the questors who acquired corporal bread when they could not have the

questors for spiritual bread. When Pope Gregory heard this, he immediately mitigated that prohibition into the hands of the general minister.[92]

At stake was the access of Clare and her sisters to Franciscan preaching. *The Legend of Clare* records the above protest in the context of recalling Clare's appreciation of preaching. Clare's reaction was quieted when Gregory IX placed the power to grant access to Clare's monastery into the hands of the Franciscan general minister.

The Rule of Hugolino,[93] allowed bishops, cardinals, and, of course, the visitor to enter the monastery under prescribed conditions. Workmen could enter, when necessary. The chaplain could enter to hear the confession and to give communion to a dying sister, and under certain conditions to perform the funeral rites. Provisions were not made, however, in Hugolino's Rule for the entrance of the Franciscan brothers to beg or to preach. Agnes needed a dispensation for the Franciscan brothers associated with her monastery to enter to do needed work within the monastery, and also to provide care for her sisters. Given the determination of Gregory IX to focus on enclosure as essential to women's religious life, the political climate surrounding the disposition of Elias, and the fact that unauthorized visitation of the poor cloistered sisters was one of Elias's alleged misdeeds,[94] receiving a bull mitigating the enclosure in order to permit the begging and preaching of the brothers would be difficult.

Agnes received her opportunity in late summer of 1240. According to two letters written by Albert Böheim, a papal legate, Pope Gregory IX needed Agnes to persuade her brother, King Wenceslas I to ally himself with the pope against Frederick II, who seemed determined to place all of Italy, including Rome, under his domain.[95] If Gregory's letter arrived in Bohemia in October/November and Agnes's response reached Gregory between December-April, a May 31, 1241 letter concerning the Friars Minor who are assigned to the needs of the monastery would be timely. Gregory's letter,

Vestris piis supplicationibus,[96] contains only the mitigation and seems almost terse. Is this because he was irritated by Agnes's request, and/or because his political vulnerability reduced time for flourishes? The letter adds little to the prescriptions of the Rule other than expressly giving the Franciscan brothers the same rights as other workmen and the chaplain.

There is no other known extant correspondence between Agnes and Gregory IX after *Vestris piis supplicationibus.* With the emperor's armies surrounding Rome, Gregory IX died on August 22, 1241. The papacy was in shambles.

Innocent IV ascended to the papacy on June 28, 1243. Most likely, Agnes immediately wrote to him to congratulate him and to place herself under him as a spiritual daughter. Innocent's response accepting her as a spiritual daughter, *Ex regali progenie*,[97] is dated summer, 1243. Upon receiving this letter, Agnes immediately wrote back to the new pontiff asking "that the two phrases which are written regarding 'the virtue of obedience' and 'the Rule of Benedict' be removed from that form and that we have those indulgences that were specially granted to the aforesaid monastery by Pope Gregory recorded in it."[98]

Innocent IV not only denied Agnes's request in his November 13, 1243 letter, *In Divini timore nominis*,[99] but, in another November 13, 1243 missive, *Piis votis omnium*,[100] mitigated the fasting laws for the monastery of Prague even further than *Pia meditatione pensantes.* He repeats the same reasons for his denial of Agnes's request for a Franciscan Rule that Gregory IX had formulated in *Angelis gaudium*, and in essence tells Agnes not to bother him about these things again. Innocent IV had not known Francis as Gregory IX had, and did not possess his predecessor's care for the Poor Ladies.

By the summer of 1244, Innocent IV had fled to Lyons and was enjoying the protection of King Louis IX. Not at all happy with the papal response, and knowing that the papacy needed the political support of the king of Bohemia, Agnes wrote again. Unmoved, Innocent IV reiterated his position in the

The Privilege of Poverty as Source

August 21, 1244 letter, *Cum Universitati vestrae*.[101] Innocent IV, however, had to revisit his entrenchment in light of the dangerous political climate, which Clare specifically refers to as the reason for not writing to Agnes sooner in her fourth letter (*4LAg* 6).[102] On September 20, 1245, in the bull, *Cum id quod*,[103] Innocent IV again asks Agnes to influence the king of Bohemia on behalf of the papal agenda.

Pressured by the political situation, and needing Agnes's support, Innocent IV capitulated, expanding the privileges of the brothers living next to Agnes's monastery. On October 21, 1245, in *Vestris piis supplicationibus*,[104] Innocent IV gave certain Franciscan clerics the permission to

> come to the aforementioned monasteries on their special feastdays and at the death of your sisters to celebrate the Divine Office on their behalf and to preach the Word of God to the people who come there at this and other times. They may also come for other reasonable and honorable matters, and may themselves approach or send brothers of their Order, when they see fit, to the doors, grills, and parlors of those monasteries.[105]

Papal Recognition of a Feminine Franciscan Charism

On November 13, 1245, in *Solet annuere*,[106] Innocent IV reissued Hugolino's Rule for the Damianite monasteries. In his November 14, 1245 missive to the friars, *Ordinem vestrum*,[107] Innocent IV amends *Quo elongati* giving permission for brothers who have a faculty from the Holy See to enter the monasteries of the nuns of the Order of San Damiano. Agnes had successfully negotiated her Privilege of Poverty, fasting norms consistent with those observed at Saint Damian, and allowances for the brothers to preach to the sisters within the enclosure of the monastery. Even with all this, there was still one obstacle remaining—the mention of the Rule of Saint

Benedict in the Hugolinian Rule. Agnes wanted her Franciscan identity confirmed in law.

The cry to be identified as Franciscan was common to a number of monasteries of Poor Ladies. On August 5, 1247, Innocent IV circulated his own version of the Hugolinian Rule, *Cum omnis vera Religio*[108] to all the abbesses and nuns of the Order of Saint Damian. In his Rule, Innocent IV deletes the Rule of Benedict and affirms for the sisters their profession of the Rule of Blessed Francis. The mitigations prescribed in *Quo elongati* and *Ordinem vestrum*, and days later in the August 19, 1247 bull, *Quanto studiosius divinae*[109] would significantly mitigate the friar's commitment to poverty. In addition, the 1247, *Cum omnis vera Religio*, proposed fasting customs gravely contrary to Clare's third letter and permitted the holding of revenue and common possessions. While Innocent IV mouthed an affirmation of the Rule of Saint Francis in his new Rule, he contradicted the Privilege of Poverty.

The accompanying papal letter, *Quoties a Nobis*[110] of August 23, 1247, clearly stated the papal intention to insist upon a unified profession for the Hugolinian monasteries and a nullification of all former dispensations. The outcry of the Damianite sisters must have been great. By June 6, 1250, in his letter *Inter personas alias*,[111] Innocent IV completely gave up the possibility of a unified profession. He ordered the Cardinal of Ostia to permit the sisters to live under either the Rule of Hugolino or his new Rule.

The former Hugolinian confederation could now be juridically viewed as two distinct groups of federated monasteries—those that held common possessions and were happy with the Hugolinian version of the Rule of Saint Benedict, and those women associated with San Damiano who lived without property and privileges and desired to be identified as Franciscans. Given that the uniformity of the Hugolinian federation was now officially broken, Agnes's political clout as a royal was no longer needed. It was easier for Clare to work directly with Cardinal Rainaldo in the composition of a Rule appropriate for the San Damiano monastery and its associates.

Poverty's Eschatological Promise

The tone of Clare's fourth letter is unmistakably eschatological. There is no reference to the papal approval of Clare's Rule, which probably indicates that Clare's final letter to Agnes was composed before August 9, 1253. In her fourth letter, Clare invites Agnes to focus her vision on the birth, public life, death, and glory of Jesus Christ. Clare takes Agnes's commitment to the Poor Christ for granted, and teaches her how to pray and depend on Jesus Christ as her sole support.

Amid the eschatological overtones, however, Clare's precious Privilege of Poverty[112] breaks through. Agnes is to run and not grow weary "until your left hand is under my head and your right arm blissfully embraces me" (*4LAg* 32).[113] The allusion to the *Song of Songs* is also found in the Privilege of Poverty given to Clare by Gregory IX in 1228: While the Lord's left hand will "uphold the weaknesses of your body"[114] his right arm "will more blissfully embrace you in the greatness of his vision."[115] The concrete struggle of Clare and Agnes to obtain for their respective monasteries a Franciscan economy following the vision of Saint Francis has an eschatological promise that Clare on her deathbed is already beginning to experience. In her last days, Clare wished to bequeath this promise "to the other half of her soul and repository of the special love of her deepest heart" (*4LAg* 1).[116]

Clare's Letters to Agnes

Notes

[1]*BF* I: 771.

[2]Sicut manifestum est, cupientes soli Domino dedicari, abdicastis rerum temporalium appetitum; propter quod, venditis omnibus et pauperibus erogatis, nullas omnino possessiones habere proponitis, illius vestigiis per omnia inhaerentes, qui pro nobis factus est pauper, via, veritas, atque vita; nec ab huiusmodi proposito vos rerum terret inopia; nam laeva Sponsi caelestis est sub capite vestro ad sustentandum infirma corporis vestri, quae legi mentis ordinata caritate stravistis. Denique qui pascit aves caeli et lilia vestit agri vobis non deerit ad victum pariter et vestitum, donec seipsum vobis transiens in aeternitate ministret; cum scilicet eius dextera vos felicius amplexabitur in suae plenitudine visionis.

[3]*Proc* 3:14. "Et mai non podde essere inducta nè dal Papa, nè dal Vescovo Hostiensi che recevesse possessione alcuna. Et lo Privilegio de la povertà, lo quale li era stato concesso, lo honorava con molta reverentia, et guardavalo bene et con diligentia, temendo de non lo perdere."

[4]aeternae felicitatis gloriam adipisci.

[5]sponsum nobilioris generis accipientes, Dominum Iesum Christum.

[6]pompis et honoribus et saeculi dignitate.

[7]sanctissimam paupertatem et corporis penuriam elegistis.

[8]Magnum quippe ac laudabile commercium: relinquere temporalia pro aeternis, promereri caelestia pro terrenis, centuplum pro uno recipere, ac beatam vitam perpetuam possidere.

[9]merces vestra copiosissima est in caelis.

[10]et fere digne meruistis soror, sponsa, et mater altissimi Patris Filii et gloriosae Virginis nuncupari.

[11]"Then, following the example of her cousin Elizabeth, she built, at the foot of the bridge in the city of Prague, the famous hospital for the sick dedicated to the most holy confessor Francis, endowed it with revenues and property, and installed in that place the Crucifers with the Red Cross and Star, in order that they would care for the sick there, and in order that whenever anyone was in need, they would solicitously provide all things that were necessary [Denique ad imitacionem beate Elyzabeth, consobrine sue, hospitale solempne pro infirmis in pede pontis civitatis Pragensis ad honorem sanctissimi confessoris Francisci construxit, quod redditibus et possessionibus amplius ditavit, cruciferos cum rubea cruce et stella ibidem collocans, qui predictorum infirmorum curam gererent, et prout unicuique opus esset, de necessariis omnibus sollicite pro(v)iderent]." The Latin text

of the Agnes legend is found in Jan Kapistrán Vyskočil, *Legenda Blahoslavené Anežky a čtyři listy Sv. Kláry* (Prague: Nakladatelství Universum, 1932). The English translations of Vyskočil's footnotes used in this text are the work of Vitus Buresh, OSB.

[12]"She also built the famous convent for the sisters of the Order of Saint Clare [nec non famosum cenobium pro sororibus ordinis sancte Clare]."

[13]Vyskočil, *Legenda Blahoslavené Anežky*, 158, note 59, comments: "The legend says that on the next feastday of Saint Martin, seven noble women entered the convent; then it adds immediately that during the next occurring feast of Pentecost (*in Penthecoste proximo sequenti*) Agnes herself entered the convent. If, then, Agnes entered in 1234, the first Poor Clares [sic] came to Prague shortly before November 11, 1233."

[14]"Five sisters of the Order of Saint Clare came from Trent; these were sent to Agnes at her own request and through the favor of the apostolic see; they were received by her with great rejoicing of spirit, and were brought with honor to the convent [Venientes autem quinque sorores ordinis sancte Clare de Tridento, que ad peticionem ipsius de favore sedis apostolice sibi fuerant destinate, cum magna spiritus exultacione ab ipsa sunt recepte, memoratum in cenobium honorifice introducte sunt]."

[15]"Soon after, on the feast of Saint Martin, seven virgins from the kingdom of Bohemia, very highly born, desiring to attain eternal victory through the union of chastity with the Spouse of virgins, were invested with the habit and admitted to life in community with the other sisters [et in proxima festivitate sancti Martini septem virgines de regno Bohemie generis valde clari, sponso virginum castitatis nexibus vinciri perpetuo cupientes, habitu et convictu adiuncte sunt sororibus antedictis]."

[16]*CDB* III:65-66.

[17]"we accept into our royal protection the cloister built at Prague in honor of Saint Francis and the hospital connected to it, which is located next to Saint Castulus, including everything that now pertains to them or will be held by them in the future by lawful title [nos claustrum Prage in honore sancti Francisci constructum et hospitale ad idem pertinens, situm apud sanctum Castulum, et omnia, que ad ipsa nunc pertinent, vel in posterum iusto sunt titulo habitura, in regiam protectionem suscipimus]."

[18]Vyskočil, *Legenda Blahoslavené Anežky*, 158-59, note 61, cites chroniclers as proposing the years 1233, 34, 35, and 36 as possible dates of Agnes's entrance. Vyskočil solves the dilemma as follows: "Perhaps the best solution to this question can be made by using the papal letters as a guide. According to the pope's letter of August 30, 1234, Agnes was then already in the convent, for the pope instructed her in that letter to recite the Office according to the Gallican Psalter and received her convent and

hospital under his protection. On the next day, he issued a letter in which he instructed John the provincial of Saxony and Thomas the custodian in Bohemia to make Agnes the abbess of the convent of Saint Francis. Before this date, there was no mention of Agnes in the pope's letters, but in 1234 suddenly four letters in succession were written concerning Agnes. From this it can be concluded that in that year, at Pentecost, Agnes entered the convent. Therefore, according to the pope's letters, issued during the second half of the year 1234, it can be concluded with certainty that on Pentecost, June 11, of that same year, Agnes entered the Order of Saint Francis."

[19]"Finally, the prudent virgin, considering that in the tempest of the present life we are constantly tossed about by the waves of our mortality, that we are not able to contemplate the things that are above on account of the bustle of worldly affairs, all the more ardently enkindled with the love of heavenly things, on the next occurring Pentecost, in the presence of seven bishops and the Lord King her brother and the Queen, with many princes and barons as well as a countless multitude of men and women of various nations, rejecting the highest rank of royalty and holding all worldly glory in contempt, together with the seven noble virgins of her native country, like an innocent dove from the deluge of the wicked world, flew into the ark of the religious state [Considerans tandem virgo prudens quod in naufraga vita presenti continue fluctibus nostre mortalitatis iactamur, nec superna contemplari valemus propter tumultum mundanarum causarum, amore celestium ardencius inflammata, in penthecoste proximo sequenti, presentibus septem epyscopis et domino rege, fratre suo, ac regina cum multis principibus ac baronibus, nec non innumera utriusque sexus diversarum nacionum multitudine, spreto regni fastigo et omni gloria mundana contempta, cum septem nobilissimis regni sui virginibus ut columba innocua de diluvio nequam seculi ad archam sacre religionis convolavit]."

[20]*BF* I:134-35.

[21]"For this reason, agreeing with the prayers of their king, bishop, and chapter, we accept the aforementioned monastery and hospital into the law, property, and protection of the apostolic see [Nos eorumdem Regis, Episcopi, et Capituli precibus inclinati praefatum Monasterium, et Hospitale in jus, et proprietatem, ac tutelam Apostolicae Sedis suscipimus]."

[22]sed pro nihilo ducens Mundi favores, et rerum affluentiam terrenarum, carnem coegisti spiritui deservire, ut abdicatis transitoriis universis, coelesti Sponso in Religione pauperum Monialium inclusarum elegeris in munditia cordis, et corporis famulari Illi voto solemni te dedicans, et Eius ancilla fieri cupiens ex Regina, qui celsitudinem

Divinitatis humilians, et formam servi suscipiens exaltat humiles in salutem.
[23]*Cum deceat principalem, BF* I:157-58. This letter is enclosed within the May 18, 1235, letter *Filius summi Regis.*
[24]cum omnibus appendiciis suis, Pratis, Pascuis, Silvis, Agris, Aquis, Tempe, et omnibus huiusmodi pertinentiis, quae retroactis temporibus dederamus Illustri Sorori nostrae Agneti Virgini.
[25]"to the hospital which was founded by her in Prague, doing what we have done at her request for the necessities of the poor staying there [ex eius petitione conferre, sicut contulimus Hospitali ab ea fundato Pragae, ad usus pauperum ibi commorantium necessarios]."
[26]"I, Wenceslas, fourth king of the Bohemians, in order to dispel all traces of doubt, wish to bring to the knowledge of all through the present document that I have confirmed with everything regarding our brother's directed charter that the estate called Rakšice, with all its appurtenances, is to be in the possession of the Hospital of Blessed Francis forever. Our renowned brother, Přemysl, margrave of Moravia, first had given this estate to his own sister, a virgin, with all its accessories, and later at the request of this same sister gave it to this hospital, which she herself founded at Prague [Ego Winceslaus Dei gratia IV. Rex Boemorum. Ad abstergenda vestigia totius haesitationis per praesens Scriptum ad notitiam omnium cupio pervenire, quod Villam Rakscesce nomine, quam inclytus Frater noster Marchio Moraviae Premizhl nomine, prius cum omnibus appendiciis suis Sorori suae Virgini contulerat, et postea ex petitione eiusdem Sororis suae donavit Hospitali Beati Francisci, quod ipsa fundavit Pragae, perpetuo possidendam, confirmavi cum omni jure in privilegio Fratris nostri praescripto]." Wenceslas's confirmation is found within the May 18, 1235 letter, *Filius summi Regis, BF* I:156-58.
[27]*BF* I:159. This letter is incorporated within *Filius Summi Regis*, May 18, 1235.
[28]"Let the present generation as well as successive generations in Christ know that we have given to the hospital of the Cloister of Saint Francis in Prague of the Lady Agnes, our dear, illustrious daughter, for the good of her soul, all the inheritable property rights, which we bought from the brothers of the Hospital of Saint Mary of the Teutonic Order, . . . We have given the aforementioned estates to the aforementioned hospital with all their fields, woods, waters, inheritable property rights, persons, and all other things pertaining to them, to be possessed lawfully and eternally, with this condition: that we wish to act there as steward of produce until the end of our life, so that we may be able to do with its goods what seems best to us according to God [Noverit tam praesens hominum aetas, quam in Christo successura posteritas, quod Nos Hospitali Claustri Sancti Francisci in Praga

Clare's Letters to Agnes

Dominae Agnetis dilectae filiae nostrae illustris, pro remedio animae suae omnem haereditatem, quam emimus a Fratribus Hospitalis Sanctae Mariae Domus Teutonicorum, . . . supradictas Villas tradidimus Hospitali predicto, cum omnibus agris, silvis, aquis, haereditatibus, hominibus, et omnibus aliis rebus ad ipsas pertinentibus, jure perpetuo possidendas; hoc salvo, quod Domina fructuum esse volumus usque ad terminum vitae nostrae, ut possimus de iis facere, quod Nobis secundum Deum videbitur expedire]."

[29]*BF* I:156-58.

[30]*BF* I: 158-59.

[31]*BF* I:156.

[32]"we have decided that the Hospital of Saint Francis situated next to your monastery, which you, daughter and abbess, built on land of the Roman church, is to be conceded to that monastery with its appurtenances forever. Also, we order that the same hospital with all its goods can not be separated from the monastery by any means or plan. Moreover, let the income of its possessions fall to the use of yourselves and those who succeed you, always recognizing the authority of the apostolic see [Hospitale Sancti Francisci, juxta Monasterium vestrum situm, quod tu filia Abbatissa in fundo Romanae Ecclesiae construxisti, cum pertinentiis suis eidem Monasterio perpetuo duximus concedendum: nihilominus statuentes, ut idem Hospitale cum omnibus bonis suis a Monasterio ipso nullo modo, vel ingenio valeat separari; sed proventus possessionum illius usibus vestris, et earum, quae successerint vobis, cedant; auctoritate Sedis Apostolicae semper salva]."

[33]*CDB* III:144-47.

[34]Preterea quascumque possessiones et quecumque bona idem monasterium impresentiarum iuste ac canonice possidet aut in futurum concessione pontificum, largitione regum vel principum, oblatione fidelium seu aliis iustis modis prestante Domino poterit adipisci, firma vobis et hiis, que vobis successerint, et illibata permaneant. In quibus hec propriis duximus exprimenda vocabulis: Locum ipsum, in quo prefatum monasterium situm est, cum eodem hospitali et omnibus pertinentiis suis, villam Glupetin cum omnibus villulis ad eam pertinentibus, videlicet Humenche et Nidoscitz, villam Borotiz cum omnibus villulis ad ipsam pertinentibus , scilicet Supencwizt et Drahtesicz, villam Ribinic cum suis pertinentiis, villam Rokschice cum omnibus pertinentiis suis et alias possessiones vestras cum pratis, vineis, terris, nemoribus, usuagiis et pascuis, in bosco et plano, in aquis et molendinis, in viis et semitis et omnibus aliis libertatibus et immunitatibus suis.

[35]Sane novalium vestrorum, que propriis manibus aut sumptibus colitis, de quibus aliquis hactenus non percepit, sive de ortis, virgultis et

The Privilege of Poverty as Source

---

piscationibus vestris seu de vestrorum animalium nutrimentis nullus a vobis decimas exigere vel extorquere presumat. [36]Pro consecrationibus vero altarium vel ecclesie vestre, sive pro oleo sancto, vel alio ecclesiastico sacramento nullus a vobis sub obtentu consuetudinis vel alio modo quicquam audeat extorquere, set hec omnia gratis vobis auctoritate nostra episcopus diocesanus impendat. [37]in summa vivere paupertate. [38]quod terreni regni fastigia vilipendens et oblationes imperialis coniugii parum dignas. [39]adhaesisti vestigiis. [40]ipse in aethereo thalamo sociabit. [41]Sed quia unum est necessarium, hoc unum obtestor et moneo per amoren illius, cui te sanctam et beneplacentem hostiam obtulisti. . . nulli credens, nulli consentiens, quod te vellet ab hoc proposito revocare, quod tibi poneret in via scandalum, ne in illa perfectione, qua Spiritus Domini te vocavit, redderes Altissimo vota tua. [42]quod praepone consiliis ceterorum et reputa tibi carius omni dono. [43]Si quis vero aliud tibi dixerit, aliud tibi suggesserit, quod perfectionem tuam impediat, quod vocationi divinae contrarium videatur, etsi debeas venerari, noli tamen eius consilium imitari, sed pauperem Christum, virgo pauper, amplectere. [44]Vide contemptibilem pro te factum et sequere, facta pro ipso contemptibilis in hoc mundo. [45]Propter quod in aeternum et in saeculum saeculi regni caelestis gloriam pro terrenis et transitoriis, aeterna bona pro perituris participes et vives in saecula saeculorum. [46]et nomen tuum in libro vitae notabitur futurum inter homines gloriosum. [47]Ancho disse che particularmente amava la povertà, però che mai podde essere inducta che volesse alcuna cosa propria, né recevere possessione, né per lei, né per lo monasterio. — Adomandata como sapesse questo, respose che epsa vidde et udì che la sancta memoria de mesere Gregorio papa li volse dare molte cose et comparare le possessione per lo monasterio, ma epsa non volse mai aconsentire. [48]Ancho disse che spetialmente epsa tanto amò la povertà, che né papa Gregorio, né lo Vescovo Hostiense, poddero mai fare che epsa fusse contenta de recevere alcune possessione. [49]*CDB* III:182-83. [50]"This will be particularly true if you will have decided with your customary kindness that the petitions of your above-mentioned special daughter and my most-beloved blood sister, which she herself has decided to offer to you now, ought to be admitted into the chapel of your kind hearing, knowing this to be sure and in every way established that, since you give satisfaction to her prayers, which without doubt are pleasing to God because they also come from him, you receive me, as I have said, with all my power under your power, which is worthy in every respect. Nor is this action surprising, since I prize your strength, as I would truly attest, just as I would prize my wife, children, and all my goods, and I put it before everything of this world in affection [Hoc siquidem deo de matura deliberacione spondeo et promitto, quod ex hoc vobis et sancte Romane ecclesie semper promptior et paratior ex animo volo esse in omni necessitate seu oportunitate publica et privata; presertim si peticiones predicte specialis filie vestre ac dilectissime sororis mee germane, quas ipsa vobis porrigere impresenciarum decrevit, intra sacrarium exaudicionis vestre solita benignitate duxeritis admittendas, hoc certum et per omnia ratum habentes, quia per hoc, quod satisfacitis votis eius, que procul dubio deo placent, quia et ab ipso sunt, me ut dixi cum omni virtute mea sub vestram omni respectu dignam redigitis potestatem]."

[51]*BF* I:215-16.

[52]Monasterium Sancti Francisci Pragensis. . .cum Hospitali vestro.

[53]secundum Deum et beati Benedicti regulam.

[54]secundum Deum et beati Benedicti regulam atque institutionem monialium inclusarum sancti Damiani Assisinatis.

[55]*CDB* III:195-98.

[56]pietatis ac compassionis intuitu ad opus infirmorum et pauperum hospitale, in quo divino estis obsequio mancipati, fecerit et dotarit.

[57]"You previously sent us a particular note through our beloved son the prior of the Hospital of Saint Francis in Prague, a man of discretion and foresight, asking with humble supplication that we take care to confirm with apostolic authority the plan that was presented to us through that man under the sign of your seal and has been created out of the aforesaid formula and certain chapters that are contained in the Rule of the Order of Blessed Damian [quam pridem Nobis in quadam schedula per dilectum filium Priorem Hospitalis Sancti Francisci Pragensis virum ubique discretum, et providum destinati humili supplicatione deposcens, ut praesentatam Nobis per eumdem sub sigillo tuo formam confectam ex praedicta formula, et quibusdam Capitulis, quae in Ordinis Beati Damiani Regula continentur, confirmari auctoritate Apostolica curaremus]." *Angelis gaudium, BF* I:242-44.

[58]*BF* I:236-37.

[59]See above, note 1.

[60]Hinc est, quod Hospitalis Sancti Francisci Pragensis Dioecesis, cum juribus, et pertinentiis suis, olim vobis, et per vos Monasterio vestro ab Apostolica Sede concessi, vestra libera resignatione recepta, vobis, quae

contemptis visibilibus, ad invisibilium delicias properantes vitare studetis obstaculum in temporalium spinis inoffensam faciem Dei, quaerentium consurgere consuetum, devicti precibus vestris, et lacrymis praesentium auctoritate concedimus, ut invite cogi ad recipiendum de cetero possessiones aliquas non possitis.

[61]*BF* I:237-38.

[62]*BF* I:240.

[63]For historical background on this Order see Milan M. Buben, *Rytíř̌ý Řád Křižovníkǔ S. Červenou Hvězdou* (Praha: L. P., 1996), and Krsto Stošič, "Naš starí rukopis o bl. Janji iz Praga," in *Bogoslovska smotra* XIX (1931): 223-29.

[64]See above, note 55.

[65]In quibus hec propriis duximus exprimenda vocabulis: Locum ipsum, in quo prefatum hospitale situm est, cum omnibus pertinentiis suis, villam Glupetin cum omnibus villis ad eam pertinentibus, videlicet Humencle et Nidoscitus, villam Borotic cum omnibus villis ad ipsam pertinentibus, videlicet Supenewici et Drahtesici, villam Ribinic cum suis pertinentiis, villam Rokschice cum omnibus pertinentiis suis et alias possessiones vestras cum pratis, vineis, terris, nemoribus, usuagiis et pascuis, in bosco et plano, in aquis et molendinis, in viis et semitis et omnibus libertatibus et immunitatibus suis.

[66]The text here is from the 1228 bull, *Cum a Nobis*, sent to the Monastery of Saint Mary of the Virgins in Pamplona. The bull is described in P. Juan R. de Larrinaga, OFM, "Las Clarisas de Pamplona," *Archivo Ibero-Americano* 5 (1945): 252-54. The text of the bull is transcribed in Ignacio Omaechevarria, OFM, *Escritos de Santa Clara y Documentos Complementarios* (Madrid: Biblioteca de Autores Cristianos, 1982), 214-29.

[67]The term *pulmenta* means "all cooked foods." See Gerard Pieter Freeman, "Klarissenfasten im 13. Jahrhundert," *AFH* 87 (1994): 217-85. The definition of *pulmenta* is found on page 225.

[68]Ieiunandi autem haec observantia teneatur, ut omni tempore ieiunent quotidie; quarta quidem et sexta feria extra Quadragesimam a pulmento et vino pariter abstinentes nisi praecipuum festum alicuius Sancti in eis occurrerit celebrandum. In quibus diebus, quarta scilicet et sexta feria, si poma aut fructus vel herbae crudae adfuerint, reficiendis Sororibus apponantur. In Quadragesima vero maiori, quatuor diebus, in Quadragesima autem Sancti Martini, tribus diebus in hebdomada, pane et aqua ieiunent, et omnibus vigiliis solemnibus, si de earum fuerit voluntate. Hanc autem ieiunii et abstinentiae legem adolescentulae vel anus et omnino corpore imbecilles ac debiles omnino corpore observare minime permittantur, sed secundum earum imbecillitatem tam in cibariis quam

---

ieiuniis cum eis misericorditer dispensetur. Omaechevarria, *Escritos*, 222-23.

[69]"Klarissenfasten," 227.

[70]*BF* I:215.

[71]*BF* I:240-41.

[72]Vobis itaque praesentium auctoritate concedimus, ut non obstante, quod omni tempore secundum eamdem Regulam in cibo quadragesimali jejunare debetis, diebus Dominicis, et quinta feria bis commedere, et lacticiniis resici valeatis. In omni vero Pascha, et solemnitatibus Beatae Mariae Virginis, ac etiam Apostolorum, sive in festo Nativitatis Domini, nec non tempore manifestae necessitatis, utpote infirmitatis, nulla vestrum ad jejunium teneatur. Et si forte aliqua ex vobis infirma fuerit, Abbatissa, vel Soror major nihilominus cum ipsa de jejunio, et cibo dispensandi habeat potestatem. Praeterea volumus, quod diebus illis, quidus in Quadragesima majori, et minori, secundum Regulam in pane, et aqua tenemini jejunare, refectionem in omnibus, sicut aliis diebus quadragesimalibus habeatis.

[73]*BF* I:242-44.

[74]The text of this bull, the Rule of Hugolino for the Monastery of Saint Francis in Prague, can be found in *Agnetis de Bohemia* (Rome: Sacra Congregatio pro Causis Sanctorum, 1987), 114-22.

[75]Secundo, quia ipsae formula praedicta postposita, eamdem Regulam a Professionis tempore usque nunc laudabiliter observarunt.

[76]Tertio, quia cum sit ita statutum, ut ubique ab omnibus eamdem profitentibus uniformiter observetur, ex praesumptione contrarii grave posset, ac importabile scandalum exoriri.

[77]ipsius Dei te iudico adiutricem.

[78]salutis gaudia in auctore salutis et quidquid melius desiderari potest.

[79]Gaudeas igitur et tu in Domino semper.

[80]nec te involvat amaritudo et nebula.

[81]pone mentem tuam in speculo aeternitatis.

[82]pone animam tuam in splendore gloriae.

[83]pone cor tuum in figura divinae substantiae.

[84]et transforma te ipsam totam per contemplationem in imagine divinitatis ipsius.

[85]illum totaliter diligas, qui se totum pro tua dilectione donavit.

[86]Ipsius dulcissimae matri adhaereas.

[87]Quis non abhorreat humani hostis insidias, qui per fastum momentaneorum et fallacium gloriarum ad nihilum redigere cogit quod maius est caelo?

[88]Noverit quidem tua prudentia, quod praeter debiles et infirmas, quibus de quibuscumque cibariis omnem discretionem quam possemus facere nos monuit et mandavit, nulla nostrum sana et valida nisi cibaria

The Privilege of Poverty as Source

quadragesimalia tantum, tam in diebus ferialibus quam festivis, manducare deberet, die quolibet ieiunando, exceptis diebus dominicis et Natalis Domini, in quibus bis in die comedere deberemus. Et in diebus quoque Iovis solitis temporibus pro voluntate cuiuslibet, ut quae scilicet nollet, ieiunare non teneretur. Nos tamen sanae ieiunamus cottidie praeter dies dominicos et Natalis. In omni vero Pascha, ut scriptum beati Francisci dicit, et festivitatibus sanctae Mariae ac sanctorum apostolorum ieiunare etiam non tenemur, nisi haec festa in sexta feria evenirent; et sicut praedictum est, semper quae sanae sumus et validae, cibaria quadragesimalia manducamus.

[89]BF I:258-29.

[90]Ex parte Carissimae in Christo filiae Agnetis Sororis Monasterii vestri, et vestra fuit propositum coram Nobis, . . . vos ad certam jejunii observantiam obligastis, videlicet, ut a Sororibus, quae sanae sunt, et validae omni tempore tam diebus ferialibus, quam festivis, exceptis diebus Dominicis, et die Natalis Domini, quotidie in cibis quadragesimalibus jejunetur, ita tamen, quod in omni Pascha, et Solemnitatibus B. Virginis, ac etiam Apostolorum; nisi forte in sexta feria venerint, jejunare minime teneantur. In quinta vero feria, praeter quam in majori Quadragesima, et minori, quae jejunare noluerint, non jejunent. Hanc enim jejunii, et abstinentiae legem corpore imbecilles, aut debiles observare minime permittantur, sed secundum earum infirmitatem, vel imbecillitatem, tam cibariis, quam jejuniis cum eis ab Abbatissa, seu majori Sorore misericorditer dispensentur.

[91]*BF* I:68-70. An English translation of this bull can be found in *Francis of Assisi: Early Documents*, vol. 1, ed. Regis Armstrong, OFM Cap., J. A. Wayne Hellmann, OFM Conv., William Short, OFM (New York: New City Press, 1999), 570-75.

[92]dolens pia mater cibum sacrae doctrinae rarius habituras Sorores, cum gemitu dixit: Omnes nobis auferat de cetero Fratres, postquam vitalis nutrimenti nobis abstulit praebitores. Et statim omnes Fratres ad Ministrum remisit, nolens habere eleemosynarios qui panem corporalem acquirerent, postquam panis, spiritualis eleemosynarios non haberent. Quod cum audiret Papa Gregorius statim prohibitum illud in generalis Ministri manibus relaxavit.

[93]See above, note 66.

[94]"After this, Brother Elias, having chosen the place of Cortona for his dwelling place, went without permission and against the general prohibition of the minister general to visit the houses of the Poor Ladies; for this reason he seems to have incurred the sentence of excommunication decreed by the pope. But Brother Albert commanded him to come to him to obtain absolution or at least to meet him at some intermediate place. When he

declined to do this, the pope heard about it; and, when he saw that the pope wanted him to obey the minister general like any other brother, not being able to bear the humiliation in as much as he had not learned to obey, he betook himself to the neighborhood of Arezzo. Wherefore, not undeservedly, he was publicly excommunicated by the pope [Post hoc frater Helias, electo ad morandum loco de Cortona, contra generalem prohibitionem generalis ministri sine licentia accesit ad loca pauperum dominarum; unde sententiam latam a domino Papa videbatur incurrisse. Mandavit autem ei frater Albertus, ut veniret ad eum gratia absolutionis obtinendae, vel saltem occurreret ei apud aliquem locum medium. Quod cum facere dedignaretur, pervenit verbum ad Papam; et cum Papam perpenderet velle, ut generali ministro, sicut alius quilibet frater, obediret, non ferens ipse humiliationem suam, quippe qui obedire non didicerat, ad partes Frederici se transtulit. Unde non immerito a Papa publice excommunicatus est]." Fratris Tomae Eccleston, *Liber de Adventu Fratrum Minorum in Angliam* in *AF* 1 (1885): 243. For the English translation used here see *The Chronicle of Brother Thomas of Eccleston*, in *XIIIth Century Chronicles*, trans. Placid Herman, OFM (Chicago: Franciscan Herald Press, 1961), 156.

[95]*CDB* III: 332 and 334, 337-38.

[96]*BF* I:295.

[97]This letter can be found in *Agnetis de Bohemia*, Sacra Congregatio pro Causis Sanctorum, 161-62.

[98]ut duo verba praemissa, quae de virtute obedientiae, et Regula Beati Benedicti dicuntur, amoveri de ipsa formula; et quaedam de novo, ac illa etiam faceremus in ipsa conscribi, quae dicto Monasterio a piae memoriae Gregorio Papa. . .sunt indulta. This passage is found in the papal letter, *In Divini timore nominis*, *BF* I:315-17.

[99]*BF* I:315-17.

[100]*BF* I:314-15.

[101]*BF* I:350.

[102]"The truth is that a shortage of messengers and the obvious perils of travel have hindered me [Hoc est impedimentum defectus nuntiorum et viarum pericula manifesta]."

[103]*CDB* II:162-63.

[104]*BF* I:388.

[105]ut ad praedicta Monasteria in festivitatibus specialibus eorumdem, et Sororum vestrarum obitu ad celebrandum in eis Divinum Officium, et ad proponendum verbum Dei Populo, qui tunc, aliisque temporibus ibidem convenerit; nec non pro aliis rationabilibus, et honestis causis; ac ad Portas, Crates, et Locutoria Monasteriorum ipsorum, cum expedire viderint,

accedere, et Fratres sui Ordinis destinare valeant, liberam concedimus auctoritate praesentium facultatem.

[106]*BF* I:394-99.

[107]*BF* I:400-402.

[108]*BF* I:476-83.

[109]*BF* I:487-88.

[110]*BF* I:488.

[111]*BF Supp.*, 22-24.

[112]*Sicut manifestum est, BF* I:771.

[113]donec laeva tua sit sub capite meo et dextera feliciter amplexabitur me, osculeris me felicissimo tui oris osculo.

[114]sustentandum infirma corporis vestri.

[115]eius dextera vos felicius amplexabitur in suae plenitudine visionis.

[116]Animae suae dimidiae et praecordialis amoris armariae singularis.

PART THREE

The Legend of Saint Agnes of Rome

The Legend of Saint Agnes of Rome

Translation by Julia Fleming, Creighton University

Lesson 1[1]

Ambrose, the servant of Christ, to the holy virgins.
Let us celebrate the feast day of a most holy virgin. On one
side, let the psalms echo; on the other, let the readings sound.
On one side, let the crowds of people rejoice; on the other, let
Christ's poor be encouraged. Let us all, therefore, give solemn
thanks to the Lord, and for the edification of the virgins recall
in how excellent a manner the most blessed Agnes suffered!

In the thirteenth year of her youth, she lost death and found
life, because she loved the sole Author of Life. She was
reckoned an infant in years, but had the wisdom of an elder;
youthful indeed in body, but white-haired in spirit; lovely in
form, but lovelier in faith.

While she was returning from school, the son of the urban
prefect fell in love with her. When he had inquired about her
parents, he began to offer many things and to make many
promises.

Finally, he brought with him extremely precious
ornaments, which were refused by Blessed Agnes as if they
were dung. As a result, the young man was spurred by a more
intense goad of love.

Thinking that she wished to receive better ornaments, he
brought with him every status symbol [including] the most
precious stones, and on his own behalf, and through his
friends, acquaintances, and relatives, began to accost the
virgin's ears to promise riches, houses, possessions, estates,

---

[1]The lessons of the legend (*AASS*, January 21) are divided according to
Regula breviary manuscript Assisi, Biblioteca Sacro Convento, 694, ff.
269r-275v.

and indeed all the world's delights, if she would not refuse her consent to marry him.

Lesson 2

To these things Blessed Agnes is said to have given the young man this kind of response: "Depart from me, kindling of sin, nourishment of villainy, food of death. Depart from me, because I have already been taken by another lover, who presented me with even better ornaments than you have, and put me under a pledge with the ring of his fidelity, [who is] far nobler than you in birth and position. He adorned my right hand with a priceless bracelet, and encircled my neck with precious stones; he hung priceless pearls from my ears, and surrounded me with glittering and sparkling gems.

He placed a seal on my face, so that I will admit no lover except him. He clothed me in a robe of state woven with gold, and adorned me with innumerable necklaces. He showed me incomparable treasures, which he promised to give to me if I persevere with him.

Therefore, I am unable to consider another, to the insult of my prior lover, or to desert him, with whom I have been bound by love: whose nobility is higher, his power stronger, his appearance lovelier, his love sweeter, and his every grace more elegant—by whom a marriage bed has already been prepared for me; whose instruments echo for me in measured tones; whose virgins sing for me with the most perfect voices. Already, I have received milk and honey from his mouth; already, I have been held fast in his chaste embraces.

Lesson 3

Already, his body has been united with my body, and his blood has adorned my cheeks. His mother is a virgin; his father has never known a woman. Angels serve him, whose beauty the sun and moon admire; by whose fragrance the dead revive; by whose touch the sick are relieved; whose wealth never fails; whose riches do not diminish. I keep faith with him alone. To him, I commit myself with complete devotion.

Having loved him, I am chaste; having touched him, I am pure; having received him, I am a virgin. Nor will children be lacking after marriage, when birth advances without sadness, and fruitfulness is increased every day."

Hearing these things, the crazed young man, harassed by blind love, and in the midst of mental and physical difficulties, was tortured by wheezing. Meanwhile, he prostrated himself on his bed, and through his deep sighs, love became visible to the doctors. What the doctors found became known to his father; and in order to petition the virgin, the father's voice reiterated the same things already said by the son.

The most blessed Agnes refused, and asserted that she would not violate the covenant with her prior spouse by any agreement. Although the father said that he had been established in magisterial authority to discharge the prefecture, and for that reason, ought by no means to give precedence [to another], however distinguished, over himself; nevertheless, he began to inquire energetically, who the husband might be, about whose power Agnes was bragging.

Then one of his toadies arose, who said she had been a Christian from infancy, and was so possessed by magic arts that she said that Christ was her husband.

Lesson 4

Hearing these things, the prefect was made happy, and when the attendants had been sent out with a great uproar, ordered her to be brought before his tribunal.

At first, indeed, he challenged her secretly with flattering statements; then he assailed her with terrors. But Christ's virgin was neither seduced by the flattery, nor shaken by fear: and what is more, persevering with the same countenance and the same spirit, in her heart, she mocked him in the same way when he threatened as when he flattered.

And so, the Prefect Symphronius, seeing such constancy in the girl, appealed to her parents. Because they were noble, and he was unable to inflict force upon them, he confronted them with their Christianity.

For on the following day, he commanded that Agnes be presented to him, and, repeating himself again and again, began to review the conversation about the young man's love. When with useless effort his entire argument failed, he ordered her again to appear before his tribunal and said to her: "Unless you are separated from the superstition of the Christians, on account of whose magic arts you flaunt yourself, you will not be able to cast off insanity of heart, or consent to extremely advantageous plans. Thus it is necessary that you hasten to venerate the goddess Vesta, so that, if maintaining virginity pleases you, you may concentrate your attention on reverencing her sacrifices by day and night."

To these things Blessed Agnes said: "If I have refused your son, who though vexed with excessive passion, is nonetheless a living man, a man at least who is capable of reason, who is able to hear and see and caress and walk, and to enjoy completely the brightness of this light with its goods—if, therefore, I am unable for any reason to have regard for him, on account of the love of Christ, how would I be able to worship idols that are mute and deaf, without perception and soul, and, to the injury of God Most High, bend my neck to useless stones?

Hearing this, Symphronius the prefect said: "I wish to have consideration for your extreme youth, and even now I give respite to your blasphemy of the gods on that account, because I consider you too young to exercise the faculty of judgment. Therefore do not despise yourself in such a way that you incur the reactions of the gods.

Lesson 5

Blessed Agnes said: "Do not so despise the childish body in me that you think that I wish to have your favor. For faith is revealed not in years but in judgments, and the omnipotent God confirms minds rather than particular ages. But in respect to your gods, whose reactions you do not wish me to encounter, let them be angry for themselves; let them speak for themselves; let them warn me about this themselves; let them order themselves to be worshipped; let them command themselves to be adored. Yet since I see that you are straining towards what you will be unable to accomplish, enforce whatever seems appropriate to you."

Prefect Symphronius said: "Choose one of these two things: either sacrifice with the virgins of the goddess Vesta, or you will whore with the prostitutes in the comradeship of the brothel. And far from you will be the Christians, who have so tainted you with [their] magic arts, that you are confident of your ability to endure this misfortune with an intrepid spirit. Thus, as I have said, either sacrifice to the goddess Vesta to your family's glory, or to the dishonor of your parentage, you will be a harlot, publicly degraded."

Then Blessed Agnes spoke with firm resolution: "If you knew who my God was, you would not bring such things from your mouth. Accordingly, because I know the excellence of my Lord Jesus Christ, I am tranquil and despise your threats, believing that I will neither sacrifice to your idols nor be defiled by others' filth. Indeed, I have with me my body's guardian, an angel of the Lord. For the only begotten Son of God, whom you do not know, is my impenetrable wall of defense, my guardian who never sleeps, and my defender who never fails.

Your gods, on the other hand, are either bronze (from which it is better to make kettles for human use), or stones (with which it is better to pave roads to avoid the mud).

Lesson 6

Divinity, then, does not dwell in empty stones, but in the heavens; it does not rest upon bronze, or any metal, but upon high royal power. However, [as for] you and those like you, unless you retreat from the worship of such things, a similar penalty will bring you to an end.

For just as these things have been melted in order that they might be cast, thus those worshipping them will be melted in perpetual fire; not so as to be cast, but to be cast into destruction for eternity and perish."

In response, the crazed judge ordered her to be stripped and led naked to the brothel, under the stimulus of the crier's voice saying: "Agnes, the virgin, who brings forward sacrilegious blasphemy toward the gods, given as a prostitute to the brothels." But as soon as she had been stripped, with her hair untied, divine grace granted such thickness to its strands that she seemed better concealed by her lovely hanging hair than by garments. Moreover, when she had entered the place of disgrace, she found there the angel of the Lord, provided beforehand in order to surround her with vast light, in such a way that no one was able to touch or see her because of its brilliance. For the entire room was gleaming like the radiant sun in its power, and to the degree that anyone wished to be more curious with his eyes, by so much was the keenness of his vision blunted.

When she had prostrated herself in prayer to the Lord, the whitest possible outer garment appeared before her eyes. Taking it, she dressed herself and said: "I give thanks to you, Lord Jesus Christ, who, counting me among the number of your handmaidens, have commanded this garment to be bestowed upon me." For the garment was so fitted to the proportions of her little body, and so remarkable for its perfect shining whiteness, that no one doubted that it had been prepared only by angelic hands.

Meanwhile, the brothel became a place of prayer, in which everyone who had entered offered petitions and veneration, and, giving honor to the great light, went out purer than he had been when he had come inside.

Lesson 7

While these things were happening, the prefect's son, who was the person responsible for this crime, came to the place, as if to insult the girl, in the company of his young comrades, together with whom he believed he would be able to indulge the derision of his lust.

And when he saw the boys who had entered before him wildly raging with passion, coming out with complete reverence and great admiration, he began to declare them impotent, and indeed to condemn them as useless, effeminate, and wretched. Deriding them, he boldly entered the place in which the virgin was praying.

And seeing so great a light around her, he did not give honor to God; but when he rushed into the light itself, before he could even touch her with his hand, he fell on his face, and having been choked by the devil, he died.

However his allies, seeing that he was dallying inside, thought that he was engaged in obscene acts. One of the young men, who was his very close friend, went inside, as if to congratulate [him] on his insult; and, finding him dead, cried out in a loud voice, saying: "Help, pious Romans, that prostitute has killed the prefect's son by magic arts!"

Suddenly the people ran together towards the theater and there was a varied outcry from the raging crowd. Some called

[her] a sorceress; others, innocent; and some shouted "impious."

But the prefect, hearing that his son had perished, came to the theater with excruciating mental anguish and lamentation. When he entered the place in which his son's body lay lifeless, with a loud cry he said to the most blessed virgin: "Cruelest of all women, did you wish to show the proof of your magic art upon my son?"

When he repeated these things, and indeed other words of this kind, and forcibly demanded the cause of his [son's] death from her, the most blessed Agnes said to him: "He whose will [your son] wished to complete, took him into his power. Why, moreover, are all those who came in to me uninjured? Because without exception they gave honor to God, who sent his angel to me, who clothed me in this garment of mercy, and guarded my body, which from the cradle itself has been consecrated and presented to Christ. Therefore, when they saw the angelic splendor, all worshiped and departed unharmed. But he was imprudent, and, as soon as he had entered, began to rant and rage with passion; when he brought his hand into position to touch me, the angel of the Lord delivered him into the base death which you perceive."

Lesson 8

The prefect said to her: "In this way, it will become apparent that you have not done these things by magic arts, if you entreat the angel himself that he restore my son to me in good health."

To him, Blessed Agnes said: "Although your faith does not deserve to obtain this request from the Lord, nevertheless, because it is time for the supremacy of my Lord Jesus Christ to be made evident, all of you go outside so that I may offer him the customary prayer."

When all had gone out, prostrating herself upon her face and weeping, she began to ask the Lord to revive the young man. As she was praying, moreover, the angel of the Lord appeared, who raised her up as she wept, and, comforting her spirit, revived the youth.

When [the young man] had gone outside, he began to cry aloud publicly, saying: "There is one God in heaven, and on earth, and in the sea, who is the God of the Christians. For all the temples are worthless; the gods who are worshiped are all unreliable, and completely unable to offer any help to themselves or to others."

At this cry, all the soothsayers and temple priests were thrown into confusion, and because of them, the people's unrest became even more violent than it had been before. Indeed, they were all crying with one voice: "Get rid of the sorceress; get rid of the evil-doer who both alters minds and changes hearts."

However the prefect, seeing such marvels, was astounded. But fearing proscription, if he acted against the temple priests and befriended Agnes in opposition to his own decrees, he left behind a deputy judge to deal with the people's uprising. However, he went away sad, because he was not able to free her after the resuscitation of his son.

Then the deputy, Aspasius by name, ordered a massive fire to be kindled in the sight of all, and commanded that she be cast into the middle of the flames. When this had been done, immediately the flames were divided into two parts, and on one side and the other the flames consumed the turbulent people. Yet in between, the blaze did not touch Blessed Agnes at all. So much more did the people assign this not to divine powers, but to black magic, that among themselves they uttered low roars and infinite cries to heaven.

Lesson 9

Then Blessed Agnes, stretching out her hands in the middle of the fire, poured out a prayer to the Lord in these words: "Almighty Father of our Lord Jesus Christ, who inspires adoration, worship, and awe, I bless you, because through your only begotten Son I have escaped the threats of impious persons and passed through the devil's impurities by an undefiled footpath. And now behold, I have been steeped in heavenly dew through the Holy Spirit: the altar-pyre near me dies; the flame is divided; and the heat of this fire is poured back upon those by whom it is supplied. I bless you, Father, who must be praised, for you permit me to come to you without fear, even in the midst of the flames. Behold, what I believed, I already see; what I have hoped for, I already hold; what I have desired, I embrace. I confess you with my lips and I long for you with my heart, with my entire inmost being. Behold, I am coming to you, the only true God; who with our Lord Jesus Christ, your Son, and with the Holy Spirit, live and reign throughout all ages forever, Amen."

And when she had completed the prayer, the whole fire was extinguished in such a way that not even any mild heat of the blaze remained. Then Aspasius, deputy of the city of Rome, unable to withstand the people's unrest, ordered a sword to be plunged into her throat.

And so by this death, Christ consecrated her, steeped in the rosy blush of her own blood, as his spouse and martyr. In fact, her parents, having no sadness at all, carried off her body with every joy and buried it on their own small estate, not far from the city, on the road called the Numentine. When the entire throng of Christians assembled there, they were ambushed by the pagans; and, seeing an armed crowd of infidels coming upon them, all of them fled. Some, nevertheless, escaped after being injured by the impact of stones.

Octave—Lesson One

When, therefore, the parents of Blessed Agnes were keeping watch with constant, night-long vigils at her grave, within the midnight silence they saw a crowd of virgins, all dressed in robes of state woven with gold, who were passing by to the accompaniment of a great light; among whom they saw the most Blessed Agnes gleaming in a similar garment, and standing at her right hand, a lamb whiter than snow. Accordingly, while her parents, and some persons who were there at the same time, were watching these things, they more or less fell into a mental stupor.

But Blessed Agnes asked the holy virgins to stop for a short time, and as she stood, said to her parents: "Take care not to mourn to for me as if I were dead: but rejoice with me, and congratulate me, because with all these [virgins] I have received a shining throne, and in heaven have been united with him whom I loved with complete concentration of heart while I was placed on earth. And with these words, she passed on her way.

This vision was spread daily by all who had seen it.

Octave—Lesson Two

As a result, it happened that, after many years, this event was described by those who had seen it to Constantia, daughter of Constantine the Augustus. For Constantia was herself a queen, a most prudent virgin, but had been so beset by wounds that from her head to her feet no part of her limbs had remained free [of them].

But having accepted the advice, in hope of recovering her health, she came by night to the martyr's grave; and although she was a pagan, nonetheless she poured out prayers with confiding attentiveness of heart.

While she was doing this, she was overcome, by the sudden sweetness of sleep, and saw in a vision the most blessed Agnes, extending to her admonitions of this kind: "Act with constancy, Constantia, and believe that the Lord Jesus Christ, the Son of God, to be your savior, through whom you will now obtain the healing of all the wounds which you suffer upon your body." At this utterance, Constantia awoke in good health, so that no sign of any wound remained on her limbs.

Having returned to the imperial residence in the best possible health, therefore, she brought joy to her father the Augustus, and to her brothers the emperors. The whole city was decked in garlands; the soldiers rejoiced, and the private citizens, and indeed, all who heard these things.

Octave—Lesson Three

The infidelity of the nations was confounded, and the Lord's faith rejoiced. In the meantime, she asked her father and imperial brothers that a basilica of Blessed Agnes be constructed, and ordered her mausoleum to be placed there. This report spread quickly to all, and as many as believed and came to her grave were healed, no matter with what infirmity they had been held captive, which no one should doubt that Christ continues to do right up to the present day.

Moreover, Constantia, the daughter of Constantine the Augustus, persevered in virginity: through her, many virgins, of middle-rank, the nobility, and the distinguished, took sacred veils.

And because faith does not suffer the losses of death, right up to the present day many Roman virgins attend the most blessed Agnes as if she remained present in body; and challenged by her example, manfully persevere uncorrupted, believing without doubt that by persevering they will obtain the palm of perpetual victory.

The Legend of Saint Agnes of Rome

These things that I, Ambrose, the servant of Christ, have found written on hidden papyrus rolls, I have not allowed to be buried in unproductive silence. Accordingly, to the honor of so great a martyr, I have written down her deeds as I have come to know them. I thought that the account of her passion had been destined for your imitation, oh virgins of Christ, and I pray to the Holy Spirit that our labors find fruit before the Lord in the similarity of your lives. Amen.

Index of Cited Authors

Index